D0360883

ON Q

Causing Quality in Higher Education

Daniel Seymour

AMERICAN COUNCIL ON EDUCATION ★
ORYX PRESS ★
Series on Higher Education
1993

Published by The Oryx Press
4041 North Central at Indian School Road
Phoenix, AZ 85012-3397

Printed in the United States of America

Library of Congress Cataloging in Publication Data
Seymour, Daniel T.
   On Q: causing quality in higher education / Daniel T. Seymour.
   p. cm. — (American Council on Education/Oryx series on higher education)
   Previously published: New York: American Council on Education: Macmillan Pub. Co.; Toronto: Maxwell Macmillan Canada; New York: Maxwell Macmillan International, © 1992.
   Includes bibliographical references and index.
   ISBN 0-89774-804-2 — ISBN 0-89774-994-4 (Paper)
   1. Education, Higher—United States—Administration.   2. Total quality management—United States.   I. Title.   II. Title: On cue.
III. Title: Causing quality in higher education.   IV. Series: American Council on Education/Oryx series on higher education.
[LB2341.93.U6S49   1993]
378.73—dc20   92-38216
                                                          CIP

To Rhonda

Contents

Preface and Acknowledgments

Kierkegaard calls them the "immediate" men.* These are individuals who tranquilize themselves with the trivial so they can lead normal, unencumbered lives. Asking the difficult questions, tackling the most perplexing problems, is unsettling. It often creates doubt and uncertainty. It muddies the water. The better approach, at least for the "immediate" men, is to avoid trouble by keeping a narrow focus on the small problems in life. This requires real concentration, an ability to block out the complexities that swirl around while keeping a trained, unwavering eye on the simplicities.

Colleges and universities are complex organizations. We have many characteristics that make us look like any other business: multi-million dollar payrolls; accounting and billing departments; computer systems; and security guards. We have diversified holdings as well: restaurants, bookstores, living accommodations, investments, and real estate. We also have a broad array of customers. These customers include not only the people that sit in our classrooms, but those who used to sit in the same classrooms twenty or thirty years ago, the local community, the employers who avail themselves of our educational services, and, at least in the case of state-supported institutions, the legislators who want to ensure that state funds are being used wisely. But at the center of all this activity is the core responsibility of every academic institution—to teach. We teach people how to analyze chemical compounds, how to construct a well-developed argument, how to calculate financial ratios, and how to appreciate the works of the Great Masters.

Given the complex nature of our higher education organizations, it isn't unusual to conclude that "immediacy" abounds on our college campuses. Faced with the crunch of skyrocketing tuitions, declining demographics, and

---

* The male pronoun is used in the Preface to reflect Kierkegaard's words. Throughout this book an attempt has been made to use non-sexist language.

strident calls for more accountability and increased productivity, the standard response has been to revisit time-worn cost containment and policy options. We have become accomplished experts in crisis management—our days filled with reacting to the most pressing problems at hand. Simple, short-run solutions are used to minimize enduring difficulties that show no intention of going away. How many more retrenchments do we have to go through, how many more early retirement programs and hiring freezes do we have to endure before we ask the question: *Is there a better way to manage higher education?*

This book is not for immediate men or women. It is not about rethinking, reworking, or reinforcing past solutions. Curing a minor ailment or bandaging a surface wound is better dealt with elsewhere. The concern here is with radical surgery—the kind that requires massive infusions of new blood and heavy doses of convention-busting procedures. The folklore of "this is how we do things around here" cannot begin to handle the demands placed on our institutions of higher education in a new global economy. We are kidding ourselves if we believe that educating people for the year 2000 is essentially the same as educating them for the year 1975. Everything has changed—technology, lifestyles, culture. Our educational institutions must change as well. Not by cosmetic retouching, one-shot consultants, or slick marketing, but by challenging the basic assumptions of higher education administration.

The "better way" I have chosen to examine in this book has its roots in industry. Prior to the Industrial Revolution, quality was embedded in the hearts and hands of skilled artisans. With the advent of mass production, the embodiment of quality was sliced and diced as different people on the production line were assigned the task of making interchangeable parts. Inspectors were hired and placed at the end of each line. Their job was to analyze each and every product with the intention of detecting errors. A small group of statisticians at Bell Telephone Laboratories was the first to recognize that variability in error rates could be understood with probability and statistics. From these somewhat humble beginnings came the idea of sampling plans and statistical process control that dominated American industrial management until well after World War II.

The next major shift of thinking began to take form in post-war Japan. With a decimated industry known throughout the world for its shoddiness, the Japanese were willing to try anything; even the radical ideas of W. Edwards Deming and Joseph Juran. These two American statisticians were invited to Japan to share their evolving views of how quality could be built into manufacturing processes. Some of these ideas defied common logic: quality did not cost more, it cost less; inspectors didn't decrease the number of defects, they increased them. Both Deming and Juran began to see quality as a management function that could be systematically improved. In fact, the management of quality in this broadened view involved not only the use of statistical tools but also consumer research, goal-setting, team work, problem solving, human resource management, and strategic planning. The philosophy of Total Quality Management (TQM), as the movement was later labeled, helped transform Japanese industry into the economic powerhouse it is today. Many American companies have since followed Japan's lead. Total Quality Management continues to grow and evolve as organizational researchers explore its effects, as firms refine its procedures, and as service industries, such as hospitals, museums, and hotel chains adapt its principles to meet their needs.

The philosophy and tools of Total Quality Management are not a magic potion able to turn a poorly-run, noncompetitive organization into one that operates with awe-inspiring efficiency and effectiveness, but the fact is that TQM has made a difference in organizations around the world. It cannot be dismissed as another management fad. It is not academic whimsy. It is too well-grounded in a scientific approach to problem solving, and it has been tested, scrutinized, and revised in thousands of organizations over a period of more than three decades. Bottom line: It works.

While teaching TQM in my graduate business classes and conducting my own research for this book, I decided to engage in a parallel line of inquiry. People are always looking for shortcuts. They want to take what works in one situation and apply it, with little thoughtful alteration, to their own situation. We are always looking for these "boilerplate" solutions. With this in mind, I concluded that it would be a mistake to merely describe how Deming or Juran's ideas might apply to a college or university. The tendency would be to plug and crank in typical boilerplate fashion. Instead, I decided to examine the nature of quality on college campuses by listening to administrators and professors. My idea was to explore the culture of quality by asking a series of questions. What does quality mean to you? How does your institution or program pursue quality? Can quality be managed? I call this my "Iron Rooster Methodology."

Paul Theroux spent a year traveling around China on trains and then reported his recollections in a wonderful travelog, *Riding the Iron Rooster*. His descriptions of the country and its people follow in the noble tradition of other oral historians such as Studs Terkel. At some point in his book, Theroux is asked how he assembled his stories. He reluctantly offers his secret strategy—"Grin like a dog and wander aimlessly." My "aimless" wanderings were not quite so exotic. No Mandarin hideaways, no sojourns to Outer Mongolia. My one hundred-odd interviewees were mostly of the convenience-sample variety, as I wandered with no conscious plan to choose "quality" schools or interview "exceptional" administrators. Nonetheless, I was thoroughly enlightened by: Joseph Fink, the president of Dominican College, while we walked along the streets of San Rafael on a sunny Friday afternoon; the University of Chicago's Norman Bradburn as we looked out over the quadrangle from his campus office; Jonathan Fife, of the ERIC Clearinghouse and George Washington University, while we enjoyed a luncheon omelette together at an AAHE meeting; Paula

Goldsmid, the dean of the faculty at Scripps College at the time, as her cat kept a watchful eye on me from its box in the corner of the office; and Bert Simon, the head of the Physician Assistant Program at St. Francis College as we shared a pizza at "Wally's" across the street from the school's Loretto, Pennsylvania campus.

My conclusion is that quality can be actively and aggressively managed into our colleges and universities. I am also convinced that accrediting agencies, program reviews, standing committees, control-minded governing boards, and the occasional well-intentioned task force will never be able to do it. Most of these traditional quality-causing mechanisms view quality from an inspection perspective. "Inspecting in" quality never worked in industry (as many American companies continue to find out), and it isn't the model that will help us successfully manage our higher education institutions in the year 2000 and beyond. What I discovered in my wanderings was that while quality management was alive on many college campuses, its occurrence was almost totally serendipitous. In some instances, there was an inspired leader with a distinctive vision. Other times there was small group of faculty members who spent extraordinary amounts of time asking the tough questions: What are we trying to accomplish? How can we measure the effect we're having? Is there a way to improve what we are doing? Quality was happening in fits and spurts, in isolated programs tucked away in the corner of a campus. What institutions were and are lacking is a comprehensive or systematic approach to quality. That is where the philosophy and tools of quality management can be useful. *Yes, there is a better way to manage higher education.*

The first chapter begins with a discussion of the importance of quality in three different types of organizations: a university, a hospital, and an automobile manufacturer. These examples illustrate the common opportunities that quality presents across a broad range of organizations. A brief description of the history of the quality movement follows, while the remainder of the chapter is devoted to an enumeration of the basic principles that underlie the management of quality.

Chapter 2 develops the argument that the strategic management of quality is a viable option for academic administrators. Four short case studies of higher education institutions are presented to illustrate the kind of approaches and planning that are beginning to occur on our campuses.

The third chapter shifts gears. This chapter, and the next five, merge the philosophy and tools of strategic quality management from industry with the thoughts of campus administrators. The approach is not an attempt to adapt industry ideas to higher education but to appreciate the specialness of a college or university while at the same time avoiding any boilerplate generalities. Each chapter examines a different quality opportunity: satisfying the customer; choosing distinctiveness; attending to process improvement; involving everyone in quality improvement; nurturing human resources; and under-standing the cost of "un-quality."

The final two chapters deserve more explanation. One of the most troubling things I discovered in researching the management of quality was the lack of appreciation for implementation issues. In example after example this "new approach to management" struggled not because of a fatal flaw in logic but because of a lack of attention to integration and institutionalization. We are talking about a "thought revolution" that challenges the *status quo*. No matter how pleasing the revolution may sound, there will always be individu-als married to the old regime. There will always be norms, policies, proce-dures, and a non-conscious ideology that defy change. Chapter 9 is concerned with the creation of a culture in which the pursuit of quality becomes the standard—"the way we work around here." It counsels both patience and persistence.

Finally, I have always been concerned by higher education's inability (or unwillingness) to communicate quality to its various publics. We expect others to appreciate our special calling: students should eagerly flock to register; legislators should willingly fund our programs; and agencies, foundations, and corporations should line up to invest in our research and creative endeavors. If quality is really an organizational goal then we need to be able to articulate how well we are doing. Chapter 10 describes how the management philosophy and tools outlined in this book can help move quality from the whispy notions of excellence that fill the pages of recruiting brochures to sharply-defined mea-sures that can shape the perceptions of our constituencies.

My sincere thanks to all those individuals on college campuses who let me wander aimlessly into their lives. Their common sense ideas about quality are what made this book exciting to write. A warm and special thank you to Bert Simon at St. Francis College. My resolve to complete this book was strengthened considerably after I talked with him that day at Wally's. I am sure that Bert never heard of Total Quality Management and was unfamiliar with the writings of the renowned Messrs. Deming and Juran. Nonetheless, many of Bert's everyday efforts to improve the quality of his Physician Assistant program were TQM textbook examples. I knew after the two hours we spent together that this book, and the ideas that I wanted to present, could be written. To Bert and the others, thank you for your voices.

I want to acknowledge the support of Macmillan Reference Division president and publisher Philip Friedman. He, along with the able assistance of Michael Sander and Jennifer Black, made this book a reality. Their suggestions improved the manuscript tremendously as it went from the "I've got this idea for a book" stage to final production. I was also lucky enough to have a small group of friends—Trudy Banta, Ellen Chaffee, Casey Collett, and Larry

Sherr—who read and commented on draft chapters. They did the best they could with what I gave them, and I am grateful for their support, encouragement, and sugar-coated criticisms. Finally, I need to single out one person who labored over my ill-constructed sentences and faulty reasoning with special care. Gisela Voss is a great editor, a sharp woman, and, most importantly, a dear friend. Thank you one and all.

Daniel T. Seymour
Los Angeles, California

1

The Incline of Quality

Bruce Gildseth has been accumulating frequent flier mileage lately. As the vice chancellor for Academic Support and Student Life at the University of Minnesota, Duluth, Gildseth goes to the same meetings and conventions attended by his colleagues. But he has also been making side trips to meet with people at Milliken & Co., 3M, and the Hospital Corporation of America (HCA). It's part of his new job description. About a year ago, the university's chancellor, Lawrence Ianni, declared that his senior administrative cabinet would become the institution's Quality Steering Committee and that the Student Life Division would launch a twelve-month pilot project to improve quality. "I knew that we had to start looking at quality in a different way," says Gildseth. "Not from my perspective, but from the perspective of someone who uses our services. So I decided to talk with people who were known for delivering quality service." The result has been an education for him, his staff, and the members of the chancellor's cabinet as they work to incorporate ideas from Milliken & Co. with lessons learned in the Student Life project into a university-wide, five-year quality improvement plan. "We're not trying for a quick fix," he concludes. "We're committed to changing the way we look at quality on this campus."

The small classroom at HCA Bayonet Point/Hudson Medical Center was nearly filled to capacity. There were some lab technicians, a group of nurses, people from the business office, others from the pharmacy section, and even a contingent from housekeeping. The occasion was one of the hospital's recent Presidential Review sessions. After a few opening remarks, J. Daniel Miller, the hospital's chief executive officer, began the session by inviting a business office worker to address the group. This employee talked about her attempts to use a new Medicare report throughout the office. She thought the report would save hun-

1

dreds of staff-hours in the future, so she worked with a team of people to analyze the situation, test a new procedure, and then start implementing it. The results looked good. They were thinking about changing a few of the steps. Experimenting a bit. Besides that, she said, everything was right on target. A question and answer period followed, then came another speaker. These sessions have been going on just about every six weeks since May 1990. Why? Because as Miller points out, "The public is clearly demanding that healthcare organizations improve clinical quality in a way that demonstrates value. Our employees know their work. They are closest to the customer, they know the problems. We have to empower them to act. That's the only way we are really going to improve quality around here."

John Grettenberg, Cadillac's general manager, was beaming as he opened his speech: "Ladies and gentlemen, I am extremely proud to be standing at the end of this long line of Cadillacs in our Detroit-Hamtramck Assembly Center to advise you of a historic announcement being made right now by President George Bush. For the first time since its inception, an automobile has been named recipient of the U.S. Department of Commerce Malcolm Baldrige National Quality Award. And *it's us. Cadillac.*" The award that caused Grettenberg's exuberance was established by Congress in 1987 to promote national awareness about the importance of improving quality, and to recognize the quality achievements of U.S. companies. Firms applying for the award must submit a seventy-five-page application which is actually a detailed examination of what their company is all about. For those passing the original screening, on-site visits are conducted by an independent board of examiners. In 1989 Cadillac was a finalist in the manufacturing category. They vowed to redouble their efforts and commitment to quality. Their determination paid off the very next year. The reward? It's fourteen inches high, weighing in at twenty pounds and bearing the seal of the president of the United States. But as Grettenberg told his workers on the assembly line in October, "This is the highest recognition for quality in our country, and, if you will, 'The National Stamp of Approval' for our unwaivering focus on the customer, the processes required to continually improve, and adherence to the simple fact that nothing can be more important than providing a quality product, service, and ownership experience."

Why has "quality" moved to the front burner in these organizations? Certainly every enterprise—football teams, utility companies, symphony orchestras—will tell you that it pursues excellence. Each one is dedicated to providing superior products or performances. No one ever says, "Well, we are committed to mediocrity around here. We strive to be as average as we possibly can." So what makes the University of Minnesota, Duluth, HCA Bayonet Point/Hudson Medical Center, and Cadillac unique? These organizations think and act differently when it comes to quality. They aren't just *talking* quality, they are *doing* quality. It is not something that is put on letterhead, it is something that is *caused* on a daily basis. Quality is being managed into operations. Attitudes are different as well. There is a sense of purpose, urgency, and excitement. People in these organizations have an individual stake in making quality products and services. Quality is part of their job descriptions. It is real to them.

The incline of quality in these organizations is anything but circumstantial. In fact, there are two distinct factors that are fueling the flames of the quality movement. The first factor is "motivation." No organization changes its operating philosophy and procedures willfully. There need to be forces, usually external, that demand a new approach or different strategies. The second factor is "means." Even with an incentive to change, there must be mechanisms or methods that can be applied to the situation. Motivation without means creates fear and denial. Along with knowing that "something must be done," there is the paralysis that comes from walking down a dark alley, or taking a blind step off a ledge. In contrast, means without motivation is a ho-hummer, evoking all the rhetoric of "don't rock the boat" and "why bother."

Let me leave the discussion of means for later in the chapter and expand upon the idea of the motivation for an incline of quality in today's organizations. I believe there are essentially four motivating forces: (1) survival in an increasingly competitive environment; (2) the escalation of the costs of doing business; (3) a trend to make organizations more accountable for their actions and outcomes; and (4) a blurring of the distinction between "products" and "services."

Perhaps the most obvious motivation prompting the incline of quality is that *survival* is the first order of business for any organization. More than a few colleges in this country can talk to you about survival—they are struggling to do just that. It is the "Age of Consumerism" in higher education, a buyer's market. For example, every study or survey in higher education that asks the question of college students, "Why did you choose this college?," evokes a similar response—good academic reputation or the quality of the faculty/institution. Consumers are searching for quality and the effects are all around us. Students apply to many more schools now than they did in the past. Once they've been accepted, they compare financial aid packages, facilities, and so on. Transfers are up as well. If one school doesn't deliver on its promises, students just pack up and move down the block. The result is an increasingly dynamic marketplace. Colleges and universities have hired public relations firms and enrollment managers to tell their quality story. Additionally, the newsstand issues of *U.S. News & World Report, Business Week,* and *Money* ranking colleges and universities have also helped foster a competitive atmosphere by comparing schools on the basis of quality indicators. Preliminary reports for the 1991–1992 academic year show some public institutions with application increases of 15 percent while many private schools are experiencing serious shortfalls—Drexel University projects a 20 percent decline in applications, University of Hartford down 16 percent, Villanova University receiving 11 percent fewer applications. "The consumer movement is moving into the college and university world with a lot of energy," comments Ernest Boyer, president of the Carnegie Foundation for the Advancement of Teaching. "My impression is that parents and students are more sophisticated and determined to get answers to questions rather than simply be in awe of the neatly manicured lawns or the record of the football team."[1] In such a competitive environment, "quality" is a discriminating feature of the healthy survivors.

The health care industry has witnessed a similar tumult in recent years. Gone are the placid days of the local or regional hospital, quietly serving the needs of the community—enter Health Maintenance Organizations (HMOs) and Preferred Provider Organizations (PPOs). Each is grabbing for a share of the $600-billion-a-year market. "Quality of care," according to health care professionals, is prompting doctor-shopping, complaints, and disenrollment from plans. Additionally, much like with higher education, rankings and consumer-related data have begun to make their way into the media. Morbidity rates and the percentage of cesarean sections performed are now among the most common figures made available to the public. Again, quality is a deciding factor in determining which facilities flourish and which flounder.

And then there is Cadillac's world. As the international automobile industry enters the 1990s, the Japanese have established a viselike competitive grip over Detroit's auto makers. More than a decade ago, the Japanese began to give customers what they wanted most—reliability. According to J.D. Power & Associates surveys (Initial Quality Survey and the Vehicle Dependability Index), the Japanese consistently produce cars that have fewer problems. United States automobile manufacturers are paying an awful price for their failure to close this quality gap as Nissans, Toyotas, and Hondas crowd our highways. The big three U.S. automakers are hemorrhaging money and the forecasts suggest that the United States-Japan trade deficit in automobiles will grow by 36 percent by 1993. The conclusion is obvious. If products are second-rate, customers will quickly turn to those that are first-rate. As one automotive analyst stated, "We are improving but so is the competition; in fact, we may just be losing the war."

Quality has become a universal criterion in a competitive environment. It is now the definitive measuring stick by which comparisons—Villanova versus Penn State, Toyota versus Buick—are made. Those organizations that have made quality their most important goal will live to fight another day. Those that haven't chosen quality as their goal face an uncertain future.

Another motivation that has affected the role of quality in organizations has to do with costs. Let's use the health care industry as the touchstone. A doctor's bill used to be something that you (either as an individual or your insurance company) just paid—quality of care was what mattered. But health spending now accounts for an unprecedented 11.6 cents of each dollar's worth of goods and services produced by the U.S. economy. Spending per person—$1,059 in 1980—reached $2,354 last year. Throughout the 1980s, therefore, cost containment became a critical public policy objective. Quality of care is not a stand-alone concept any longer. Implicit in the concept of quality of care is the idea that services should be provided in a cost-efficient and cost-effective manner, because unnecessary, excessive, or inappropriate services waste the patient's resources and do not contribute to the patient's well-being. The frustration and concern that everyone feels are evident in the words of Carl Schramm, the president of the Health Insurance Association of America: "There is no firm evidence that Americans are healthier than a decade ago, although they are spending vastly more for health care."[2]

Colleges and universities are also having to defend quality vis-à-vis the increasing cost of higher education. In fact, higher education institutions risk becoming the "hospitals of the 1990s" with regard to cost containment. Tuition increases rose faster than the Consumer Price Index throughout the 1980s. Journal articles, books, conferences, and symposiums have analyzed, examined, inspected, and investigated the situation. Scarcely an issue of the *Chronicle of Higher Education* goes by without a story about tuition increases or how a particular institution is freezing vacancies or evaluating sick leave policies in order to contain costs. The flip side to cost concerns is the notion of value to the student—or "What am I getting for my buck?" Increasingly, there is a stridency in the tone of the question that seems to be paralleling the health care situation. Aims McGuinness, the director of higher education policy at the Education Commission of the States, puts the situation into perspective when he states, "When there are pressures for tuition increases, students are going to come down with a vengeance about [the quality of] what they are getting [for their money]."[3]

In addition to competition and costs, a third force driving the quality movement is accountability. Certainly the performance of an automobile manufacturer's management is directly accountable to its board and stockholders. This bottom-line orientation is nothing new in the business world. But in recent years, health care and higher education—parts of the service industry—have faced an increasingly vocal "show me" attitude from their overseers and constituents. As organizations staffed with autonomous professionals, they have traditionally relied upon physicians and professors to define, measure, and deliver a quality health care or educational service. No more. In response to dwindling confidence in these organizations' ability to provide quality services at a reasonable cost, there has been a broad-sweeping attempt to increase external control through legislation, investigation, and policy mandates.

In the health field, everyone wants a piece of the "quality assurance" action. In addition to hospitals' and HMOs' own programs, state governments exercise licensure authority over individual practitioners and health care institutions, and the federal government imposes conditions of participation for facilities wishing to qualify for reimbursement through Medicaid and Medicare. Private quality-certifying organizations, such as the Joint Commission on Accreditation of Healthcare Organizations, have instituted external review and certification standards. These agencies are literally stumbling all over each other to establish jurisdictional control by developing and imposing quality standards and data requirements.

In the higher education arena, concerns over the decline of student performances in standardized exams (e.g., the Graduate Record Exam) and professional licensing exams (e.g., state bar exams), the dilution of the liberal arts, and the steady climb of tuition, have all called into question the value of a college degree. The result has been an ambitious set of activities and mandates: a majority of the states have convened blue ribbon commissions to examine various higher education issues (e.g., Rhode Island's Blue Ribbon Commission on productivity), legislators have passed bills (e.g., the Colorado Higher Education Accountability Act), and coordinating and governing boards have greatly expanded their staffs in order to quench their seemingly never-ending thirst for institutional data. In addition to these issues, the key quality assurance device to emerge in higher education has been the assessment movement. Most states have undertaken comprehensive programs of assessment based upon the belief stated in the 1986 National Governors' Association report that assessment would be the "central strategy for improving the quality of undergraduate education." The call to arms has been effective. The American Association for Higher Education's (AAHE) Annual Assessment Forum draws standing-room-only crowds, and regional and disciplinary accrediting associations are scrambling to develop and include student outcomes measures and "value-added" criteria in their evaluation procedures.

No one should be under the illusion that any of these external bodies—stockholders, federal agencies, state governments, accrediting agencies, or governing boards—are being driven by selflessness. They operate largely on the basis of self-interest, whether that is politics, personal frustration, well-meaning oversight, or self-aggrandizement. But regardless of the intent, the plain fact is that the accountability push has been a light switch that has caused many organizations to illuminate their concern for quality.

A final factor that seems to be adding to organizations' focus on quality is a subtle but inexorable shift in how they pursue quality. Historically, we have made hard distinctions between organization types: profit versus non-profit, product versus service. But more recently there has been a realization that the consumer does not think in terms of categories and types. Regardless of whether they are dealing with a college, a hospital, an automobile dealer, or the local hardware store, people want their needs met—*all of their needs*.

Quality is more than making a good car, performing a successful appendectomy, or receiving a glowing accreditation review. Take an automobile, for example. American car companies have found out through their market research programs that even if they build the highest quality product in the world, the customer may still not be satisfied. As one of Ford's executives recently stated: "When we got down to specifics, we discovered that roughly 60% of our customers' satisfaction with our products could be attributed to the vehicles themselves—their quality, reliability, ride, fuel economy and so on. The remaining 40% of how well customers were satisfied depended on how they were treated during the sales and service experience at the dealership."[4] The point, of course, is that satisfying the customer's technical requirements is simply a prerequisite to staying in business. The consumer wants more, much more.

The health care industry has seen a similar broadening of the notion of quality. For years, the principal dimension of the quality of care was also "technical"—or how well the science and technology of medicine were applied to diagnosing and treating patients' problems. It has been a notion of quality with which the health care provider was most comfortable. More recently hospitals and health care providers have begun to understand, and devote energy and resources to, a second dimension of quality—"interpersonal" quality. Unlike technical quality, interpersonal quality depends on how well each patient's personal needs are accommodated. As an example, "quality" may depend on whether the physician communicates well with the patient and whether the physician understands how much the patient wants to participate in decisions about his or her care.

Colleges and universities also tend to define quality in their own, technical terms: the number of terminally qualified professors on the faculty, the size of the library holdings, and securing and maintaining good standing with the appropriate accrediting associations. These are quite literally the nuts and bolts of education, not unlike the fuel economy of an automobile or the procedures for treating a broken leg. But it has become evident that students, the primary customers of the institution, need and want more than library books and an impressive set of faculty degrees enumerated at the end of the college catalog. A front-page story in the *Chronicle of Higher Education,* "Undergraduates at Large Universities Found to Be Increasingly Dissatisfied," is a notable example of the need to develop a service orientation on our college campuses. A disenchanted University of Texas at Austin sophomore perhaps said it best: "Here, it's not what the system can do for you, but what you can do to make the system work for you. You have to fight it."[5] Students want "quality" to extend beyond the size of the endowment or the research credentials of senior faculty in a way that affects their daily lives as education consumers.

Manufacturers and non-profit companies are no longer separate entities. Everyone, including colleges and universities, is in the same business—

the service business. And everyone needs to have an expanded notion of quality that goes beyond fulfilling the technical requirements of the customer.

Competition, costs, accountability, and a service orientation, then, are the driving forces—the motivation—behind the incline of quality across a broad set of organizations. They share a common interest in the quality movement. The status quo has been challenged. Conditions have changed. Demands are different. The bar is being raised to a new standard with greater expectations and an increasing unwillingness to tolerate ordinary performances. The motivation is now clear. Either respond to the call for quality or step aside because others will be more than happy to move to the front of the line.

———————◆———————

As I have already pointed out, *motivation* is not sufficient to generate change. The *means* must also be present. An alternative pathway needs to exist so that a conscious choice can be made—the status quo versus something else. That "something else," in the case of the University of Minnesota, Duluth, HCA Bayonet Point/Hudson Medical Center, and Cadillac, is "strategic quality management." It is a management philosophy and structural system born out of American industry, exported to Japan after World War II, and then reintroduced into this country more than a decade ago. David Garvin traces the history of this trans-Pacific evolution in his book *Managing Quality*. He contends that there have been four major quality eras, starting with "inspection" and moving to "strategic quality management" (see Table 1.1).

Prior to the Industrial Revolution, quality was viewed as the natural result of the application of individual skills of an artisan or skilled crafter. But with the advent of mass production and the need for interchangeable parts, the responsibility for quality shifted to another individual who stood at the end of the production line—the inspector. "Inspection" was primarily concerned with "detecting defects" and involved a simple set of activities such as counting, grading, and repairing. The era of "statistical quality control" began in 1931 with the work of W.A. Shewhart, a statistician at Bell Telephone Laboratories. Shewhart was the first to recognize that variability in industry could be understood using the principles of probability and statistics. He observed that no two parts were likely to be manufactured to exactly the same specifications. Raw materials, operator skills, and equipment would all vary to a degree. From a manager's point of view, therefore, the issue was no longer whether variation existed but whether the variation was inherent in the production process (common cause) or whether it could be assigned to something specific (special cause). This distinction enabled the people at Bell Telephone to question whether the inspection of 100 percent of the output of a process was an efficient way of sorting good products from bad. Instead of "inspecting in" quality after a unit had been fully assembled, the idea was to "control in" quality by using sampling and statistical techniques (e.g., the

TABLE 1.1 The Four Major Quality Eras

Identifying Characteristics	Inspection (Pre 1930s)	Statistical Quality Control (1930s–1950s)	Quality Assurance (1950s–1980s)	Strategic Quality Management (1980s–1990s)
Primary concern View of quality	detection a problem to be solved	control a problem to be solved	coordination a problem to be solved, but one that is attacked proactively	strategic impact a competitive opportunity
Emphasis	product uniformity	product uniformity with reduced inspection	the entire production chain, and the contribution of all functional groups, to preventing quality failures	the market and consumer needs
Methods	gauging and measurement	statistical tools and techniques	programs and systems	strategic planning, goalsetting, and mobilizing the organization
Who has responsibility for quality	the inspection department	the manufacturing and engineering departments	all departments, although top management is only peripherally involved	everyone in the organization, with top management exercising strong leadership
Orientation and approach	"inspects in" quality	"controls in" quality	"builds in" quality	"manages in" quality

Source: From *MANAGING QUALITY: The Strategic and Competitive Edge* by David A. Garvin. Copyright © 1988 by David Garvin. p. 37. Reprinted by permission of The Free Press, a Division of Macmillan, Inc.

process control chart). As Garvin points out, "These breakthroughs were instrumental in improving the quality of telephone equipment and service. Inspection costs fell, quality improved, and with fewer defects to correct, employees became more productive."[6]

Statistical quality control became recognized as a discipline during the 1940s and 1950s. The War Department established a Quality Control section, staffed largely by statisticians from Bell Laboratories, to increase the quality of arms and ammunitions for the war effort. Colleges and universities began teaching courses on the subject and the American Society for Quality Control (ASQC) was formed in 1945. But the thrust of quality control was still primarily statistical and narrowly confined to manufacturing. The new era, "quality assurance," changed all that. The prevention of problems began to expand beyond statistics and the factory floor, to a management function. Three individuals were especially influential in leading this transformation: Joseph Juran, Philip Crosby, and W. Edwards Deming. Juran was a colleague of Shewhart's at Bell Labs. His initial contribution, highlighted in his *Quality Control Handbook* (1951), was to show that the *entire* production chain—from new product design to the marketing function—had an effect on quality. He was also the first to explore fully the planning function and the economics of quality. For example, Juran suggested that the costs of achieving a specific level of quality could be divided into avoidable and unavoidable costs. Avoidable costs were the expenses related to defects—scrapped materials, the time and effort to repair mistakes, complaint processing, and losses resulting from dissatisfied customers. Unavoidable costs were the quality control initiatives associated with preventing defects from happening in the first place.

Philip Crosby, corporate vice president of IT&T for almost fifteen years, also helped broaden the scope of the quality movement. He advocated that "managers of any operation or function can take practical, non-technical steps to improve quality" and mapped out a quality improvement program and a Quality Management Maturity Grid in his popular 1979 book, *Quality Is Free.* Crosby also popularized the notion of zero defects (ZD) which suggested that quality was as much a part of expectations as it was anything else. According to Crosby, in addition to lack of knowledge and lack of proper facilities, a third common cause of worker error was lack of attention. The overriding goal of zero defects, then, was to promote a constant, conscious desire to do a job right the first time.

Finally, there was W. Edwards Deming, who began his career with the Department of Agriculture in the 1920s. An advocate of Shewhart's work in statistical process control, Deming went on to bring a new sampling program to the Census Bureau in 1940. Deming's real influence, however, didn't begin until he was asked to visit with the Union of Japanese Scientists and Engineers as a private consultant in 1950. Mary Walton, the author of *The Deming Management Method,* described Deming's first visit with the Union group:

The situation was desperate. Japan could not grow enough food to feed its people. It was clear that they needed to export goods for money to buy food. But not only had Japan lost traditional markets like China and Manchuria due to the war, but the industrial production that did exist was almost worse than none at all because it had given Japan what Dr. Deming would call a "negative net worth." MADE IN JAPAN stamped on a piece of merchandise was a synonym for junk.[7]

Deming's initial set of lectures on statistical techniques was delivered to Japanese businessmen who had nothing to lose. His charts and checklists were quickly adopted by the technical people. But more important, the message that "building in" quality was more than a set of statistical tools also began to hit home with the management of most of Japan's largest companies. He encouraged the Japanese to adopt a systematic approach to problem solving and, along with Juran, continued to broaden the message to include consumer research, goal-setting, and organizational issues. The Japanese not only listened, they learned. They also adopted, innovated, and produced a few of their own quality gurus. The quality assurance era flourished in Japan.

While Garvin suggests that the fourth quality era, "strategic quality management," cannot be dated precisely, I would contend that its origins have a *very* specific time and place—9:30 P.M., June 24, 1980, on NBC. Hosted by Lloyd Dobbins, American audiences for the first time got a real glimpse of Deming's quality message in a documentary entitled "If Japan Can ... Why Can't We?" Deming explained that by increasing quality, a company reduced scrap and rework, thereby decreasing costs and increasing productivity. On the broadcast he hammered away with the same message that he had been preaching for decades—*quality is the most highly leveraged investment an organization can make and there is a system for making it happen.* Mary Walton described the response to the message he delivered that night:

> The next day, the telephone rang relentlessly in Dr. Deming's basement office. "We were bombarded with calls," recalled Cecelia Kilian [Deming's secretary]. "It was a nightmare." Many of the callers sounded desperate. "They have to see him tomorrow, or yesterday, or their whole company will collapse."[8]

America's leadership in quality had been almost imperceptibly eroding for years. While U.S. companies were showing an interest in quality, foreign competitors were making it a religion. From motorcycles to microwaves, from pianos to premium beer, consumers were turning their backs on U.S.-manufactured products. A new standard had been set. The *motivation* to respond had finally become clear and, just as important, Deming's message gave many the hope that there was also a readily available *means*.

Unfortunately, as is often the case, many wanted a quick fix. Junkets to Japan were formed. Consulting practices blossomed overnight. Of course, off-the-shelf versions of Japanese quality assurance programs were not what was needed. What we needed, and what eventually began to evolve, was the next era in the quality movement. Strategic quality management, as described by Garvin, acknowledges the role of statistical analysis and other quality control and quality assurance advances. But these earlier eras carried a certain set of assumptions that were limiting the way organizations viewed quality. For example, quality was still perceived in a negative light—something that could damage a company if ignored. The main objective, therefore, was to rely on a specific set of individuals (i.e., a quality department) to prevent defects. What began to emerge was a perspective on quality that was a good deal more robust, more comprehensive, and, in effect, more meaningful to management than any of the earlier practices. Specifically, for the first time, quality was perceived to be a leadership function that could be "managed in" to the daily affairs of an organization. Other departures also began to emerge. Quality was being included in the strategic planning process and in financial planning—linking it directly to profitability. The definition of quality also underwent a transformation from an emphasis on fixed, internal standards to consideration of quality from the customer's point of view. And a final distinction: Quality could be a powerful competitive weapon.

This final broadening of the quality concept ensured that the message could jump beyond manufacturing firms such as Hewlett-Packard, Motorola, and Ford to insurance companies, utilities, hospitals, city governments, and colleges and universities. Hewlett-Packard had their total quality control (TQC) program called *Quest for Total Quality* and now The Paul Revere Insurance company has its *Quality Has Value* approach. Motorola had its *Six Sigma* defect-reduction strategy and now, Florida Power & Light has its wonderfully successful *Quality Improvement Program* (QIP). Ford developed its *Total Quality Excellence* program and The University of North Dakota System has recently initiated its own total quality management (TQM) plan. Quality, it seems, has evolved from a narrow set of shop floor statistical tools to a management philosophy and structural system that has adapted well to organizations of all types and sizes.

The University of Minnesota, Duluth, HCA Bayonet Point/Hudson Medical Center, and Cadillac had the *motivation* to change. Each was faced with concerns over competition, costs, accountability, and the increasingly vocal needs of its customers. What was lacking was a *means* to respond to the challenge. The means that they chose, and are continuing to choose every day, is the *strategic management of quality*.

◆

Strategic quality management—TQC, QIP, TQM, or any of the other dozen titles or acronyms used to describe the principles that have evolved from Shewhart's early work on statistical quality control—is an integrative concept. While each of the leading advocates has his own notions—Deming has "fourteen points and seven deadly diseases," Juran has the "quality trilogy," and Crosby has the "absolutes of quality management"—there is still more agreement than disagreement among the three. Any concept that can be successfully adapted to the operations of a car company, a hospital, and a college must have a strong set of well-defined underlying principles. These principles, or basic themes, can be divided into three groups: philosophy, management, and tools. The following section includes a series of "general philosophical principles."

Quality is meeting or exceeding customer needs.

There is an old saw around college campuses that goes, "If it weren't for the students, this would be a great place to work." It is an attitude that is prevalent in the way that many people, in many organizations, do their jobs. Everyone has experienced the store clerk, the insurance adjuster, or the government bureaucrat who seems to be doing you a favor by just acknowledging your presence. You want to scream, "I pay your taxes!" or "Can I get a little attention around here?"

The Quality philosophy follows a simple rule: The first priority of an enterprise and everyone in it must be knowing and satisfying the customer. This is not sloganeering; it is common sense. In a competitive environment, if you don't satisfy the customer, someone else will. The Japanese have 40 percent of the car market in California because they build something that the car buyer wants. They understand that the customer—not design engineers or executives—defines quality. They gain this understanding through their ability to listen. Unfortunately, organizations often don't operate this way. In fact, many organizations do not have the foggiest idea what happens to their product or their service once it leaves their hands. Just build it, box it, and ship it—and, if you're lucky, someone will pay money for it.

Quality is also understanding who your customers are *inside* the organization. Everyone produces things for someone else's consumption. We analyze data and pass the material along. We make widgets and send them down the line. We produce reports and disseminate the results. In every case there is a person at the other end of that transaction. That's a customer. You had better be talking with that person—often. Quality is what *he or she* needs and wants, not what *you* think is needed or what's convenient for you to deliver. The logic is, then, that every person in an organization is both a producer and a consumer. In your role as a consumer, wouldn't you like the producer to present you with a perfect product or service? Would that make your job easier—more enjoyable, more rewarding? Now picture a whole series of need-satisfying producer/consumer linkages throughout your organization. That's quality.

Quality is everyone's job.

Placing the customer on a pedestal creates a real problem for most organizations. Many people in organizations, especially front-line people, have a pretty good idea of what the customer needs and wants because they hear about it almost daily—praises when things go right and complaints when they don't. These people want to do a good job. They want to be responsive. They even know what has to be done in most cases. But they are caught between the desire to satisfy the customer and systems that make it impossible. Most systems are based upon control. This "control mentality" is characterized by the person *up* the chain of command who thinks that she or he is being paid to issue orders to those *down* the chain of command. The responsibility for quality resides in the manager's office at the end of the hall. Unfortunately, more often than not, the person in the office is too far removed from the customer to know what really matters. By the time he or she has responded to the obligatory "What do you want me to do?" question from the front-line, the timely resolution of a customer-satisfying moment has passed.

I like the interpretation of Robert Galvin, Motorola's chairman of the board. He talks about quality as being "very first person." He suggests that an organization needs to be saturated with people, from the chair down to the night shift janitor, who speak about quality in terms of "I dids."[9] The idea is that quality is not a functional or departmental responsibility, it's an organizational goal. It shouldn't be pigeonholed or "assigned" to a specific person or area. Quality is everyone and everything within an organization.

Quality is continuous improvement.

After Xerox Corporation won the 1989 Malcolm Baldrige National Quality Award, it ran full-page ads in newspapers across the country praising and thanking its own employees . . . "the real winners of this award—TEAM XEROX." Yet the most important "quality" message in the ad was a quote from David Kearns, Xerox's chairman and CEO. It read: "In the race for quality there is no finish line."

Kearns was reinforcing an important point at the very heart of the quality philosophy. Quality is not a place or a prize. Just the idea that you have finally "made it"—whether that means gaining accreditation for an academic program or reducing defects to only three hundred per one million parts—is unhealthy. Quality is an eternal struggle. "Good enough" is simply not good enough. There is always a better way, a simpler approach, a more elegant solution. The challenge is to develop an organizational culture in which people accept the notion that change—or striving—must be constant. It is a culture that is always asking itself, "Why do we do things like that?" and "Is this the best we can do?" The idea is not unlike the geometry exercise of halving the distance between a curve and a straight line. By cutting the distance in half, the curve gets closer to the line. No matter how far out you extend the curve and the line, they never meet. But you can always get closer. Or, in our case, you can always improve the quality of any product or any service. Always.

Quality is leadership.

Think of an organization as a collection of arrows. If the arrows are generally pointing in one direction, their effect is intensified and the organization begins to move in that direction. Call it synergy or alignment. If as is true in most organizations, the arrows are pointed in somewhat random fashion, the net effect is a lack of motion.

There is no substitute for leadership when it comes to quality. The leader of an organization must cause the arrows to align. No one else can do it. The job cannot be assigned or assumed by someone else. The leadership must build a strong consensus regarding quality and take every opportunity to reinforce that consensus. Quality must be entrenched in the rhetoric of the leadership—in speeches, in vision statements, in organizational goals. Most importantly, the quest for quality must be given meaning through actions. The Hospital Corporation of America, of which HCA Bayonet Point/Hudson Medical Center is a member, learned this lesson early in its pursuit of quality. The nation's largest hospital chain methodically trained hundreds of hospital executives—both on-site and at its headquarters in Nashville, Tennessee— with moderate success. But it wasn't until headquarters changed the ground rules that things really took off. The new procedure was as follows: "Only after a CEO and his direct reports have attended the Nashville sessions will the HCA Quality Resources Group in headquarters dispatch trainers to do on-site training in hospitals, and then only when the CEO agrees to teach part of the course."[10] The CEO, in the new arrangement, was making a statement. She or he was saying, "Quality is the most important thing we can focus on. And to show you how much I believe that, I'm going to learn as much as I can about it, and I'm going to help teach you what I've learned." The CEO becomes due north, the compass arrows begin to align, and a unifying theme emerges.

I can now state what I consider to be the *philosophy of strategic quality management*.

> *The leadership of an organization must, by word and deed, convey the message that customer satisfaction, through a process of continually improving quality, is the responsibility of every member of the organization.*

Although a philosophy is a necessary (albeit insufficient) condition to bring about real change, there also needs to be a structural system for creating organization-wide participation in quality improvement. The next set of principles then, reflects the "critical management methods" needed to implement the new quality philosophy.

Quality is human resource development.

Think of Japan. What does it have going for itself? It has limited resources. No iron and no coal, no oil, and no copper. What it does have is people. The Japanese, as a culture, understand this and willingly make investments in this very human of natural resources. Strategic quality management, also, sees the people who populate an organization as its key resource—one that is a good investment.

Somehow management in the West has developed a negative view of organizational education and training. Here are some typical attitudes taken by management representatives: "It's for my people, not for me"; "We expect people to know how to do their job"; "If poor performances continue, we'll have to institute some training"; and "We can't afford the expense." This type of attitude is anything but productive. First, no one really has an education in the final analysis. Just because we hold a certain title—full professor, plant manager, chief surgeon—it doesn't mean that we can't improve the skills that we bring to our jobs. Second, no job is, or should be, a set routine. People need to be trained in ways that enable them to respond to new conditions. Third, education and training is not a punishment to be inflicted when things go wrong. It's giving people the skills that they need to prevent things from going wrong in the first place. And last, education is not an expense. It is an investment in the human capital of an organization. It empowers the people who breathe life into a quality philosophy. *People* identify customer needs. *People* implement continuous improvement. *People* make things happen. It is, or should be, their job. And so, it must become a part of the management function to help people learn their jobs and perform them better.

Quality is in the system.

Most of the things we do in organizations have to do with input-process-outcome. That's what we do. We change things. We convert, transform, or assemble. In foundries we convert iron into steel. In hospitals we transform sick people into healthy people. In factories we assemble little things into bigger things. In education we change people through a talent or skill development process. Of course, within each of these organizations there are literally hundreds of more detailed input-process-outcome systems in operation—the emergency room is a system, the accounts receivable office is a system, the kitchen is another system.

When things go wrong in systems quality suffers. We know this because outcomes are sometimes poor. Perhaps a cold meal gets sent back to the kitchen or a product breaks within sight of the store from where it was purchased. Researchers have concluded that approximately 85 percent of these quality-killing problems are caused by common variation, the remainder by special variation. What this means is that the vast majority of problems that occur are not assignable to a specific person or a specific event. Instead, the system that converts input into outcome is flawed. The system itself is either too complicated, redundant, or replete with technical errors. And it will continue to create problems at regular intervals, regardless of the person or persons placed within the system. Workers become frustrated laboring in a system that management has created and rules. The bottom line is that the common cause of variation is system problems, and management traditionally *owns* the system. If improved quality is the goal, then the way to achieve it is to ask the people who work *in the system* to join with management to work *on the system*.

Quality is fear reduction.

Working to improve a system is difficult. If a sales-person doesn't make his or her quota, it's easier to blame laziness or stupidity than it is to question the sales training procedures or the system designed to identify prospects. If a custodian doesn't maintain a building well, it takes less effort to conclude that he or she is lazy than it does to review staffing needs or to analyze the cleaning equipment and supplies. "Management by fear" is how we operate best.

At the very core of strategic quality management is the procedure of locating shortcomings or defects, scrutinizing them, tracing the sources of the problem, and making corrections. This critical procedure for continually improving systems has a few important preconditions. You cannot solve a problem unless you admit that it exists. You cannot improve a system unless you admit that there is room for improvement. In a "management by fear" environment people are afraid to point out problems for fear they will start an argument, or worse, be blamed for causing the problems. Moreover, so seldom is anything done to correct problems that there is little incentive to expose them. Why admit a mistake, why suggest a new way of doing something if the only thing that is going to happen is that you will be labeled as being incompetent or a loud mouth? Maintaining a low profile, hunkered down, is the only sane way to go. Or is it? In a keynote address, Thomas Murrin, the deputy secretary of commerce stated: "No quality movement in this country can succeed without the participatory efforts of its workers." He then added a sobering footnote—the average number of suggestions per employee per year in Japanese corporations is twenty-two. That's not management by fear, that's fearless management!

Quality is recognition and reward.

Recognizing or rewarding a good effort increases the probability that something good will happen again. Yes, this is Psychology 101 stuff. And, yes, it is essential to "managing in" quality. And, no, we don't do it. Recognition, gratitude and celebration are powerful concepts that need to be used by management to reinforce the principles of strategic quality management. Say a person goes out of their way, at some inconvenience, to satisfy a customer's needs. Maybe once, then a few more times. She or he really tries to make it a regular part of the job. But no one notices. Instead of commenting on a job well-done, a remark is made about spending too much time on "the Jones account." Exactly how long is a "customer-orientation" going to last in this kind of environment? Some organizations give awards for suggestions, others give cash prizes. Recognition can also come in the form of creating heroes; that is, telling stories about a coworker's great idea. Oftentimes a simple "thank you" is enough. The most important recognition or reward that management needs to consider is "implementation." Let me give you an example. Oregon State University concluded its pilot quality program in 1990 and then spent some time analyzing its findings. According to Ed Coate, OSU's vice president for Finance, perhaps the most significant finding was that once people began to see most of their ideas for improvement being implemented, they became enthusiastic. They had spent years working in a system that was broken. They always had a pretty good idea of how to fix it. Now they were being asked to speak out—*and someone was listening.*

This, then, is the operating approach that *management needs to take in pursuing quality:*

> *The management of an organization should make a conscious investment in helping people perform their jobs better by reducing their fears and rewarding their quality-causing efforts.*

These principles, combined with the philosophy that we have already discussed, create a powerful dynamic for influencing the way in which an organization conducts its business. Still there is one final grouping that needs to be described in order to complete the picture. These are "the tools of strategic quality management."

Quality is teamwork.

Every organization has its pigeonholing practices. These practices include inquiring secretaries who ask "Who may I say is calling?", rigidly-enforced reporting lines, offices with closed doors guarded by vigilant gatekeepers, and titles that designate our spot in the organizational structure. Our eyes are focused straight ahead, intent upon dealing with the issues that fall within our territorial wind tunnel. It is unfortunate that most quality problems aren't paying attention. If they were, they would divide themselves up, nice and neatly, so that they would fit into the little boxes that we have constructed.

In a hospital the anesthesiologists talk to the anesthesiologists. The nurses to nurses. Doctors to doctors. How can you improve the critical care unit in a hospital with these kinds of barriers? The same is true in a college, a bank, or a manufacturing plant. We speak about continuously improving the quality of a process by involving everyone. So we have to organize ourselves into teams of people who work *both in and on* these processes. This means building cross-functional relationships, giving up the power to control people, and working more as a facilitator and a coach. It also means having teams of people suggest new ways of simplifying systems and new ideas for preventing problems. There are benefits to using teams as a management tool that are apparent to even a nine-year-old. In a delightful book called *Real People, Real Work* by Lee Cheaney and Maury Cotter, Adam Cotter, Maury's nine-year-old son is asked by his mom why it's such a good idea to work together in teams. The following is what transpired:

> He pondered briefly, lying in his water bed, snuggling his old grey bear. Then he said, "Well, you can get done faster, because you are all working together." Bingo. "That's right, Adam," I said. "Can you think of any other reasons?" He thought again, and said, "You can do better. Because if you all work together, you should agree on what you're working on." Bingo. I asked, "Why is that good if you all agree?" He said, "Because if you all agree, there is a better chance that you are right." BINGO!![11]

Quality is measurement.

I listened to a speech delivered last year by Xerox's David Kearns. "We benchmark everything," he said. "There are hundreds of metrics that we measure. We measure how we do against the best in the world as part of our on-going quality improvement efforts." The logic here is quite simple. You can't improve a process unless you have hard evidence of how you're doing. There has to be a system that raises the little red flags or that let's you know you're on the right track. This measurement system can include customer satisfaction surveys, complaint data, the number of returns, or rejects. The system can generate numbers such as the cost per unit of an item, lost-days from injuries, or the time that it takes to process a customer's order. As Kearns states, there are hundreds of metrics. Every organization, and every process within that organization, has a different set of metrics that could, in effect, reveal how well it is doing. It is also important to understand that such measurement must be institutionalized into a management information *system*. There are no one-shot, "let's crunch some numbers," deals here. *Continuous* quality improvement requires a *continuous* flow of data.

There is a lot of fear in measurement and statistics. This fear exists because we have always treated it as a stick to beat people with—"That's the third month that John's been below quota," or "Professor Seymour, you do realize that promotion is highly unlikely with such atrocious student evaluations?" Assessment is a good example. In spite of its obvious benefits, assessment continues to be held with deep suspicion by many people on campus because of the "accountability" threat they feel is implied in assessment data. Measurement works best when the people working *within the system* contribute to deciding what gets measured. That's because measurement within the context of strategic quality management is feedback for improvement. It is not a mechanism to affix blame, a way to allocate merit pay, or a routine management task that just fills up dust-covered black binders. It is the basis for a knowledge-driven organization.

Quality is systematic problem-solving.

You can weigh yourself ten times a day. It's a way to know whether you're gaining or losing. It's a way to bench mark—an objective. Nevertheless, the information doesn't reduce the weight; you have to do that. That requires a procedure or a "system." Working systematically does not come naturally to most people. Problem solving is a messy business. So when faced with a series of problems, the tendency is to tackle the easiest problem first by opting for the most obvious solution. More often than not, such quick fixes tend to recur because the root cause of the problem is never addressed. The weight keeps coming back.

Strategic quality management requires a proactive approach to problem solving that can be learned and applied to process improvement. Perhaps the most basic approach involves a simple plan-do-check-act cycle. Take widget complaints. An organization is receiving numerous complaints about its widgets. One way to handle the problem is to employ a few more telephone operators and send out "replacement" widgets when the chorus of complaints gets too loud. Of course, this also requires hiring more widget makers to increase the production of widgets—both good and bad. Another way would be to develop baseline information about the complaints (e.g., type of complaints) as well as full understanding of the widget production process. The complaints can then be analyzed for common causes and a plan proposed to improve the widget-making process. The plan is then tested and data collected to see if widget defects decrease. If the number of defective widgets decreases the new process is implemented, if it doesn't, a different plan is proposed. Systematic problem-solving skills are needed throughout an organization like this to ensure that the goal is: getting good at making widgets, not getting good at fixing widgets.

A strong philosophy coupled with sound management practices are fundamental to this new quality era. Strategic quality management also *requires hands-on tools.*

People need to work together to generate objective data concerning the processes in which they work and then apply that wisdom to a systematic methodology for improvement.

EXPENSE & REIMBURSEMENT RECORD

PHONE CALLS

2200	10
2100	9
2000	8
1900	7
1800	6
1700	5
1600	4
1500	3
1400	2
1300	1
1200	12
1100	11
1000	10
0900	9

TO BE DONE TODAY (ACTION LIST)

0800	8
0700	7

APPOINTMENTS & SCHEDULED EVENTS

HOURS — NAME • PLACE • SUBJECT

FRIDAY

27

DECEMBER, 2002

4 Days Left

DECEMBER 2002

S	M	T	W	T	F	S
1	2	3	4	5	6	7
8	9	10	11	12	13	14
15	16	17	18	19	20	21
22	23	24	25	26	27	28
29	30	31				

JANUARY 2003

S	M	T	W	T	F	S
			1	2	3	4
5	6	7	8	9	10	11
12	13	14	15	16	17	18
19	20	21	22	23	24	25
26	27	28	29	30	31	

NOVEMBER 2002

S	M	T	W	T	F	S
					1	2
3	4	5	6	7	8	9
10	11	12	13	14	15	16
17	18	19	20	21	22	23
24	25	26	27	28	29	30

DIARY AND WORK RECORD

REF.	NAME OR PROJECT	DETAILS OF MEETINGS • AGREEMENTS • DECISIONS	TIME HRS. 1/10
1			
2			
3			
4			
5			
6			
7			
8			
9			
10			
11			
12			
13			
14			
15			
16			
17			
18			
19			
20			
21			
22			
23			
24			
25			
26			
27			
28			
29			
30			
31			
32			
33			
34			
35			
36			
37			
38			
39			
40			

26
THURSDAY
DECEMBER, 2002
360th Day
52nd Week
BOXING DAY (AUST, CAN, NZ, UK)

Taken together, the philosophy, management, and tools of this approach to quality provide a powerful set of *means* to respond to the *motivation* for change in organizations—including higher education.

◆

Many of the colleges and universities in this country have been around for one hundred years. Harvard University and the College of William and Mary for more than three hundred. And it is certainly reasonable to assume that the majority may be able to survive for at least another decade or two without the gracious help of a Deming, Juran, or Crosby, or insightful lessons from Xerox, Motorola, or the Ford Motor Company. That's not to say that there isn't pressure. Of course there is. In fact, I've described a few strong motivators like competition, accountability, and cost containment. But do these reasons justify peering over campus walls for aid and comfort? Perhaps not. Still, the situation that colleges and universities find themselves in as we close out this century is one that is causing some people to question the way in which we conduct the business of higher education. John A. White, the Assistant Director of the National Science Foundation, recently chided a roomful of educators with the following questions:

> How long would a firm be in business if it rejected parts, materials, and subassemblies at an overall rate of 35 percent and rejected a critical component at a rate of 65 percent?

> How long would a firm be in business if it consistently failed to meet its advertised delivery dates by 25 percent?

> How long would a firm be in business if its products failed to satisfy more than half of its customers?

> How long would a firm be in business if it paid little attention to its cost of production, but instead raised prices at a rate considerably above the cost of living while competitors were entering the market with lower prices?[12]

White's unique perspective on the quality of higher education in this country should cause us all to ask—"Is there a better way to manage our colleges and universities?" While the roots of strategic quality management come from industry, it should be clear that its most basic principles are not simply rules for running a factory. In fact, beneath the biz-speak lexicon is a general back-to-basics approach for operating any organization. This approach focuses on the power of individuals to improve. It is not unlike the way in which skilled crafters or artisans approached their jobs before we started "inspecting in" quality—without the suffocating policies of traditional bureaucracies. It is working together with tools, pride, and a close knowledge of the customer without fear and denigration. It is an approach that respects and encourages people to become masters of their own work.

2

Strategic Quality Management on Campus

It is so easy to say no to a new idea. We tend to assume that tomorrow is an extension of today; the ideas that got us where we are now are the same ones that will take us far into the future. After all, we already know what works, so why bother with something else that isn't "tried and true?" All of us are guilty of staying with an old pair of shoes just because they're comfortable. Everyone has practiced routines for managing their own affairs; every office or organization has a set of norms—"That's how we do things around here." The academically enlightened term for this phenomenon is a "paradigm." The dictionary definition of "paradigm" refers to it as "something serving as an example or model of how things should be done."[1] In *The Structure of Scientific Revolutions,* Thomas Kuhn describes a paradigm as a rule or regulation that establishes boundaries and shows us how to be successful by solving problems *within* those boundaries. A paradigm, therefore, is extremely useful because it acts as a pattern and allows us to perform a task with greater efficiency. But there is a difference between doing things right and doing the right thing. A paradigm excels at the former, not necessarily the latter.

People in higher education, like people in any other endeavor, establish regular patterns for solving problems. Oftentimes a pattern is evident in the assumptions that pervade their thinking. The following quotations from an article in a recent edition of *Academe* and from the *Chronicle of Higher Education* are illustrative:

> Our students are not our product, nor are our research and scholarship. Therefore, a college or university's 'profitability' cannot be measured. Even if higher

education is regarded as providing a service, no reliable method for measuring the quality of that service exists.[2]

I have been particularly disturbed as I listen to governors, legislators, and executive officers of state boards speak of 'quality' and 'excellence.' It struck me that all of these issues discussed by public officials are—or *should* be—within the domain of college faculties.[3]

These are not the isolated thoughts of extremists. In fact, I would venture to say that the authors' comments are fairly representative of the prevailing "quality" paradigm on campus—"quality is *ours* to define and manage, even if we are not quite certain what it's all about." Many of the issues relating to quality, therefore, are processed *within* the boundaries of this paradigm; one that provides comfort and stability to professors, administrators, and staff in the course of their daily decisions.

Of course those of you familiar with Kuhn's famous treatise know that he also goes on to suggest that paradigms act as filters that screen data from entering the scientist's mind. Information that agrees with the paradigm has an easy pathway to recognition. It is seen in sharp relief. But data that don't match the expectations created by the paradigm are usually ignored, misinterpreted, or distorted until the proper fit is found. In fact, Kuhn suggests that at times the individual may be physiologically *unable* to perceive the data—it is invisible. Joel Barker, the futurist, uses a deck of cards in his videotape entitled *Discovering the Future* to further illustrate Kuhn's point.[4] Eight playing cards are rapidly flashed on the screen. The viewers are asked to write down the card after each one is shown. Invariably (I know because I have had many groups of people perform the task), the viewers miss three cards; in fact, they miss the same three cards—the queen of spades, the six of spades and the nine of hearts. Just those. You see . . . the deck has been altered such that the color of the two spades is not black but red. The heart, in turn, is not red but black. Such trickery doesn't change the correct answer, it just makes it almost impossible, as Kuhn and Barker suggest, for people to see the cards the "correct way" according to their "card deck paradigm."

Much of what was discussed in the first chapter regarding strategic quality management was a frontal assault on our quality paradigm in higher education:

Quality and costs are inversely related?

Inspection doesn't help quality, it hurts quality?

People aren't the problem, it's the administration?

We can measure quality?

This is a service industry?

Governors, legislators and others customers' opinions about quality are worthy of our attention?

These ideas don't necessarily fit within the boundaries of our operating paradigm. They do not offer any easy pathway to recognition. Indeed, strategic quality management in higher education has a great deal in common with a red queen of spades.

———————◆———————

I am not suggesting that the University of Southern California should be run like General Motors or that the professors at Occidental College should see themselves as the organizational equivalents to the employees at Federal Express. What I am suggesting, however, is that the challenges that face higher education today and in the near future require a new set of philosophies and methods. Our work environment is in a continual state of flux. Many of the operating assumptions of the past simply don't apply now. New demands are screaming for attention—decaying infrastructures, soaring tuitions, increasing calls for accountability, falling levels of public confidence. The list is seemingly endless, and challenges are everywhere. In such an uncertain environment there are two generic responses to these demands. One is to redouble our efforts. This approach sees success as a direct function of sweat and recommitment to the institution's founding vision. It is the equivalent of the oil drilling company that drills to 1,000 feet and, upon finding no oil, puts all of its effort into pushing for the 2,000 foot mark—digging the same hole, only deeper. If you are certain as to your location such persistence can eventually pay off. In an uncertain environment, however, there is a good chance that you may be drilling in the wrong spot. If that's the case, then no amount of inspiration or prespiration will enable you to reach your goal. The second, more appropriate response then is to be flexible and to commit to a plan for drilling other test wells. Don't just dig the same hole deeper, dig other holes. In the unstable world of higher education, chances are that *all* of the responses to *all* of the challenges will not be found *within* our campus walls. We need to shuck our arrogance—"if it isn't our idea, it can't be good"—and get on with the task of examining other ideas, other perspectives.

What I am advocating is that American colleges and universities should consider the benefits of "creative swiping" when it comes to strategic quality management. Tom Peters uses this term in *Thriving on Chaos* to describe the process of looking beyond your own organization for other ideas, other test wells, that may be adapted and enhanced to fit your special circumstances.[5] After World War II, Japanese industrialists reached out to another culture, the United States (a culture they had been taught was inferior and that had just defeated them in war), for new management methods. Many of the basic ideas of Deming and Juran found fertile ground in Japan at the same time that they were being eschewed here. The techniques and tools of statistical process control were refined and adapted to fit with the conditions of postwar Japan. Over the next 40 years the philosophy and methods have been further enhanced by Japanese companies and, in the last ten years, American organizations as well.

The questions, then, are simple. In a changing environment in which flexibility and a broadened set of choices (or drill holes) are required of our colleges and universities, does strategic quality management offer any help to the challenges that we face today and tomorrow? Are there any ideas worth swiping and adapting to higher education? Is there a fit between the tools and techniques of strategic quality management and the culture of the campus? Like a venn diagram, is there any overlap between the philosophy of strategic quality management and our current approach to administration? Does this new paradigm make sense for your institution? The next few pages examine the common ground. In fact, I propose three solid connections that make strategic quality management a viable model for a college or university: one is definitional, another is organizational, and the third is operational.

> *Definitional—Quality extends beyond the interaction between the professor and the student in the classroom or the meeting of accreditation standards: strategic quality management is a set of multidimensional principles that embrace this broadened definition.*

Discussions about quality are dependent upon one's perspective. For example, Robert Pirsig in *Zen and the Art of Motorcycle Maintenance* offers an oft-cited perspective. After four or five pages of tussling with the question, Pirsig states: "Quality . . . you know what it is, yet you don't know what it is."[6] Another perspective is that of the self-described realist who sees quality in concrete terms: the number of volumes in the library, the price tag on a new car, the wattage of a stereo system, and so on. These perspectives don't offer much help in terms of operating philosophy and they certainly do not recognize that quality is a multidimensional construct that is defined differently by different interests.

Perhaps the best way to explore this broadened nature of quality is to review the five definitions of quality that are described by David Garvin in *Managing Quality.*[7] Let's begin with the notion of *transcendent* quality since it might be called an occupational hazard that is associated with professional people. Transcendent quality is innate excellence derived from the close association between the producer and the product. Artisans or crafters have years of apprenticeship to hone their skills. They then use that knowledge base to produce a superior product. Medical doctors and college professors have similar professional pathways and standards: both the quality of health care and the quality of education can be seen as the direct result of their expertise. For example, according to Harold Enarson in an *Educational Record* article, quality is something that we in higher education know "in our bones."[8] While transcendent quality is important to the professional integrity of higher education, it has little or no clout beyond the campus walls. Indeed, state legislators, governors, and the trustees of colleges and universities are less than enamored with higher education's use of the "in our bones" defense when they are attempting to make investment judgments (i.e., higher education versus roads, police, jails, K–12 education).

A *manufacturing-based* definition of quality is closely related to Philip Crosby's notion of conformance to requirements—"We decided we were in the business of causing and measuring conformance to the requirements. Therefore, quality means conformance. Nonquality is nonconformance."[9] In spite of an orientation that would appear to come directly from the floor of a General Motors assembly plant, the fact is that accreditation—in both institutions of higher education and hospitals—is a quality control mechanism that is based upon conformance to requirements. The conformance perspective has a number of advantages in higher education. First, it neutralizes, at least in theory, a limited reputational view of quality. Stanford University is not necessarily any better than Lane Community College if they both do an outstanding job of accomplishing their stated missions. Second, one of the purposes of institutional accreditation is to provide public confirmation that what the institution is doing is of acceptable quality. All of higher education, then, benefits to the extent that the public has confidence in our ability to self-regulate. However, a conformance perspective, like transcendent quality, is not without its problems. For instance, just meeting the minimal standards for accreditation provides little strategic advantage for an organization since issues like "distinctiveness" are not a part of any accrediting evaluation. Conformance is internally focused thus disregarding the importance of the competitive environment while at the same time minimizing the importance of the consumer. And while institutions may meet the standards of accrediting associations, there has been little evidence that the associations are concerned with the quality standards used by students, parents, employers, and so on.

The next definition of quality, according to Garvin, is essentially a *product-based* definition. It views quality as a precise and measurable variable such as 18-karat versus 14-karat gold, 25 versus 55 miles per gallon in a car, or 300 versus 3,000 REM of a computer. Differences in quality, then, relate to differences in quantity of a particular attribute. Perhaps the greatest value of this perspective, as we have seen, is that it moves away from the "swampish" notions of Pirsig to dry land. Quality is no longer a matter of whimsy or insight, but rather a definitive state that reflects the presence or absence of a specific ingredient. One of the areas of dry land in higher education is located within the assessment movement. For example, an institution's assessment practices reflect its values; that is, the values of an institution are revealed in the information it gathers about itself and pays attention to. An institution can evaluate critical thinking skills or communication skills in a first-year student and do it again in his or her senior year. Subject-matter competency, vocational competency, aspirations, and expectations are all "product-based" attributes or ingredients. These are measurable attributes. The clear advantage of this approach to quality is that it is decidedly strategic. The methods of learning are continuously being scrutinized in terms of their ability to affect desirable changes. With this in mind, assessment spotlights values or goals and provides an institution with an integrative framework for marshalling its resources and concentrating its energies on achieving its stated aims.

Quality can also be seen as conformance or performance at an acceptable price or cost. A *value-based* approach to quality sees the actual cost of a good or service as being relevant to the quality equation. In essence, a high performing service with a reasonable price is of greater quality than the same service with a very expensive price tag due to differences in value. In fall, 1990, the Department of Education released a report entitled "The Escalating Costs of Higher Education" in which the reasons for tuition increases were dutifully enumerated in great detail. For the consumer of higher education services, however, the important point was not in the fine print of analyses but in the simple declaration that the cost of attending college had increased faster than family incomes in the 1980s. Interestingly, during the same time period *Money* magazine premiered its issue of "America's Best College Buys." The core of the issue centered around a statistical analysis that determined how much each school might be expected to cost, based upon seventeen measures of academic performance, and then compared that figure to each school's actual cost. The result was a "value ranking" of the top 200 schools that delivered "the best education for the buck."[10]

A final approach to defining quality can be described as *user-based*. This perspective is grounded in the preferences of the consumer and consists of the singular capacity to satisfy wants. A user-based approach is highly subjective and idiosyncratic. Each individual decides what product or service has the greatest quality by determining, as Joseph Juran notes, its "fitness for use."[11] It is a personal view of quality based upon one's own perspective. While the notion of fitness for use has a certain common sense appeal to it, I have saved it for last because it is the most threatening to professional people. The threat is clearly evident if we refer back to our initial definition of transcendent or "in our bones" quality. From such a vantage point—that of the professionally trained college professor or medical doctor—quality is an integral part of accomplishment. But what happens when we suggest that the student or patient might have an opinion?

Perhaps the best way to answer the question is to offer an example. In the book *The Quest for Quality* by Lewis Mayhew, Patrick Ford and Dean Hubbard, the authors agree that the transcendent approach mirrors the historic view of quality education. They go on to comment on a *user-based* definition of quality: "Of course, such an approach has appeal for those undergraduate students who judge their education only in terms of how well it facilitates securing their first job and those adult part-time learners who

TABLE *2.1* "Best Indicators" of Top-Quality

	STUDENTS	PARENTS
High admission rates of its graduates who apply to top graduate or professional schools	41%*	69%
Large variety of courses and programs	32	26
Advanced laboratory equipment and library resources	26	26
Faculty spend as much time teaching as on their research	25	39
Students who were high achievers before college	23	14
Many small classes	22	24
High starting salaries for its graduates in fields that interest them	21	19
Faculty spend a lot of time with students outside of class	15	10

* Percentages indicate the incidence with which respondents selected each indicator.
Source: Table 2.1 adapted from "In the Eyes of Our Beholders" by Larry H. Litten and Alfred E. Hall, *Journal of Higher Education*, Vol. 60, NO. 3 (May/June 1989), p. 315. Reprinted by permission. © 1989 by the Ohio State University Press. All rights reserved.

only select courses which appear to be immediately applicable to their current job."[12] Unfortunately, such time-honored traditionalist thinking ignores a few relevant facts. For one, in spite of the condescending "we-know-what's-best-for-them" inference, studies of students' and parents' perceptions of institutional quality do not reflect such vocational narrow-mindedness. Table 2.1 reports the results of a *Journal of Higher Education* study on how high school students and their parents view quality in colleges: A view with limited short-term vocationalism.

A second fact ignored by the traditionalists is that a "user" is not limited to a student or a parent. Higher education has many consumers, both internal and external. The campus personnel department has its consumers, as does the career placement center (e.g., both students and employers). They have their publics as well: the local community, state legislators, alumni, and so on. Each and every one of these groups, whether we like it or not, has its own legitimate "fitness for use" view of quality.

Herein lies the definitional argument for strategic quality management on campus. *Higher education no longer has the luxury of using narrow definitions of quality.* The public isn't buying it. The legislators aren't buying it. Indeed, one Colorado legislator recently expressed the feelings of probably many others when he said, "the university is more run for the faculty than the students—particularly in respect to freshmen and sophomores."[13] Derek Bok has made similar statements regarding colleges' and universities' lack of responsiveness to societal needs. The difficulty is that many in the higher education community continue to reject all definitions of quality that are not simply "in our bones," or that do not conform to accreditation standard's definitions. Reliance on such narrow definitions of quality is a paradigm problem. It forces us to focus on a limited, rigid set of outcomes at a time when we need to think in broader operational terms. Strategic quality management, in contrast, is not so much concerned with debating definitions or arm wrestling for territorial claims as it is with developing and understanding systems for improvement. Strategic quality management is, in effect, a day-to-day operating philosophy that can accommodate definitional differences. It is a basis for action, a comprehensive decision-making framework. It is a never-ending quality journey, not a narrow, self-determined quality destination.

> *Organizational—A college or university seeks to advance learning: strategic quality management is a structural system that creates a learning organization.*

Let me ask a question—"How can your institution be made better?" Understand that the question is not "How well is your institution doing?" All of us can reel off a set of statistics or engaging anecdotes that describe the current situation in the most flattering light. But that's not the question. The question relates to *improvement*. The core idea of strategic quality management is that the administration needs to take responsibility for understanding the system (delivering educational services on your campus) and for empowering everyone in the organization to work on improvement. Now that's a big chunk of responsibility, so the first step in implementing strategic quality management is to disaggregate the existing system into critical processes. For example, in higher education there is the advising process, the payroll process, the registration process, the general education process, and so on. Within each of these processes there is also a group of relevant subprocesses. Improving the system (higher education at a college or university) is accomplished by improving these processes. It is not unlike a game of chess. A chess player does not try to win by simply asking, "How do I win at chess?" Instead, the player asks, "How should I use my pawns, my rooks, and my bishops?"

Let's move on to a second question—"What is your job?" Now most of you will probably answer by saying—"I'm the dean of Arts and Sciences," "I'm an English professor," or "I'm the vice president of Student Affairs." Again, that isn't the question. The question doesn't say anything about your letterhead, it asks you about your job—*what you do*. In spite of the fact that our colleges and universities are entrusted to advance learning in the physical sciences, the arts, and so on, this is not how the institutions themselves are operated. We do not run "learning" organizations. As institutions, we do not seek to systematically gain knowledge or skills concerning how we operate. Colleges and universities tend to be static and descriptive. We spend an extraordinary amount of time and money every year describing the programs and courses we offer, when and where they will meet, and who will teach them. We then describe what happened—that x number of courses were offered in a specific semester, taught by y number of professors, for z number of students. We take these numbers and divide them, multiply them, make pie charts and detailed tables that fill various documents and reports. Other areas of our higher education institutions can be just as descriptive. Library personnel can tell you in the blink of an eye how many volumes they have. The cafeteria can show you a menu for all of next month and provide you with cost-per-meal calculations. We describe.

A strategic quality management approach would suggest that the function of the administration is not merely to describe what has happened, or to control what will happen, but to foster improvement (i.e., "How can your institution be made better?") *by encouraging people to really understand the processes in which they participate* (i.e., "What is your job?"). Perhaps the best example of this systems thinking is the seven-step problem analysis that is prevalent among total quality management (TQM) advocates in industry. It goes like this:

1. Reason for improvement: To identify a problem situation and the reason for working to improve it.
2. Current situation: To select a problem, describe the current situation, and set a target for improvement.
3. Analysis: To identify and verify the root causes of the problem situation.
4. Countermeasures: To plan and implement countermeasures that will correct the root causes of the problem situation.
5. Results: To confirm that the problem situation and its root causes have been lessened and the target for improvement has been satisfied.
6. Standardization: To prevent the problem and its root causes from re-curring.
7. Future plans: To plan what can be done about any remaining problems and to evaluate the effectiveness of the process that has just taken place.

Does the director of food services operate this way on your campus? How about the head librarian? Does anyone? Perhaps the closest thing we have to a real learning system on our college campuses is assessment. As all assessment experts will tell you, assessment is not a matter of methods and control but a way of thinking about learning. The focus of student assessment, for example, is thinking—and I mean *really* thinking—about a series of very basic questions:

What do I want my student-customers to achieve?
Are they getting it?
Exactly *how* are they getting it?
What do I need to change?

What the individual professor is doing here is studying the learning process and assessing the effects of her or his actions. I am especially fond of the terminology used by Pat Hutchings to describe this process. She often talks about assessment in terms of "the way we work."[14] Improving student learning is the goal, but how to improve student learning is like asking "How do I win at chess?" In effect, professors, like chess players, need to think hard about *the way they work*. Assessment is a learning system to help them do just that. In the same way that assessment involves learning how to improve teaching, strategic quality management involves learning how to improve the registration of students and learning how to improve campus maintenance. It is a structural system that helps create a true learning organization.

> *Operational—A college or university operates as a collection of isolated individual parts; strategic quality management is a unifying force that advances an integrated, purposeful whole.*

More than a decade ago I ran across, what was to me, a disturbing interview with Robert Maynard Hutchins in the *Chronicle of Higher Education*. Let me quote one section:

> The only way you can criticize a university, the only way you can appraise it, the only way you can determine whether it's good or bad or medium or indifferent, is to know what it's about, what it's supposed to be, what it's supposed to be doing. If you don't know these things, you haven't any standards of criticism . . . [Universities] haven't any . . . clear ideas of what they're doing or why. They don't even know what they are.[15]

Over the years I have been sensitive to discussions and statements regarding this lack of cohesion—and there have been many. Some have come as informal comments made at conferences or in hallway chats with colleagues and friends. Oftentimes there is a sense of frustration and unease surrounding our ambiguities or fuzzy purposes. Take, for instance, the comments of a professor of Philosophy at the University of California at Riverside which appeared in an op-ed piece: "Students today see themselves as collecting credits for degrees. Faculty see themselves as primarily researchers. Administrators see themselves as regulators. It's a triumvirate of forces driving off in different directions. What is conspicuously lacking . . . is the sense of belonging to a common enterprise."[16] At a more formal level, I have also been attracted to the research and writings of organizational behaviorists. Henry Mintzberg characterizes colleges and universities as "professional bureaucracies" in *Structure in Fives: Designing Effective Organizations*. He suggests that the work in such organizations is highly specialized in the horizontal dimension typified by a series of independent entities that operate in relative isolation—in pigeonholes: "It is this pigeonholing process that enables the professional bureaucracy to decouple its various operating tasks and assign them to individual, relatively autonomous professionals. Each can, instead of giving a great deal of attention to coordinating his work with his peers, focus on perfecting his skills."[17]

While the term "pigeonholing" does not necessarily evoke the most flattering imagery, it does reflect the same notion that Karl Weick, another organizational behavior researcher, advances when he suggests that schools are "in the business of building and maintaining categories" by operating as loosely-coupled systems.[18] Irrespective of the terminology, the fact remains that the professional autonomy resulting from this organizational structure is both a tremendous source of strength as well as an underlying weakness. Professors and individual academic units are relatively free of the policy-controlling constraints that are endemic in other types of organizations. Such freedom, of course, is critical to the creative process and has not escaped the notice of many American corporations. Indeed, the whole notion of "skunk-works" popularized by 3M, Ford, and other companies which involves insulating a small group of people from the corporate infrastructure so that they can pursue "ideas," has an uncanny similarity to the academic department.

Autonomy, however, does not come without a substantial cost. And that cost is that the organization often operates like a seemingly random collection of elements "driving off in different directions" with no unifying purpose, common ambition, or as Hutchins remarked, "clear ideas of what they're doing or why." Consequently, professional bureaucracies suffer from problems of innovation and problems of coordination. It should come as no surprise that colleges and universities tend to be conservative bodies, hesitant to change established procedures. In a stable environment with few competitive challenges or dynamic changes, this lack of innovation is of minor consequence. Organizations can survive quite well by merely responding or reacting to problems as they come along. But a disconnected, isolated system of pigeon-holes also has little capacity or incentive to respond to the many opportunities and threats that are part of the changing scenery that dots higher education's landscape in the 1990s. Even if our professional bureaucracies had the *will* to change, they often don't have the *way* to change because of coordination problems. To work as a cohesive whole necessitates some loss of autonomy, which in the higher education community is akin to the pulling of teeth without the luxury of novocaine. The trick, then, would seem to be to retain the strengths of a loosely-coupled system while developing means or methods to ameliorate the problems of innovation and coordination.

I have an absolute conviction that there is a single organizational dynamic that makes professional bureaucracies move in a specific direction— *and that is synergy.* Simple mathematics tell us that 2 + 2 = 4. A stereo contains hundreds of electronic parts that are capable of almost nothing as individual components yet, together they form a working system able to reproduce the music of a symphony orchestra. An organization, such as a college or university, can also be more than the sum of its parts—2 + 2 = 5. It requires, however, a shared ideology or a collective mind such that individuals are united by a common intention. There is an inescapable feeling or mood—perhaps a kind of chemistry—that permeates a company or an organizational unit that has developed a strong ideology. In fact, the "atmosphere" that results from synergy is to an organization what personality is to an individual.

Many of the basic axioms of strategic quality management, as enumerated in Chapter 1, have synergy-causing influences in organizations. For example, Deming's notion of "constancy of purpose" provides a consistent philosophy and a unifying focus by emphasizing a long-term commitment to a vision. It inspires confidence in everyone when the organization is able to articulate its goals and practice day-to-day decision making that is consistent with those goals. Giving people the tools and techniques, the training, and the responsibility for causing quality creates a feeling that the organization is *investing* in its own people. Encouraging a perception of quality that extends beyond transcendence or conformance to accrediting standards helps break down the barriers between departments and disciplines. The strong orientation toward teamwork that is inherent in the strategic quality management philosophy enables individuals to work at common purposes instead of at cross purposes. Finally, the ability of strategic quality management to create synergy on a college campus serves one additional function of a purely political nature. In recent years the focus of the discussion about quality in higher education has moved off campus. Why? Is it that most state boards of education or legislators are power mongers? Probably not. The answer, most likely, is that professional bureaucracies are often unable to articulate their purposes, their definition of quality, and their quality-causing activities. The result is a predictable vacuum. The words of Henry Mintzberg, in his discussion of professional bureaucracies, can be applied to the current state of affairs in higher education:

> What responses do the problems of coordination . . . and innovation evoke? Most commonly, those outside the profession—clients, non-professional administrators, members of the society at large and their representatives in government—see the problems as resulting from a lack of external control of the professional and of his profession. So they do the obvious: try to control the work with one of the other coordinating mechanisms. Specifically, they try to use direct supervision, standardization of work processes, or standardization of outputs.[19]

Certainly some ill-conceived assessment initiatives by state agencies fall into the category of "standardization of outputs," while productivity measures and the desire for performance data by the ever-expanding staffs of education boards are attempts at "standardization of work processes." Increasingly, such agencies and boards fail to distinguish the difference between what is policy and what is management—that is, "direct supervision." Strategic quality management enables an individual institution to respond to the challenges of a changing environment in some other way than by spouting tiresome, territorial rhetoric. It enables an organization to regain the high ground by assuming responsibility for causing quality in a systematic and comprehensive manner.

◆

Strategic quality management on campus is in its infancy. But in spite of its youth, there have been a few, tentative, first steps by several dozen colleges and universities. There are no definitive conclusions yet, so it would be inappropriate to offer a series of case studies for analyses and review. Also, this book is not meant to be a strategic quality management "how to" manual. It is worthwhile, nonetheless, to offer a number of snapshots of institutions (and in one case, a higher education system) that are applying the strategic quality management philosophy and techniques to the way they operate their organizations.

The University of Wisconsin–Madison. [20]   In October 1990 the University of Wisconsin–Madison introduced a draft plan to implement the "principles and methods of Total Quality" into its operations and philosophy. The plan defines Total Quality Leadership (TQL) as "a comprehensive management approach which uses the scientific method and the contributions of everyone in the organization to continuously improve everything the organization does in order to consistently meet or exceed customer expectations," and offers a framework and an action plan. The framework describes the resources and interrelationships deemed to be instrumental in the transition process. It includes the following eight groups:

RESOURCE FRAMEWORK

1. The Leadership Team—The role of the leadership team is to develop a vision for the TQL transition: to develop broad goals and objectives, to determine measures of success, to address major policy issues, and to begin to develop TQL methods.
2. The Office of Quality—The mission of this group is to guide, facilitate, and coordinate the implementation of the philosophy and methods of Total Quality.
3. The Implementation Team—This group consists of staff within the University who have expertise or knowledge to contribute to the implementation efforts.
4. Transition Departments—These are departments targeted for early TQL efforts.
5. Internal Network—This includes a monthly meeting with speakers on Quality topics and other efforts to inform people and departments of training and information opportunities.

6. Advisory Team—A team of experts from public and private organizations is to be appointed to meet twice annually and be looked to for advice.

7. Corporate Sponsors—The University will seek support from corporations that have implemented quality. Supporting contributions may come in the form of funding, training resources, or consulting.

8. External Network—The Office of Quality will continue to make contact with other colleges and universities implementing Quality, private consultants and corporations, state agencies and other groups across the nation.

The action plan that the university has developed for initiating their Total Quality Leadership program includes an initial effort to build a data collection system to define its customer (internal and external) needs and to define a set of appropriate benchmarks. Additionally, the Leadership Team has begun the process of generating a vision statement as well as a five-year plan. Michael Williamson, the director of the Office of Quality, strongly believes that while the impetus to initiate the TQL program came from the tightening of fiscal resources and a need to do more with less, "the immediate effect is being seen in the better use of our human resources."

North Dakota University System.[21]   The open letter to the people of North Dakota that prefaces the North Dakota University System's "Partners for Progress Plan for 1990–1997" begins with this statement: "This seven-year plan marks the beginning of a new era for the North Dakota University System—an era of dedication to constant improvement in quality, productivity, and efficiency in serving the people of North Dakota as a unified system." Indeed, the North Dakota University System is the first higher education system in the country to embark on a strategic quality management effort. The impetus for this ground-breaking action is spelled out in the plan's executive summary: total revenues fell nearly $40 million short of inflation during the 1980s while serving an increasing number of students. The strategies for the 1980s included a tripling of the tuition, equipment and capital cutbacks, larger classes, an increase in part-time faculty, fewer student services, salary freezes, and "other desperate measures." The conclusion is blunt: "Such strategies have reached their limits. Continuing them into the 1990s would decimate higher education. North Dakotans would ultimately pay less to attend out-of-state universities and possibly get a better education there." Given the situation, the board's willingness to explore a new operating paradigm seems a logical step:

> The State Board of Higher Education and its staff have been learning about a management approach that has had great success in increasing quality, increasing productivity, and decreasing cost in business. North Dakota businesses using Total Quality Management (TQM) include Lucas Western, Melroe, Great Plains

Software, and American Crystal Sugar. . . The Board believes that TQM holds great promise for higher education institutions, although colleges and universities throughout the country are just beginning to use it.

The Plan goes on to state an overarching standard for quality: setting and achieving constantly improving standards of service that meet the needs of students, citizens, economic enterprises, and colleagues in education, as appropriate for each operating unit and level of the system. It then details 1997 goals for TQM in four areas: graduates, faculty, research, and public service personnel, creating a campus community, and ensuring quality. And finally, the Plan concludes that, "By 1997, every component of the system will be actively involved in constant improvement of quality." In discussing North Dakota's initiatives, Ellen Chaffee, the vice chancellor for Academic Affairs, concludes: "TQM gave us a reason for hope when we hit bottom. At first our board said, 'This is too good to be true.' As someone here says, TQM is organized common sense—it's so obviously *right.* Then the board said, 'Somebody must have a copyright on this. Can we afford it? Who'll get rich if we commit to it?' When they understood that the 'price' was their leadership and personal commitment over the long term, they began to get on board."

Delaware County Community College.[22] DCCC is one of the first colleges in the United States whose management and philosophy is based on the concepts of continuous, systematic improvement as embodied in the principles of Total Quality Management. In 1985, the president of DCCC, Richard DeCosmo set the college on its present course by enrolling himself and his executive staff in a year-long seminar about TQM that was sponsored by the Philadelphia Area Council for Excellence—a subsidiary of the Philadelphia Chamber of Commerce. After a year of planning, study, and introspection, DCCC established three goals:

- To transform its philosophy of administrative management to Total Quality.
- To develop a training curriculum and programming in Total Quality for business in its service area.
- To incorporate the concepts and philosophy of Total Quality into its credit curriculum and into classroom management.

Over the ensuing three years, the college made significant strides in accomplishing these goals. For example, all administrators at the college received awareness training in TQM. Meetings were held to identify and prioritize college systems and processes in need of improvement. Subsequently, 80 percent of these administrators and their staffs have been actively involved in improvement projects. The college presently supports contracts with eleven local industries, state agencies, and federal government offices. The college is listed as a vendor on the Federal Supply Schedule. Additionally, representatives from more than fifty local companies attend open introductory seminars on TQM at Delaware County Community College each year. Faculty members are beginning to experiment with the use of the TQM philosophy in the management of their classrooms. The college's nursing faculty, for instance, is using TQM tools to revise instructional procedures for teaching the administration of medications in a clinical setting. A support group of faculty interested in incorporating TQM into their classes has also been recently established. Finally, a certificate program in Total Quality Technology will be offered by DCCC beginning with the winter 1991 semester. In summing up their experiences to date, Susanna Staas, DCCC's Total Quality Projects coordinator says, "Total Quality Management requires cultural change and changes in management techniques. It is a change that is not undertaken lightly, nor is it one that takes place quickly. We are convinced, however, that Total Quality Management will be instrumental in ensuring that DCCC meets the challenges of the nineties and beyond."

Oregon State University.[23] While a philosophy department or a dean's office has no parallel in industry, some areas of colleges and universities such as facilities, billing, and security have very similar counterparts in other types of institutions. Wouldn't it be nice to reduce the average duration of remodeling jobs by 23 percent, or to decrease the number of journal vouchers returned to departments for error correction by 94 percent, or to increase the number of daily building security checks by 17 percent? These are just some of the Total Quality Management (TQM) pilot team results recorded at Oregon State University. Early in 1990, OSU set out to find its own answer to the question being asked by some colleges and universities across the country: How adaptable are the quality management methods of W. Edwards Deming, J.M. Juran, and Philip Crosby to higher education? After an initial period of research, consultation, and cogitation, the following model was adopted (see Figure 2.1).

The purpose of the first (1) phase is to provide a critical mass of top management people who understand what TQM is and its use to the university—in this case, a bibliography was compiled and site visits to Ford, Hewlett-Packard, and Dow were conducted. A pilot study team (2) was formed (e.g., a physical plant) to address a specific, high priority issue. At the same time, an organized system to identify and prioritize customer needs (3) and translate them into university priorities was initiated—surveys, focus groups, complaints/feedbacks, and so on. Breakthrough planning sessions (4) were conducted to integrate a distinctive vision with a customer focus and an understanding of critical processes. The same approach to planning (5) was being conducted in the divisions and colleges. Study teams (6) were formed with people who normally work together on a process to be reviewed. These study teams include a team leader and a facilitator who are given instructions

FIGURE *2.1* The OSU Total Quality Management Implementation Model

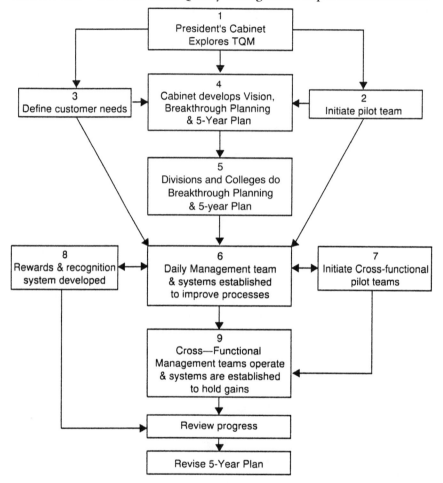

on problem solving techniques and TQM tools. A cross-functional pilot project (7) is developed with the intention of converting many university committees (9) to Total Quality Management. And finally, the institution develops a system of reporting and an awards program (8) to recognize both outstanding individuals and teams.

According to Ed Coate, OSU's vice president for Finance and Administration, the first year's experience has some valuable "success" lessons: (1) a firm commitment to TQM from the president is essential; (2) a person of considerable authority must champion TQM from inception to implementation; (3) the essence of TQM is team study devoted to process improvement;

and (4) the administrative services side is easier to start with than the academic side.

Somehow higher education has gotten into a tug-of-war over quality that continues to miss the point. We seem to equate quality in higher education with two things: funding and jurisdiction. If you give us plenty of money and leave us alone, we'll deliver quality. Cutting the budget of any college or university will bring a swift reply from the president—"You're endangering the quality of this instituion." The faculty and the rest of the campus community not only encourage this reaction, they expect it. I do not mean to suggest for a minute that funding is irrelevant. I think we can all agree that there is a very good chance that we can *do more if we have more.* But the fact remains that there are some awfully good institutions with far fewer financial resources than some entirely mediocre, well-funded ones. Money guarantees nothing when it comes to quality.

As you recall from the beginning of this chapter, quality is also associated with a territorial imperative. Many on the side of academe would agree with the state legislator that Frank Newman quotes in *Choosing Quality:* "The harsh fact that our state government has forgotten is that there are no great universities run by governors or budget analysts or legislators."[24] In an even-handed fashion, Newman presents the other side of this debate by also stating: "Left totally to its own, the university will evolve toward self-interest rather than public interest."[25] The responsibility for supposedly ensuring quality, then, is an active part of the tug-of-war. But this is not the end of it. The topic of quality and the debate over quality-related issues rages in other areas as well. Do the practices and procedures of accrediting agencies (both institutional and disciplinary) ensure quality in our institutions? Is student outcomes assessment a quality-causing system or a political weapon? Are the changes being made in the name of improving the quality of a college education threatening accessibility?

While these are legitimate concerns and worthy of our attention, none address the more fundamental issue: *How can we, as academic administrators, do a better job of managing quality into our campus operations?* This is the key challenge that we face in the 1990s and beyond. Increased funding will not improve quality if we don't allocate it wisely, if we don't use it to promote distinctiveness, and if we aren't able to create customer satisfaction. We can improve accreditation procedures all we want but that won't enable us to improve the way in which we analyze problems on a day-to-day basis. While an emphasis on student assessment is necessary—and long overdue— it doesn't help us upgrade library and computing services on campus. In short, what our institutions need is a new operating philosophy—a new approach to managing their human and fiscal resources.

Some may see the next eight chapters as a frontal assault on higher education administration. It is not. In fact, as I noted in the Preface to this book, I spent a considerable amount of time on college compuses speaking with administrators about quality—not Total Quality Management, or Deming's fourteen points, just their understanding of what quality was to them and how best to achieve it. What became obvious to me was that quality was being actively pursued at St. Francis College, Nebraska Wesleyan University, the University of California, Berkeley, and the other colleges and universities that I visited in much the same way as prescribed by the quality gurus. The common-sense philosophy, if not the tools and techniques, were evident in the words of many I had the opportunity to interview. The difference was that the *management of quality* was not a comprehensive, coordinated effort. It happened in fits and spurts; Or it was tucked away in wonderfully successful, but isolated programs—here and there across the campus. Quality, as an organizational goal, was not being pursued in a strategic fashion—in spite of what the mission statement said.

The time is right for us to quit talking about quality in ubiquitous terms. It is not like air and water. We don't have it just because we say we have it. It is in no sense a self-fulfilling prophecy. *We need to cause it.* And we can because the responsibility for quality lies with each individual at your institution. Work with them to articulate a distinctive vision and to identify customer needs. Help them describe the key processes involved in their work. Give them the tools, training, and incentive to improve those processes continuously, and then get out of their way. They will reward you for your confidence in their abilities. They will respond to your leadership challenge. They will show you what quality in higher education is all about.

3

Satisfy the Customer: Everything Else Follows

I like to write in margins. With Tom Peters' book, *Thriving on Chaos,* a pencil is a flat-out necessity. In one chapter, Peters describes the activities of Deluxe Check of Minneapolis, a company that did $1 billion worth of business in 1989 alone. Deluxe Check is a supplier to commercial banks, thrifts, and credit unions and chances are, that when you opened up a new checking account or placed a reorder, the checks were printed and shipped to you courtesy of Deluxe. Peters contends that "wildly profitable" Deluxe Check does a consummate job of attending to its customers and cites two simple statistics: in 1986, Deluxe shipped 97.1 percent of orders within one day of their receipt and 99.6 percent of those orders were error-free. I made a notation next to the following paragraph:

> How is this achieved? While appropriate automation marks Deluxe's sixty–two plants, simple, visible systems are the essence of success. For instance, each day's order slip is a different color. Tuesday's is orange, and one plant manager comments. "At 4:30 Wednesday, I don't want to see any orange around here."[1]

My penciled note said "grades" and the name of a small college that I had taught a few courses at the previous year. The anecdote that my brain had jogged loose had to do with a number of students that had given me postcards following the final examination. They wanted me to send them their grades in the mail. While this is an occasional practice at larger schools where the glut of grades for tens of thousands of students can cause a delay, smaller schools are usually more responsive to this end-of-the-semester challenge. Nonetheless, my students were merely reacting to the fact that the registrar's office at this college took six weeks to deliver grades—hence the postcards. I took the obvious action and attempted to post the grades (by social security number) on the office door. They were promptly, and efficiently, removed by a keen-eyed secretary who informed me of a campus policy against the posting of grades.

The connection is clear. The bank customer deposits his or her money and wants the checks to access the funds—not in six weeks but as soon as possible. Deluxe recognizes this need and responds with a customer-driven passion—"I don't want to see any orange around here." The student, in contrast, pays money for the course, buys the book, attends classes, writes reports, studies, takes examinations, and wants a grade. This is important to the student—the customer—and yet the college responds with indifference.

Admittedly, it is a small point. Harvard's or Stanford's quality reputation's are not based upon how quickly its students receive their grades. No student will transfer because of it. The local newspaper is not going to run a revealing exposé. But the fact remains that it is important to students. Perhaps it doesn't fall into a column headed "most important," but it still could be one of the many things that says how much the college cares about them and their needs.

> *Developing a lot of happy, satisfied customers—whether they are students, parents of students, alumni, professors, or industry employers—should be a primary goal of causing quality in higher education.*

◆

A recent cover of *Business Week* (March 12, 1990) leaves no room for doubt. It simply says, "KING CUSTOMER." The inside article is a description of how to organize entire companies—from research to manufacturing, from information systems to pay incentives—around giving customers what they want. Why this regal status? Why are companies becoming so slavishly submissive? There are a number of reasons. The obvious one is that in spite of all the trappings of success such as soaring stock prices, a solid balance sheet, and a corporate jet, a company owes its good fortune to the customers' willingness to give up something (money) to get something (a product or a service). The key, then, is to grasp—and hold tightly to—a simple truth: Customer-driven companies are successful because they have a unifying focus and understand that need-satisfaction is the Holy Grail. Indeed, one executive, PepsiCo Worldwide Beverages' president Roger A. Enrico, comments in the *Business Week* article, "If you are totally customer-focused and you deliver the services your customers want, everything else will follow."[2]

A second point: In the competitive environments of every industry—including higher education—customers have options. Consequently, getting people to try your product or service is only the opening gambit. The more difficult task is keeping them as loyal customers.

Some studies indicate that it takes twelve positive experiences to make up for one bad one. So the expensive part of doing business, making someone aware of your product or service and getting them to the trial stage, can be quickly negated by a single unpleasant experience. And don't think that you can easily make amends ... For every constructive complaint you get, perhaps twenty or thirty people just walk. For them there are no second chances.

A customer orientation relies upon a user-based definition of quality. From this perspective, quality is defined by the user in terms of "the capacity to satisfy wants." Quality is a perception, and that perception becomes the user's reality. Further, there is no singular, all-encompassing definition of reality. Reality is merely what each individual decides it is. Perhaps the best description of this user-based quality is the title of an article in a January, 1985 issue of *Across the Board*—"Quality Is Between the Customer's Ears."[3] Of course, such an approach leaves one with the problem of how to aggregate widely varying perceptions, given that there is no one "average" customer. Indeed, there are whole groups of customers. The manufacturer of children's toys is interested in how the user—the child—defines quality. That same manufacturer must also be concerned with how parents, or the influencers and, in most cases, the purchasers, view quality. Even the government is a customer since various agencies (e.g., the Consumer Product Safety Commission) have their own performance standards.

This same pressure to understand quality in consumer terms is growing in higher education. There is the tug and pull of the perceptions of professors, students, administrators, state legislators, board members, accrediting agencies, employers, and so on. Each constituency creates its own reality. Students, for example, are notorious for making choices about quality by voting with their feet. A professor who is poorly organized, unable to articulate his or her thoughts, or who treats the students with contempt will end up lecturing to empty seats. Students will transfer out of programs that are weak or that they feel don't deliver a quality education. They will stay, they will learn, and they will graduate if they *perceive* that the time, effort, and money are worth it. Indeed, when the representatives of the Association of Independent Colleges and Schools (AICS) asked Deming, "What is a quality school?" he answered from the perspective of the student by saying that the first thing you have to ask is whether a person is "better off having gone to that school."[4] This is a value-added or talent development slant. It can come in many shapes and forms. As an example, Joseph Duggan, Associate Dean of the Graduate Division at the University of California–Berkeley, spoke to me about the importance of "mentorship" in graduate education: "I was in charge of placement for three or four years in my department–Comparative Literature. I think a very good way to find out what people never learned is to be in charge of placement. You call a meeting and say, 'Okay we're going to go to the Modern Language Association meeting. Now, how many of you have given papers at a meeting?' One hand will go up."

Why is this important? Duggan went on to say, "Well, this is something you ought to do if you're coming from a major university. But students haven't been told this. It gives them a bit of poise and then if they go up for an interview, it's probably going to be less intimidating than having delivered a paper to a room full of people—all of whom know something about that subject." Educational outcomes refer to changes in the individual—his or her intellectual growth and development, changes in values, skills and so forth. In this case, the idea is that each and every professor takes a personal responsibility for adding value—experience in delivering a paper—to the service that is delivered to the student/customer.

Cognitive and affective outcomes are influenced by more than the nature of the student/faculty member relationship. There are a whole slew of campus experiences that shape the attitudes and educational experiences of the student. Failure to keep appointments with students sends a message to students. Abrupt and discourteous treatment by secretaries sends another message. Uninformed advisors and counselors are clear messages and the failure to take the prompt delivery of students' grades seriously is also a message. According to Thomas Plough, provost at Rochester Institute of Technology, the quality of a program or institution is communicated every day in a thousand and one small acts:

> The professor who takes time out to explain criticism of student work in a constructive way, the health service nurse who visits the hospitalized students, the president who sits down at a table in the cafeteria with a group of students, the computer services department that responds, in writing, in its newsletter to every comment and suggestion made to them by students for improving the service, the dean who writes a short note to students who appear in the campus paper as sponsors of a community service project, the professor of television production and the residence hall adviser who sponsor a group of students to develop a documentary on residential life, the ombudsperson, dean of undergraduate students, or director of student life research who clearly presents valid data which supports improvement in the lives of students, the student leaders who initiate a process to shadow incoming students for several weeks as they become acquainted with the college as an organization, and the secretary who takes the time to smile and track down the answer to a question of moment for a student—these are the agents of the university responsible for the quality of student life.[5]

Many of the standard quality measures used by accrediting agencies, legislative bodies and faculty committees mean little to a student. This particular purchaser of educational services can and does apply his or her own "between the ears" quality test. The test is given every day in hallways, offices, and classrooms. Jan Carlzon, the president of Scandinavian Airlines (SAS), another service company, likes to call these opportunities "moments of truth." And when the institution doesn't make the grade, when they repeatedly fail these moments of truth described by Thomas Plough, a student responds like any other consumer. The manifestations are everywhere: low retention rates, weak alumni support, poor student attendance at campus events, high incidence of vandalism, and academic dishonesty.

For the most part, colleges and universities fail the "between the ears" test. The notion of KING CUSTOMER is alien to the college campus for a number of reasons. The most obvious is that some people on campus reject the notion that we have customers; that is, that college students are individuals who purchase our services. For example, in an issue of *Academe,* Roger Rollin, an English professor at Clemson University, dismisses the idea that the "business" of higher education has anything in common with the business of business. In his indignant diatribe against "biz-speak," he suggests that "when such modes of thinking [the language of business] become current, it is only a short step toward perceiving faculty as "employees," and students as "customers" at best, at worst as mere "revenue producers."[6]

I am reintroduced to another reason on a fairly regular basis. For more than a year I have been giving workshops on "managing for quality" at colleges and universities. The workshops are usually tied into a planning session or retreat and include both administrators and faculty members. After reviewing the methodology of my research and a snapshot of the quality movements in industry and higher education, I spend ten or fifteen minutes on each of the areas covered in this book. I have yet to make it through one of these workshops without having a dean or professor stand up and, in a bit of a huff, proceed to query, "What does this have to do with me?" Their point is that they do a good job in the classroom. They know their material, they make their classes interesting, they are available during office hours and beyond, and they have just completed a draft of a book. That's quality. Period. End of discussion. Our approach to educational quality is very much an "I know it when I see it in my classroom" perspective. In a contest of definitions, this transcendent definition seems regularly to beat out a user-based perspective.

In many regards, the day-to-day approach that we take to higher education is not that much different from the processes put into place at the *beginning* of the Industrial Age. As was noted in Chapter 1, the need for interchangeable parts in manufacturing required the division of labor. Each person on the production line was responsible for a specific task—one nut attached to one bolt. Is higher education that different today? We pigeonhole quality in much the same way. Each professor has a territorial right to a few classes and is encouraged to do the best possible job of transferring knowledge within that limited landscape—"That's quality. Period. End of discussion." But how often do we take responsibility for more than our own pigeonhole? How often does a department sit down (together) and wrestle with the holistic notion of what its program intends to accomplish? How much time do we spend evaluating whether the sum of our efforts in individual classrooms will suit our customers' requirements for lifelong learning and earning skills? Of course there are always people and programs that defy the general sweep of stereotyping, so I can't let the notion of "pigeonholing" pass without mentioning one convention-busting individual. During my interview with Tom Maher, the vice president of Academic Affairs at St. Francis College in Loretto, Pennsylvania, he told me that I *had to* talk with Bert Simon, the head of the Physician's Assistant (PA) Program. I did—for two hours. Here's one of Bert's little gems:

> *We work as a group. We do all kinds of things as a group. Because we have outside accreditation agencies to answer to, we have to do self-studies and all kinds of other things that other departments in the school have never even thought of doing much less being required to do. But even with other programs that do go through accreditation procedures, the program director sits down and he writes the self-study or he writes a grant. We do all of it in groups. We have brainstorming sessions, we all write different sections, we all review those sections as a group, and make it work as one document—as one thought. It takes a lot of time but I really believe that it makes the individuals feel as though they have responsibility for the "whole" program, not just the course that he or she teaches.*

Besides pigeonholing, another factor underlying the lack of a customer orientation in higher education comes from the "terminal degree" sacrament. Once the mantle has been draped over our shoulders, a certain transformation occurs. As terminal degree holders, our lecturing skills begin to far outpace our listening skills. This trait ends up getting more deans, vice presidents, and presidents into trouble than anything else. The scenario goes as follows: A new president is chosen, arrives on campus, brings in a few outside consultants, and announces that the future of the "college" is based upon its becoming a "university"—change the name, add three new programs, and build some dormitories. We lecture. In the industrial world this is known as a "production orientation." Engineers or designers develop products that *they think* have unique features. Such features are often more sophisticated from an engineering point of view, but have little to do with what the customer needs or wants. A customer orientation, in contrast, replaces this "I've-got-all-the-answers" syndrome with a perspective that intimately involves the end-user. The customer is seen as a partner in the process of developing and delivering a product or service. Is it really so hard for us to see students, board members, high school teachers, industry executives and others as "Partners in Progress" (the title of the North Dakota University System's quality-driven seven-year plan)?

This "I've-got-all-the-answers" syndrome is part of the culture of higher education. We practice it and we pass it on to others. For example, Allan Tucker and Robert Bryan's book, *The Academic Dean: Dove, Dragon, and*

Diplomat, coaches the academic dean on being production oriented, the glories of isolationism and the evils of listening. In a chapter appropriately entitled "Dealing with the Students," the authors discuss the rising tide of student consumerism. They describe the role and the responsibilities of a unit's student personnel officer: course scheduling and advising, the latter encompassing not only degree program guidance, but also matters relating to academic failure or success and academic probation, as well as problems relating to student-faculty interaction. Finally, they note, *"If the dean has a good assistant or associate dean in charge of these activities, the chances are slim that a student will ever get as far as the dean's office to discuss such matters."*[7] [italics added] The customers' "between the ears" notion of quality is not something to be *dealt with.* It is, or should be, the very core of the enterprise. I am reminded here of a story told by SAS's Jan Carlzon.[8] According to Carlzon, once Scandinavian Airlines focused on being the best "business class" airline in the world, the issue of punctuality became manifest. As a core need of their business customers, SAS resolved to set a goal that 100 percent of their planes would depart on time. Punctuality went from being something that was no one person's responsibility, to everyone's responsibility. Carlzon had a computer terminal installed on his desk to update him *every five minutes* on this critical quality indicator. I can think of no more important real-time, quality indicator for a student than his or her own "academic failure or success." It seems axiomatic that the dean, the professor, and the student would all have a common interest in the educational process.

Finally, the fact remains that more often than not, administrative convenience takes precedence over customer orientation. While discussing the topic of customer orientation at a college last year, one professor, said with some reluctance, that he often wondered what message we were sending to students. His example came from the registrar's office. He noticed that the windows where the students talked to the office workers had bars across them. One day, in passing, he asked the registrar about it and was told that they were installed because the office had confidential student records. The bars were for protection. This small revelation inspired another professor, just new to the college, to recall her first trip to the library. It had taken her several minutes to find the main card catalog. She finally found it in a large alcove toward the rear of the building. The back of the catalog cabinets were facing the main lobby while the front faced a row of offices—those belonging to the catalog librarians. Other professors and administrators quickly followed with their own examples.

The obvious point is that many of the things we do in higher education—both large and small—lack the unifying focus that a customer-driven organization naturally strives for. A customer-driven organization would find another way to protect the records without forcing the customer to speak through an iron-barred window. Such an organization would position a card catalog where access was easiest for the customer, not the staff. Such is the stuff of customer-driven organizations where quality really is "between the customer's ears," rather than being organized for the sake of administrative convenience.

So far I have taken a limited view of how "customer orientation" relates to the issue of causing quality in higher education. The view has focused on students as customers. We need to open the aperture to observe a somewhat broader panorama. The discussion has also been almost entirely descriptive. Consequently, the next several sections of this chapter are forceful prescriptions for the academic administrator.

Higher education must understand, appreciate, and respond to its "multi-customer" environment.

Perhaps the greatest "quality" problem that higher education faces is imbedded in the earlier story about the dean or professor who wanted to know "What does this have to do with me?" The intellectual center of a college campus is its academic programs, and at the heart of those programs are faculty members. Each faculty member, in turn, has her or his own transcendent definition of quality. Professors read, write, and do research or consulting in their specialities. This process not only increases their information base but also allows them to gain a deeper and richer "wisdom" as they grapple with more difficult discipline-specific questions. The quality of their research is the degree to which they advance their discipline. The quality of their teaching is the degree to which they can impart that wisdom to others. This perspective on quality parallels the one defined by Barbara Tuchman, as quoted in David Garvin's book on quality: "a condition of excellence implying fine quality as distinct from poor quality. . . . Quality is achieving or reaching for the highest standard as against being satisfied with the sloppy or fraudulent."[9]

While this quality perspective is critical to higher education, it remains singularly grounded in the narrow, historical view of a teacher—the artisan, the crafter. Socrates, discussing philosophy with several students on an Athens street corner, has moved inside a new $12 million "Humanities" building. The students go from his class to one in computer programming to another in cost accounting. They come from all over the world to attend the university—owned and operated by the state, and paid for by the students, their parents, and subsidized by the citizens of the state. Industry also supports the university through research grants and hires the most talented graduates. Each of these modern-day constituencies brings a unique "quality" perspective to higher education; their competing views present a real challenge to today's colleges and universities. Nonetheless, institutions and programs must develop clear understandings of each customer-constituency. The best way to do this is to stretch the standard definition of "customer" to include all persons or organizations who are affected by our service and process (see Figure 3.1).[10]

FIGURE *3.1*

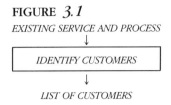

EXISTING SERVICE AND PROCESS
↓
IDENTIFY CUSTOMERS
↓
LIST OF CUSTOMERS

Seeing the service of education as a process reveals that every transaction has a customer (receiver of a service) and a supplier (provider of something that goes into a service). For example, a student in an advanced accounting course is a customer because he or she receives a service from a professor (the supplier). But that professor, in turn, is also a customer of the *introductory* accounting professor since he or she provides something (the student) that is part of the service. One of the fundamental principles of the strategic quality movement is related to this notion. Upon seeing the "process" as a "stream," it is logical to suggest that product or service quality *downstream* is best assured by maintaining quality *upstream*. The entire educational process (or stream), therefore, is a series of "quality-related" service transactions between a supplier and a customer.

To make it easier, let's divide the world of customers into two groups: internal and external. Within a college or university, groups or individuals can play different customer/supplier roles depending upon the nature of the service transaction. John Bennett provides an illustrative case study of the professor-professor transaction in his book, *Managing the Academic Department.*

THE COURSE SEQUENCE

Harry Jones was wondering why he had ever sought the position of department chairperson. One reason for his black mood had just walked out the door. Roger Grimm was a tenured associate professor of history responsible for a key course in the development of American economic institutions. The course was the second in a series of three, and it was important that the objectives in the syllabus be fully met. Otherwise students would be unprepared for the final course and the integrity of the whole sequence was threatened.

That was, in fact, precisely what was happening, for Grimm was failing to meet these goals. Several students had come by to complain to Jones about the course. Invariably, it seemed, Grimm would get bogged down along the way and the end of the semester would come before all of the material was covered. In defense, Grimm argued that the issues that diverted the course were important ones and that one should be free to follow wherever inquiry led. That, after all, is academic freedom, and nobody has the authority to intrude.

Jones had met with Professor Grimm several times on this issue. While rather stubborn and inflexible as an individual, Grimm had always enjoyed a reputation as a sympathetic instructor—concerned enough to meet the students "where they were" and to move ahead only when convinced that all or most were ready. At the last meeting Jones had rather forcefully stated to Grimm that the students were not well served if the class had not prepared them for the third course in the sequence. While Grimm seemed to agree, he could be rather enigmatic, and Jones had no confidence that he would improve.[11]

Each professor in the three-course sequence is both a supplier and a customer in the students' educational development. "Causing quality" requires that each professor works closely with her or his downstream "customers." Avoidance of this responsibility is disastrous for Professor Grimm's fellow professors in the same way that it would be in a manufacturing company. In Robert Waterman's book, *The Renewal Factor,* he describes a similar phenomenon referred to as "tossing it over the wall" by the people at the Ford Motor Company: "Design works on a project, tosses it over the wall to engineering, which tosses it over the wall to production, and so on. But engineering might not like whatever design tossed; production might not like what engineering had done, and so on."[12]

These same customer-supplier linkages occur all over the campus. You may recall some of the results described in the Oregon State University profile in the previous chapter. One Total Quality Management team in the physical plant worked on decreasing the time to complete a remodeling project with the intention of increasing efficiency and customer satisfaction. Another TQM team, in public safety, examined the security delivery process with the idea that increasing the frequency of security checks would thereby reduce the frequency of thefts. Currently, Facilities Management is an ongoing customer of the Office of Public Safety (supplier) as it works to ensure that thefts do not occur in the physical plant buildings. In the future, the Office of Public Safety (customer) may be the recipient of a customer-satisfying remodeling job performed by Facilities Management (supplier). The linkages are everywhere.

External customers are those individuals or groups who are affected by our service but are not a part of the college or university. Each of these customers has a different slant on quality. For example, in a recent article entitled "The Political Meaning of Quality," James Mingle, the executive director of the State Higher Education Executive Officers, says, "Quality, by the academician's definition, comes from the accrual of prestige *within* the academy. But state leaders are unimpressed by this measure of quality; they want concrete *service to the state*—basic skills, job training, and applied research being three such services."[13] The state is the customer. States and their citizens pay good money to support its colleges and universities. They, in effect, "purchase" an educated citizenry to support a democratic system. They purchase consulting and research services to help run the government. And they purchase the graduates of higher education institutions to fuel economic development. Consequently, they have every right to set quality standards—especially in light of concerns over the decline in student performances on standardized exams (e.g., the Graduate Record Exam) and professional licensing exams (e.g., state bars), the dilution of the liberal arts, and the steady climb in tuition rates. The unfortunate result, exacerbated by higher education's continued parochialism and defensiveness, is an ambitious set of mandates: a majority of states have convened blue ribbon commissions to examine higher education issues and have made the terms "productivity," "accountability," and "assessment" a common, if unwanted, part of the campus lexicon. Clearly, dismissing this customers' perception of quality is a mistake. It is this mistake that Frank Newman points to in *Choosing Quality: Reducing Conflict Between the State and the University:*

> The university needs a considerable degree of autonomy and flexibility so that it has the freedom to teach and research without politicized interference, so that creativity and imagination are encouraged and so that resources (including the time and energy of faculty, staff and students) are used efficiently. The university also needs the involvement of the state as a force for meeting the public's needs, as a force for change and as a force for accountability. The problem, therefore, is not to eliminate the state's role, but to perfect it.[14]

Industry is an external customer with yet another view. For example, as businesses become less hierarchical, the importance of team-playing skills begins to emerge. Specifically, lateral relationships (working with people and groups at the same level) are becoming at least as important as the traditional superior/subordinate vertical relationships. One aspect of a recent study by Porter and McKibbin on management education concerned the amount of emphasis given to *people* vs. *technical* skills in the business school curriculum. The authors suggest that "organizations are becoming, on average, more participative with diminished reliance on the exercise of 'top down' autocratic authority. Such tendencies, which probably become accentuated in service organizations, have the effect of increasing the need for effective 'soft' (i.e., people) skills even more than has been the case in the past."[15] But deans and faculty members—the suppliers to industry—offer a strikingly different perception (see Table 3.1). Clearly, business schools are still not "people" oriented enough for the business schools' customers (the CEO and VPHR). Equally clear is the fact that the schools that provide students with such skills will be viewed as being of higher quality.

In general, each customer group (including ones that I haven't mentioned such as the local community and alumni groups) uses its own defini-

TABLE *3.1* Perspectives on "People Skill Training" in the Business School Curriculum

(percentages)

	DEANS	FACULTY	ALUMNI*	CEO*	VPHR*
Too much	11	17	6	9	7
About right	68	60	48	24	21
Too little	21	23	46	67	72

*Alumni are recent undergraduate business school graduates.
*CEO are chief executive officers.
*VPHR are vice presidents of human resources or the chief personnel officers.
Source: Lyman W. Porter and Lawrence E. McKibbin, *Management Education and Development: Drift or Thrust into the 21st Century* (New York: McGraw-Hill, 1988), 69. Reprinted with permission of McGraw-Hill, Inc.

tions and perceptions to judge quality. Professors use one, students use another, accrediting agencies and members of the state legislature use still others. Consequently, a college or university must become increasingly savvy about the tug and pull of these competing customer groups. Let me offer an illustration:

THE TALE OF TWO CUSTOMERS

The Association of College and Research Libraries (ACRL), a division of the American Library Association, first issued its Standards for College Libraries in 1959. The most recent version, approved in 1986, has eight sections: objectives, collections, organization of materials, staff, services, facilities, administration, and budget. Within some of these sections, the quality "standard" is defined in terms of a formula. Specifically, the quantity of materials that should be in a collection is derived from Formula A. A basic collection requires 85,000 volumes and is supplemented by a 15 volume allowance per FTE [Full-time equivalent] student, a 100 volume allowance per FTE faculty member, a 25,000 volume allowance per doctoral field, and so on. Formula B looks to enrollment, collection size, and collection growth to determine the number of librarians required. One librarian is necessary for each 5,000 volumes that are added per year. Formula C derives the space requirements for users, staff and books. The space allocated for books, for example, is estimated to be 0.10 square feet per volume for the first 150,000 volumes. The next 150,000 volumes require 0.09 square feet per volume and so on. Finally, it should be noted that the ACRL Standards even have a grading system to accompany the formula. In regards to space, libraries that provide 90 to 100 percent of the net assignable called for by the formula shall be graded A; 75–89 percent shall be graded B; 60–74 percent shall be graded C; and 50–59 percent shall be graded D.

The William Patterson College library conducted a self-study that was designed to (1) identify the impact of library weaknesses on users, (2) evaluate functions by patrons, (3) be feasible, and (4) serve as a management tool, not as an academic exercise. The approach was to survey selected users regarding the purpose of their search, the steps they took, and the outcome. Librarians then reviewed failed outcomes via a branching analysis to determine the source of errors—e.g. acquisition error, catalogue error, circulation error, retrieval error, and so on. Also, other selected users were directly observed in their search efforts. An extensive analysis of the findings revealed six categories of failures (of which fully 63 percent were considered library errors)—i.e., shortcomings in library routines. For example, the study concluded that several physical plant idiosyncrasies, such as signage, influenced patron success rates. The recommendation: "Directional signs that have become 'invisible' to staff members who 'see' them at the time, may be woefully inadequate. An assessment of signage by an outside party may help improve patron access to materials."[16]

The criticalness of understanding the multiple perspectives on quality is evident in the "Tale of Two Customers." The ACRL, an external customer, uses a manufacturing-based definition of quality similar to that proposed by Philip Crosby—quality defined as "conformance to requirements." Hence, a high quality library receives "A" marks if it can meet or beat the 90 percent level on its various standards. But there is an obvious problem with relying on "standards" as a single, comprehensive measure of quality. Students and professors apply a decidedly different measure. For example, in the same year that the new ACRL standards were issued, Hernon and McClure reported the results of their study on library use. Based upon their unobtrusive testing of reference services (the process of asking reference questions—for which answers have been predetermined—of staff members who are unaware that they are being evaluated) and previous studies in the area, the authors concluded that college reference staff generally answer just 50–60 percent of the questions correctly. In addition, these staff members also make infrequent referrals, either internal or external, to other libraries, fail to negotiate reference questions, and conduct ineffective search strategies. Hernon and McClure further conclude: "For approximately 20 years now, the library community has been aware of the 55% accuracy rate, yet few tangible strategies have been developed to address the finding."[17] Conformance to standards, therefore, may be a necessary but certainly not a sufficient condition for quality in libraries. The internal customer is less interested in standards and formulas than they are in a user-based definition of quality—"fitness for use."

It is incumbent upon the college or the program to research the
needs of its specific customer groups.

Knowing who your customers are (upstream-downstream, internal-external) is not enough. Generating the list, by itself, is a routine exercise. Even having a "general idea" or "gut feel" about needs is inadequate. Only understanding, in the truest sense of the word, will do. But knowing what quality means to different customer groups is not an easy assignment. Empathy is not a commonly-occurring human characteristic.

The intellectual roots of customer-based understanding are found in anthropology and sociology. Their emphasis on human culture and interaction requires that the phenomena be described in an individual's natural language. The resulting approach, phenomenology, stands in stark contrast to the characteristics of the scientific method. For example, the traditional empiricist sets up preconceived realities that he or she seeks to test, whereas, the phenomenologist begins with the data and inductively forms conclusions to fit that data. The procedure is from the bottom up, with the researcher attempting to reduce preconceptions of the subject to a minimum. By beginning with specific observations and building toward general patterns, the researcher is able to develop an understanding of the situation as it emerges from the data. I particularly like the view expressed by Schwartz and Jacobs in *Qualitative Sociology* when describing a research subject: "He lives there; he knows better than we do what it is like and how best to describe it."[18] With a slight alteration it serves our topic quite well: The customer lives there; the customer knows better than we do what quality is and how best to describe it (see Figure 3.2).

Stripped down to its street-language basics, phenomenology is listening—*really listening.* From the industry side, ineffective listening costs American businesses billions of dollars annually. Because of poor listening skills, reports have to be retyped; unnecessary conflicts disrupt daily operations; shipments have to be reshipped; ideas are distorted as they travel through communication channels; *and individuals and organizations are unable to understand and respond to customers' needs.* Management experts have sounded the trumpets. Tom Peters devotes an entire chapter to the topic—"Become Obsessed with Listening," in *Thriving on Chaos.* Robert

FIGURE 3.2

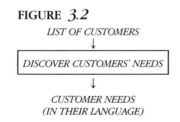

LIST OF CUSTOMERS
↓
DISCOVER CUSTOMERS' NEEDS
↓
CUSTOMER NEEDS
(IN THEIR LANGUAGE)

Waterman recalls the following story in a section on listening in *The Renewal Factor:*

> William Colby, former director of the CIA, was speaking to a group of American businessmen, and his remarks were on the listening theme. 'The trouble with the way you run your businesses,' he said, 'is that you don't listen. Looked at one way, American business has one of the most wonderful intelligence-gathering networks in the world. Branches, divisions, and subsidiaries everywhere. But the communication goes one way. You talk to them, tell them what to do. You don't listen.'[19]

And in *Commit to Quality,* one insurance industry executive, Patrick Townsend, discusses in detail the notion of "listening down—and out."[20] Townsend claims that in spite of American industry's agreement that listening down is desirable, all too often the common mode of communication is "listening up." All of their lives, managers have been told implicitly and explicitly that wisdom comes from further up the corporate ladder. It is an unfortunate part of the culture that one listens up and gives orders down.

Although we don't have such rigid hierarchical structures in higher education as in many businesses we are not any better listeners. Professors are paid to lecture. Administrators are paid to develop and implement policies—top down. Directors of housing and computer services seem to issue memos at the same rate as corporate America. We all have something to say, and we keep searching for someone who will listen to it. It's part of our culture, too. When you think of it, students are the only ones on a college campus who are really encouraged to listen. In fact, they are graded on their ability to listen and to repeat what they have heard or read. To a great degree we parallel Colby's view of the corporate world. We have wonderful listening networks—college classrooms, advisory boards, alumni groups, and so on. But we talk to them. We don't really listen.

There are a number of different ways in which we can improve our hearing. One of the most effective ways is by informal listening. It merely involves creating the opportunities to discover our customers' needs—*in their language.* Michael Weber, the vice president of Academic Affairs at Duquesne University, uses informal get-togethers to tackle the dozens of little things that people see as problems too frivolous to bring up at a formal meeting but which "are the little ticks that bother people and make it tough for them to do their job." Every month or so he has breakfast with his deans. Bacon and eggs, problems and peeves. In one meeting a couple of deans got onto a topic. The tick: "I can't read those damn budget sheets. Can't you get somebody in the budget office to do something different so that I can make some sense out of it?" The solution: "So I said fine and I called the budget director and said "How about joining us for breakfast?' " According to Weber, all it took was a simple change. The budget sheets had been set up that way because of "administrative convenience" but once the director saw that it really was a problem—through the eyes of his customers—he was willing to change. The key to informal listening, then, is to get out from behind the cozy confines of the office furniture. Peters and Waterman stylized the concept— "Management by Walking Around"—in *In Search of Excellence*. A president will learn more about the important issues on the minds of the students during a dormitory "study break" than from a biweekly, 2:00 to 3:00, sit-behind-the-desk, office hour. A dean will understand the hopes and dreams of a professor far easier from a series of after-hours chats in the professor's lab than from a formal, first-thing-in-the-morning meeting in the dean's office. A director of Public Safety will appreciate the problems facing her or his officers by occasionally working a car or foot patrol shift.

Formalized listening also has its benefits. St. Francis College's Bert Simon had a great example for me. His Physician's Assistant Program is tough and he knows it: "Most of these students have never been pushed. And maybe sometimes we push a little too hard and then we have to ease off. But we push. We want to make sure that they see what they can do. Most of them don't realize what they can do. They've never been challenged to the extent that we challenge them." Under such conditions, he and his colleagues feel it's necessary to have a formal listening mechanism—"We have an hour a month where we have a psychologist come in with the students. The faculty is not allowed in the meeting. And the rules are that the students can say anything to the psychologist that they want and that none of that will leave the room unless they want it to. So they can have a chance to really bitch and moan about us or anything and get it off their chest. If it's important, we'll hear about it."

Colleges and universities need to consider all sorts of listening devices. Exit interviews should become a common practice. Pick 15 graduating seniors and spend 30 minutes with each of them. Ask them about their best experiences and their worst. How about first-year students? Take a group of them to lunch and ask them about their impressions of college life. What were their expectations? A professor at a small, private college recently told me of his own little "listening" session. He asked a few first-year students from his classes how they felt about the college after one year. One student was positively effusive. It turns out that she hadn't been sure she was "college material," after spending the prior semester at a large university. Then she transferred to this smaller school, and on the first day of her first class a professor wrote his home phone number on the chalkboard saying, "If you ever need help on classroom work or just someone to talk to, I want you to know that I am always available—night or day." Quality, in her case, included the need to feel as though there was a safety net. Giving out a home phone number was a symbol of the degree to which the professor cared. The professor never knew, until he listened, how important such a simple act really was.

And let's not focus just on the student interviews. Does your school conduct interviews with professors, administrators, and staff persons who choose to move on to other institutions? Most people leave a position for a "better one," not necessarily for more money. Why is it better? What did the other institution offer the individual that you didn't? What would have made him or her consider staying?

Do customer surveys. Jerrold Pritchard, the associate vice president for Academic Programs at California State–San Bernardino, has been a disciple for years: "We did marketing surveys, asking students in the area, high school teachers, counselors, community leaders—"What did they see as the strengths of our programs?' The thing that initially came back very clear was that they didn't know we were here at all. We were invisible to this community. And that's one reason why the institution didn't grow. We had been here twenty years and still were only 3,000 students." Things have changed, however. "Now we are close to 10,000. But that didn't happen by accident. We not only opened up our doors but we actually brought the institution out to the community. We got very well plugged in with the planning commissions, chambers of commerce, got people put on city council boards, worked in regional meetings with school administrators—to let them know that we were here and that we were interested in providing a service."

I will leave this section with one short quote. It's a favorite of mine by Philip Crosby: "Listening. You can convey no greater honor than to actually hear what someone has to say."[21] High quality colleges, universities, and corporations are better at listening, at researching the needs of their specific customer groups, than the hordes of mediocre institutions that they compete with. They have more people listening and they listen harder to what their customers have to say. They are in the enviable position of being able to cause quality because they are uniquely aware of the quality indicators as described by their customers.

You need to engage in quality deeds, not just quality words.

This final prescription is the third leg of a customer-orientation stool. One of the most important aspects of listening is not only to hear the words voiced by your customers but to react to them. There is, perhaps, nothing worse than a suggestion box that fills up, generates polite responses, but nothing else. The message is clear to those individuals who make the effort to offer suggestions: their perceptions of quality are interesting but don't really count.

Customer needs are not warm fuzzy notions. They are identifiable: you know what you want in a new car, an airplane flight, and a night at the theater. In a recent article entitled "Winning Customer Service," the author gives an example to which all of us can relate: "When a customer is turned down for a loan by a bank, he's not nearly as interested in why the bank won't loan the money as he is in what his options are. So, instead of turning people away when they don't 'qualify,' we'd be better off helping them find the best alternative solutions."[22] Empathy or intentions are not enough. Listening is, again, a

FIGURE *3.3*

CUSTOMER NEEDS
↓

DEVELOP AND REFINE SERVICE

↓

SERVICE FEATURES

necessary but insufficient condition for causing quality in higher education. Listening to the complaints of a student who has decided to transfer will not change that person's mind. Quality deeds are what counts. Locate shortcomings or defects, scrutinize them, trace the sources of the problem, make corrections, and then standardize the new approach so that quality problems don't reoccur (see Figure 3.3).

Jerrold Pritchard happened to describe a wonderful illustration of translating a customer need into service features. California State–San Bernardino's surveying of students who had dropped out of college revealed that one of the main reasons was finances—the car broke down and they couldn't commute any longer. It was decided that a key goal of their STOPOUT program should be to "maintain these people as part of the university community." The service features? According to Pritchard, "We keep them on the mailing list for university events, we still advise them, give them library privileges, and they don't have to reapply for admissions. We need to help them persist." Understanding is great. Customer-driven solutions are better. And the way to generate such solutions is by listening, learning, and then taking action.

Finally, nothing, and I mean nothing, attracts customers—top notch students who send in their tuition deposits early, great professors who stay in spite of being offered more money elsewhere, local citizens who vote for a university construction bond, employers who can't get enough of your graduates—like quality. Customers tell us every day what quality means to them. Sometimes they pound the table while shouting it, other times they whisper it to each other in hallways and parking lots. Those of us in higher education just need to listen and act.

4

Choosing to
Be Distinctive

The story which I heard from Jerry Kissler, former vice provost at UCLA and now at the University of Oregon, was virtually the same story that had been described to me on other college campuses. It seems a particular program was struggling: It lost its chairperson and was in the process of losing several of its better faculty members. According to Kissler, they organized a retreat with the purpose of rebuilding a sense of cohesion within the department: "As part of a brainstorming activity, one of the stronger members of the department said to his colleagues, 'I want you to tell me what you think are some of the most important research questions in our field.'" What he had hoped to do was to uncover a common denominator or recurring themes and coordinate special groups to pursue them. There was also the possibility of outside funding for these projects. Nice idea—theoretically. Unfortunately, there stood a major hurdle in this new pathway to respectability. Kissler noted, "It turned out there were thirty different themes. No overlap. No cohesion. Nothing. Three years later and it's [the program] still floundering." With an accreditation review on the horizon, the steady loss of students and the constant bickering having been adopted as the cultural norm. The program has no prospects for a quick reclamation.

Thousands of miles away, in a hotel conference room on the East Coast, a management consultant is using an organizational behavior exercise to shake up a room of confident, qualified executives. The exercise goes as follows: First the individuals write, in twenty words or less, what makes their organization, or unit, "distinctive." This causes mild heart palpitations and various twitching reflexes among many of the executives. The individuals' "comfort zones" are further disturbed when the consultant asks them to compare their descriptions with others in the room. Next, every person is asked to call, sometime during the day, another person back at the office—

not a same-level colleague, but rather a secretary, a junior executive, a receiving clerk, or so on. They are to ask that person the same question: "In twenty words or less, what makes us distinctive?"

Of course, in cases like the program at UCLA, we don't need a management consultant to tell us a problem exists. The signs are everywhere. But in many other situations, programs or institutions just stumble along, propelled forward by sheer momentum rather than a sense of direction or purposefulness. Those working in these programs are content to muddle their way through a daily set of activities. Their decisions are reactive and lack focus or passion. The bottom line: If you, your colleagues, and other members of your institution don't use virtually the same words to describe your distinctiveness, your individuality, you have a problem that *necessarily* affects the quality of your operation.

> A *unifying, guiding, and distinctive vision is the foundation on which a "house of quality" is built.*

The previous chapter presented an ordered view of the world—identify customers, discover customers' needs, and develop and refine your services. It would be nice if "causing quality" was so straightforward: Just satisfy the customer's needs and let everything else fall logically into place. Unfortunately, reality is a good deal more knotty than that. For example, let's assume for a moment that each customer-constituency (i.e., students, professors, legislators, accrediting agencies, and so on) uses more than one criterion or service attribute (e.g., class size) to form an attitude about quality. An individual student could use, in addition to average class size, other criteria such as selectivity and job placement success to make quality judgments about a specific program or college vis-à-vis another program or college. Furthermore, the various criteria or attributes are not of equal importance to the student—selectivity may be more important than class size, and class size, in turn, may be more important than job placement. These quality judgments could be quantified by asking the student to rate three different colleges (from 1 = worst to 10 = best) on each of the attributes. In addition, the attributes could be assigned a weight (from 1 = very unimportant to 10 = very important). Table 4.1 displays the results of our student's evaluation exercise.

Now, what can we surmise about this student's "between the ears" perception of quality? Is College A better? How about B or C? Martin Fishbein pioneered a model that specifies how individuals combine evaluations of an object across multiple attributes to arrive at a single overall attitude toward that object.[1] The Fishbein model (as detailed in note 1) applied to our student's perceptions results in an overall score of 184 for College A, 214 for College B, and 152 for College C. Obviously, the model is compensatory

TUESDAY
DECEMBER 31, 2002

31

DECEMBER 2002

S	M	T	W	T	F	S
1	2	3	4	5	6	7
8	9	10	11	12	13	14
15	16	17	18	19	20	21
22	23	24	25	26	27	28
29	30	31				

NOVEMBER 2002

S	M	T	W	T	F	S
					1	2
3	4	5	6	7	8	9
10	11	12	13	14	15	16
17	18	19	20	21	22	23
24	25	26	27	28	29	30

JANUARY 2003

S	M	T	W	T	F	S
			1	2	3	4
5	6	7	8	9	10	11
12	13	14	15	16	17	18
19	20	21	22	23	24	25
26	27	28	29	30	31	

APPOINTMENTS & SCHEDULED EVENTS

HOURS	NAME • PLACE • SUBJECT
7 0700	
8 0800	
9 0900	
10 1000	
11 1100	
12 1200	
1 1300	
2 1400	
3 1500	
4 1600	
5 1700	
6 1800	
7 1900	
8 2000	
9 2100	
10 2200	

TO BE DONE TODAY (ACTION LIST)

PHONE CALLS

EXPENSE & REIMBURSEMENT RECORD

REF.	NAME OR PROJECT	DETAILS OF MEETINGS • AGREEMENTS • DECISIONS	TIME HRS. 1/10
1			
2			
3			
4			
5			
6			
7			
8			
9			
10			
11			
12			
13			
14			
15			
16			
17			
18			
19			
20			
21			
22			
23			
24			
25			
26			
27			
28			
29			
30			
31			
32			
33			
34			
35			
36			
37			
38			
39			
40			

DIARY AND WORK RECORD

MONDAY
30
364th Day
DECEMBER, 2002

TABLE *4.1*   One Student's Opinion

ATTRIBUTE	IMPORTANCE WEIGHT (0 = 10)	RATINGS		
		COLLEGE A	COLLEGE B	COLLEGE C
Selectivity	10	9	8	6
Average class size	8	8	10	7
Job placement	6	5	9	6

because it assumes that an overall attitude toward a college is determined by the weighted sum of the ratings for that college on all relevant attributes. Thus, a poor evaluation on one attribute is compensated for by a strong evaluation on another attribute. So while College B receives a lower rating on the most important variable (selectivity), its overall rating is still the highest.

We have identified a customer (our student), discovered his or her needs (what quality means), and now all we have to do is refine our services accordingly. If we are College A for instance, we might want to consider putting our energy into reducing class size. College B could improve its quality, between our student's ears, by becoming more selective. But this is still oversimplified. First, chances are the student uses more quality attributes than the three mentioned above. Second, not every student views the world the same way. It is futile to use our solitary student as a cookie-cutter stereotype for all other students. There are clusters of students who use a different array of attributes and/or they attach different importance weights to those attributes. Each and every customer-constituency uses different attributes and/ or different importance weights to generate their perceptions of quality. For while class size may say "quality" to some students, it may say something quite differently to members of the state legislature—specifically, "a lack of productivity." Job placement (i.e., economic development) may be key to legislators' view of the world while selectivity may be critical to professors. Each constituent group, therefore, may contain numerous subgroups or segments—all of which have competing, and in some cases contradictory, views of quality.

How do most colleges and universities address this conundrum? In the midst of such complex, opposing views, how do institutions of higher learning choose the quality attributes on which they will compete? For the most part, they don't. Our institutions don't fashion a vision statement based upon systematic attitude research, internal analyses of strengths, and societal needs. They don't use TQM tools like the affinity diagram to collect the attributes of the "ideal" institution or program and organize those attributes into sets of related information. They don't study the barriers to achieving the vision. In short, quality attributes are not "managed in" in any sort of strategic fashion. This is not a conscious choice. For colleges and universities tend to avoid choices by straddling as many different quality attributes as possible. Take a brief look at three illustrations of this institutional non-decision making: homogenized vision statements, program proliferation and a broadened commitment, and competition for resources (not quality).

Most colleges, universities, and academic programs or centers, have vision statements. These statements are intended to be the written manifestations of an organization's unifying focus. The vision statement is also an attempt to formulate and communicate "key values" as well as a view of the future. A vision statement is a sense of purpose . . . *this is why we exist.* How many of you reading this book know your institution's vision statement? How many of you think that half the employees in the institution know it as well? I suggest that the reason so few people have a clear understanding of their institution's vision is because there is really nothing in it worth remembering. Benjamin Tregoe and Peter Tobia provide an example of this phenomenon from one of the companies they studied for their book, *Vision in Action.* The company defined its business as "the creation of machines and methods to help find solutions to the increasingly complex problems of business, government, science, space exploration, education, medicine, and nearly every other area of human endeavor."[2] This "sense of purpose" sounds as if it were devised by a committee of politicians who, knowing that whenever they take a stand on an issue they risk disenfranchising a segment of the electorate, choose instead, to spread a blanket of . . . rhetoric. When faced with the task of choosing a unifying focus, colleges and universities and their sub-units, tend to act exactly like a committee of politicians. By attempting to couch vision statements in terms suitable for public consumption, they often end up with apple pie generalities; that is, statements that, in effect, mechanically enumerate what the institution has *in common* with other institutions, rather than seeking to explain and describe its "specialness." Just listen to the words of Glenn Irvin, the associate vice president for academic affairs at California Polytechnic State University–San Luis Obispo (Cal Poly–SLO):

> *I've been on a lot of campuses and they're homogenized. They're shopping center institutions. If you were to walk around most campuses and talk to the faculty and administration and say, 'What's your vision?,' you'd be greeted with common platitudes but they really don't get at anything special. Because once you do that you are necessarily shutting some doors. And most people are very reluctant to shut any doors. The resulting statements are eminently forgettable.*

Another manifestation of non-decision making has occurred in the area of academic programs. With no unifying focus to guide the process, the development of new academic programs within institutions of higher education has been a growth industry throughout the 1970s and the 1980s. Each year, seemingly irrespective of admissions data, internal financial conditions, or other possible constraints, college catalogs become a few pages longer, a few ounces heavier. Like the automobile industry, each model year our colleges and universities introduce a new line of programs with the appropriate number of options, configurations, bells, and whistles. The resulting diversification strategy often creates a proliferation of programs—a menagerie of unrelated academic courses that dilutes any guiding quality theme.

Several years ago I conducted an empirical "resource" test of this hypothesis by analyzing three sets of ratios—the average number of undergraduate students per program, the average number of faculty per program, and the average amount of funding per program—at a set of institutions in 1975 and again in 1985. The conclusion was that the "average" program of 1985 had fewer students, fewer faculty members, and a smaller budget than it did a decade earlier:

> Popular or politically relevant programs are developed, some of which relate to the vision of the institution, others of which do not. Few, if any, programs are dropped. Resources, budgetary and personnel, are stretched to meet new needs while causing many existing programs to survive on a subsistence level. This forced-resource diet jeopardizes both the quality of the stronger programs and the future needs of the newly added programs. Indeed, the very mission of the institution is compromised, resulting in a collection of courses and programs—hodge-podge.[3]

This knee-jerk proliferation necessarily results in an ever-broadening commitment to academic areas. Allan Bloom in his treatise, *The Closing of the American Mind,* labels this process a "democracy of disciplines:"

> The university now offers no distinctive visage to the young person. [She or he] finds a democracy of disciplines ... Each department or great division of the university makes a pitch for itself, and each offers a course of study that will make the student an initiate ... So the student must navigate among a collection of carnival barkers, each trying to lure him into a particular sideshow ... This democracy is really an anarchy, because there are no recognized rules for citizenship and no legitimate titles to rule. In short there is no vision....[4]

The issue of program proliferation should be of special concern to administrators in an era of demographic decline. The '90s decade has brought weakened admissions standards and some deep digging into application pools in order to fill the first-year student class. At the same time, the cost of doing research in many disciplinary specializations has skyrocketed. In the *Fortune* article, "Why Universities Are Shrinking," the author states, "Research, for one thing, has become uncontrollably expensive—even Classics professors use costly computer technology. Smarter university administrators are catching on that they must conduct research in fewer fields so they can afford to provide a quality education." He goes on to quote Columbia's provost Jonathan Cole: "No university is capable of covering all areas of scholarship anymore."[5] The fact is that colleges and universities have wonderful mechanisms and incentives for creating new programs, institutes, and cen-

TABLE *4.2*   Administrators' Views of Challenges Facing
Institutions In the Next Five Years

PERCENTAGE OF ADMINISTRATORS CITING EACH CHALLENGE:	
Maintaining enrollment	44%
Facilities and technology	42
Adequate resources	39
Maintain quality	28
Fund raising	21
Recruitment and retention of good faculty	19
Serve new needs and populations	18
Strengthen curriculum	15
Diversity	13
Other faculty issues	11
Effective faculty	9
Enrollment growth	7

Source: Reprinted with permission of the American Council on Education from
"The Nation," *Chronicle of Higher Education Almanac,* September 1989, p. 24.

ters. But they have few processes that allow for or reward the efficient reallocation of resources in any meaningful way. We push forward, advancing on all
fronts, until we face overwhelming resistance. We then declare fiscal exigency
and announce a retrenchment plan or a series of cost containment exercises
as I discussed in Chapter 1.

The third and final manifestation of our colleges' and universities' unwillingness or inability to choose is a natural outcome of the prior two. With
no unifying vision and a democracy of diversified disciplines, institutions
become mired in the day-to-day problems of survival. A recent edition of the
Chronicle of Higher Education published the results of an American Council
on Education survey of over 350 college and university senior administrators.
Among the topics covered was the issue of challenges facing higher education
in the coming years (see Table 4.2).

What these numbers in Table 4.2 say, in effect, is that our colleges and
universities have created an infrastructure ("Facilities and technology") that
requires students ("Maintaining enrollment") and resources ("Adequate resources" and "Fund raising"). Instead of "quality" driving the equation, we are
stuck in the role of reactionaries—dashing to solve the most pressing problem. The tail is wagging the dog! There is absolutely nothing strategic about
this set of priorities. It is entirely tactical and decidedly reactive.

There is a crucial implication in all of this for the academic administrator. According to strategy expert Michael Porter, there are only three successful generic strategies that an organization can adopt to position itself within a
competitive environment: (1) "overall cost leadership," (2) "differentiation"
(by which he means leadership in quality or service across a broadly defined
market), and (3) "focus" (a niche strategy).[6]

"Cost leadership" is the clearest of the three strategies. An organization competes on the basis of a cost advantage that translates into high value. In higher education, community colleges and some comprehensive state colleges have this value-based position firmly staked out. They offer a "no-frills" education that often translates directly into marketable skills. With "differentiation" an organization seeks to be unique in its competitive environment along several dimensions (according to Porter an organization must choose dimensions that differentiate it from its rivals). This broad-based excellence is exhibited by Harvard, the University of California, Berkeley, and Stanford. Tom Wasow, the dean of Undergraduate Studies in the College of Humanities and Sciences, explained Stanford's unique dimensions to me:

> One thing I should say about this place, that almost goes without saying, is that we have a world class research university with people who are famous as researchers. And we are trying to run a topnotch undergraduate program as well. There's tension I suppose in every research university between those two things. But I like to think that we have more than our share of faculty members who, as research scholars, take undergraduate teaching seriously. It's a delicate balancing act to maximize the advantages of both a research university and a small, liberal arts college. But I think we probably do as good a job as anyone in achieving that balance.

The final competitive strategy, "focus," is different from the others because it rests on the selection of a segment or group of segments in the marketplace and involves tailoring a strategy to serve that segment *to the exclusion of others*. Wade Gilley, Kenneth Fulmer, and Sally Reithlingshoefer discuss a numbers of these "focused" institutions in *Searching for Academic Excellence*. This includes the age-integrated approach of Aquinas College, Northern Arizona University's emphasis in education, forestry, hotel and restaurant management, and so on.[7]

There is one additional aspect of Porter's thesis that is critical to this discussion. He suggests that organizations failing to adopt one of these three strategies are "stuck in the middle." What are the implications of being stuck in the middle? Well, if the industry is growing, the effects may be minimal. But in virtually all other situations, the organizations that are caught in the middle will struggle. Why? Because they are *average*—and who wants to put down good money on something (whether it's a car, a concert, or a college) that's average? It's common sense according to Tom Peters, who observes in *Thriving on Chaos,* that, "The average consumer doesn't go to the yellow pages and say, 'Where can I find a product with an average number of defects at an average price?' You either want something great, and you'll pay for it. Or if you don't care excessively about the quality [or can't afford it], you want it as cheap as possible."[8] Being stuck in the middle implies that the organization has no special qualities that would enable it to raise its head above the din of the competition. Those in the middle must be content to survive on whatever share of business the market tosses their way.

How many colleges and universities can offer the cost advantage of a community college, or the across-the-board excellence of Stanford, or the focused uniqueness of Aquinas College? Very few. The rest are in contention with one another trying to sell "average" to a decreasing supply of first-year students. They are also having to justify mediocrity while at the same time making a case for an increase in spending to their state's legislature. Additionally, they are challenged to generate an *esprit de corps* or an ideology suggesting one should care about the work one does in an environment that minimizes any sense of specialness. They are "stuck in the middle."

Becoming stuck in the middle is usually a manifestation of an organization's unwillingness (or inability) to make choices about how to compete. Such reluctance necessarily results in a "regression to the mean," or a generalized contentment with mediocrity. This, in turn, creates a significant barrier to the strategic management of quality. In contrast, a more assertive approach—a desire to differentiate a product or service from the crowd—has a number of practical benefits. One set of benefits is external while the other set occurs on the college campus.

A distinctive vision allows a college or university to establish a unique position in the higher education environment.

The major advantage of a customer orientation, as we noted in the Chapter 3, is that it enables us to begin to understand the critical dimensions of quality as perceived by our customer-constituencies. Knowing how an accrediting agency, or the state legislature, or industry, or parents perceive quality is a basis for developing or modifying our service features. These are the actual attributes of a product or service that we, as academic managers, can manipulate (i.e., the degree of selectivity or class size). But quality is relative. A customer believes that one make of automobile or stereo is "better" than another. Why? Because the customer has determined, through his or her own internal decision making model, that the overall evaluation of brand X's "quality" attributes rate higher than brand Y's. Products and services are not judged by customers as isolated, independent attitude objects. Instead, quality judgments are made via a matrix of trade-offs—attributes on one axis, attitude objects on another, and relative "ratings" (how well each attitude object does on that particular attribute) filling in the matrix.

It can be argued that people don't scurry around applying Fishbein's model to every can of tuna, television, or college. They don't whip out a pencil and begin practicing their multiplication tables at the first sign of a

FIGURE *4.1* An Accounting Firm's Perceptual Map

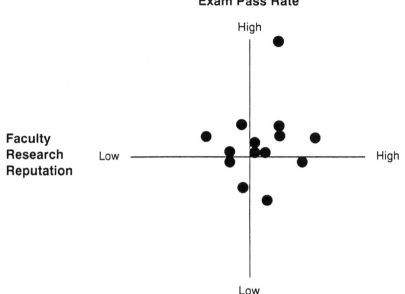

decision. But the fact is that, as customers, they do "position" products and services on a perceptual map.

Take, for example, an accounting firm's view of collegiate accounting programs. Two quality dimensions might be (1) the preparedness of undergraduates, and (2) the research reputation of the faculty. Schools might be positioned as follows (see Figure 4.1).

Most schools are perceived to be pretty "average"—average exam pass rates and average faculty research reputations. Such institutions (those that cluster together) are in the words of Cal Poly SLO's Glenn Irvin "eminently forgettable." But how about the school that has managed, by generating superior exam pass rates and a solid faculty research reputation, to separate itself from the rest? It has staked out a memorable position in a very competitive environment. Luckily, for our purposes, it isn't a fictitious school. It exists. Northern Illinois University's accounting program has *chosen to be distinctive* and Kendall Baker, NIU's vice president and provost, told me why and how:

> *Over time the department recognized that the thing that was most important, in terms of establishing its reputation, was to produce undergraduate students that would be very successful with Big 6 accounting firms. One of the things that it discovered that it needed to do was make sure that its students were well prepared and did well on the accountancy exams. And that is exactly what it did. The department put together a program, that is kind of a tutoring program, for the accountancy exam, which is superb. NIU students pass that test at a higher rate*

than any other institution in the country. . . This is an undergraduate program. The faculty do a good deal of research. Many of them have superb reputations as accountancy faculty but the reputation of the department is not really built on the research reputation of the faculty, or the quality of its Ph.D. students because we don't have a Ph.D. program. This is basically an undergraduate program that produces absolutely great accountants—students that are successful in passing the exams, students who are successful in the firms, students who move through the firms into key positions, and who then become excellent alumni for the department. . . This is a department that defines 'quality of program' not in terms of the research accomplishments of its faculty, although those are substantial, it defines it in terms of the accomplishments of its undergraduates.

NIU's Accounting department deserves the "quality" reward—a distinctive position among numerous competitors—for daring to push hard at being different and for creatively allocating resources to those attributes (quality measures) of the service that are relevant to customers. In strategic quality management, therefore, one can easily see "strategy" as a means of identifying where an institution or program locates itself—its niche—in a competitive environment.

A distinctive vision is an organizational rallying force.

Forget for a moment that colleges and universities compete for students, professors, grants, state funds, alumni gifts, and so on. Shifting our attention away from the advantages of establishing a strong quality position in the external environment, let's look at the advantages that "choosing to be distinctive" has within the campus walls. On the most general level, "choosing" necessarily involves a great deal of healthy introspection. Developing "distinctiveness" is more than just deciding what the organization would like to do; *it is also taking advantage of what it can do.* In other words, by listening to customers and understanding their dimensions of quality an institution generates a wide range of opportunities. Furthermore, by knowing how customers view an attitude object (e.g., accounting programs) along a set of product or service attributes (e.g., exam pass rates, faculty research reputation, and so on), the institution can consider focusing on those attributes that will make a difference vis-à-vis the competition. Finally, opportunity must coincide with competence. Conducting an assessment of the institution's strengths and weaknesses is one of the key elements in the strategic planning process as described by George Keller in *Academic Strategy,* and by Barbara Townsend in *A Search for Institutional Distinctiveness,* to name a few. In conducting the introspective exercise institutional members gain a better understanding of their possibilities and limitations. Kendall Baker described this introspection as part of the development of NIU's accounting program—"The faculty came to some conclusions about where they thought they could go and what they thought they wanted to become. To me, the thing that we are always battling as academic administrators is this sense of purpose, direction, and competency—defining who and what we are and what we can become—and it seems that if those matters can be settled, then departments can achieve excellence." *The key to developing distinctiveness: Know thyself.*

Following introspection, a second advantage of "choosing" is commitment. Organizational commitment has been hypothesized as having three components: (1) belief in the organization's goals and values, (2) willingness to extend effort on behalf of the organization, and (3) desire to remain in the organization.[9] Everyone wants to be part of something special. Everyone wants to be able to chant—"We're number one!" No matter if it's baseball, chess, accounting, or theater. Patricia Ewers, who has since moved on to become president of Pace University, was the vice president and dean of the faculties at Depaul University when she spoke to me about theater programs:

> *The excellence of a program really comes when there is a click between the institutional agenda, the programmatic vision and the person who comes in to achieve it. I see it in something as different as the Theater School here at DePaul. It has a very different function—it's a conservatory program—within the university. But there is a shared vision. There is a commitment to be one of the top programs in the nation. There is a willingness on the part of the faculty to make enormous sacrifices in the number of hours that they work and the individual attention paid to travel all over the country to do auditions that assures them they are getting students who can make it.*

Pat Ewers didn't mention the third component of commitment, "desire to remain in the organization," when we spoke, but Smith Holt, the dean of Arts and Sciences at Oklahoma State University did—"We've got some people in our institution that can go anywhere they want. They don't, because they have bought in so totally to that program—that enterprise—and where it's going." Commitment to a cause, to a vision that evokes an emotional response, is a powerful rallying force in any organization.

I offer one final advantage of "choosing to be distinctive": "Choosing" creates a framework for decision making. One of the most vocal advocates of "choosing" has been Richard Cyert, the retired president of Carnegie-Mellon University. Cyert's notion of "comparative advantage" has been well documented in Keller's *Academic Strategy* and Gilley, Fulmer and Reithlingshoefer's *Searching for Academic Excellence.* This notion is, essentially, the process of carefully choosing a few key intellectual areas to work in and then "trying to do them as well as anyone in the nation." When I spoke with Cyert on the topic of comparative advantage he had a specific emphasis: "The key to achieving excellence, in my view, is finding some level of comparative advantage and then concentrating your resources on the advantage—refusing to try and be everything to everybody—but concentrating on a particular area." In other words, choosing to be distinctive has specific implications in resource allocation and day-to-day decision making. It has a practical value beyond

FIGURE *4.2* A Vision Execution Matrix

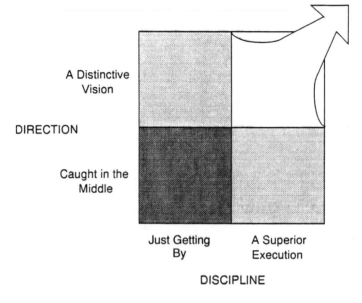

"positioning," "introspection," and "commitment." It becomes a plan of action for the institution and everyone in it. And it is this philosophy that is at the very core of the "managing in" orientation of strategic quality management.

◆

This chapter is about both direction and discipline. The direction is the distinctive vision (the end) while the discipline is the action steps we must take to reach that end (the means). W. Edwards Deming refers to this way of thinking as creating "constancy of purpose" within an organization. Deming says, "Do you know that doing your best is not good enough? You have to know what to do. *Then* do your best." It is a very simple yet very important point. Consider a two-by-two matrix with "direction" on one axis and "discipline" on the other (see Figure 4.2).

The Direction axis has two elements: a distinctive vision and a vision that has no specialness or focus—"caught in the middle." The Discipline axis has two elements as well: putting forth a superior execution and an effort that could be described as "just getting by." Obviously, an organization that is lacking in both direction and discipline is facing a dark and difficult future. But two of the other three cells have problems as well. For example, if everyone is doing his or her best without knowing what to do, as Deming points out, the results will not be terribly impressive. In contrast, a well thought out vision statement without a strong sense of execution is all talk and no action. The notion of "constancy of purpose" is the special-case scenario (a distinctive vision and a superior execution) when a vision has been articulated and then everyone focuses their energy on achieving or implementing that vision. The arrow in the upper right-hand cell of Figure 4.2 is really speaking to the issue of synergy that was discussed in Chapter 2. John White, the president of Nebraska Wesleyan University, believes in the importance of synergy and talked to me about how synergy and vision relate to each other:

> *A college or university, no matter what size or what type, is such that there are constant interactions happening, constant things going on, and all of them having spin-off effects on everything else. And the key to institutional direction is the cumulative results of all of those synergistic reactions. So if that's true, then the way to pursue quality is to try and get control of the synergy. That is, to try to do whatever is necessary to make all the synergistic reactions move toward a specific direction rather than in all directions. You see everyone talks about vision. You can find 100 books and articles—what is the president's role?—to project a vision. Projecting a vision is irrelevant if you don't know how to move the institution toward the vision.*

How can we create the synergy that White speaks of, or the constancy of purpose that Deming is attempting to achieve? How can we do a superior job of executing a distinctive vision? Although there is no fully-detailed road map for this leg of our strategic quality journey, we can at least discuss a few of the necessary signposts along the way.

First, I think we can agree that every college or university has a vision committing it to excellence. Sadly, more often than not, such statements are the grand trappings of institutional exaggeration. It is unfortunate that college administrators find it necessary to engage in such hyperbole because the likelihood of a vision statement being transformed into daily reality depends upon how much inconsequential fluff it contains. David Nichols, in an issue of *AGB Reports,* comments that most collegiate visions are, "rarely read and even more rarely acted upon. Budgetary allocations often provide concrete evidence of this. It is one of the abiding scandals of academia that these . . . statements are so hypocritically ground out and so blatantly ignored in all but a few exceptional organizations."[10] It's hard to disagree with Nichols. We do seem to miss the point. The purpose of a vision statement is to articulate, clearly and concisely, our institutional intent. It should focus on values, guiding principles, and distinctive competencies to the exclusion of almost everything else. The statement should reinforce the image of an institution as something people can identify with and something that deserves admiration from employees, customers, and the community. Visions are rallying points. But visions—especially great ones—don't simply appear in a flash of blinding light. They are not faith-inspired apparitions. Instead, they are the end product of a tremendous amount of self-reflection, listening, consumer research, competitive analysis, and informed discussion. Let me offer Oregon State University's vision statement as an example:

It is OSU's vision to be recognized as a premier international university. We want each student to have at least one additional language, to have at least one quarter's experience in a foreign country, and to be computer literate. We want our faculty to have international experience and to increase our international research programs by 100 percent (from 26 countries now to 52). We want to increase foreign undergraduates from 10 to 15 percent of the student body.

We also want our university to be the best university in which to study and work. We want to be a university that knows what its clients will want ten years from now and what it will do to exceed all expectations. We want to be a university whose employees understand not only how to do their jobs but also how to significantly improve their jobs on a regular basis; where problems and challenges are met by a team of the most appropriate people, regardless of their level or jobs in the university.[11]

If you recall from Oregon State University's TQM Implementation Model profiled in the second chapter, this vision is the result of a great deal of concerted effort. There is no hyperbole about quality or excellence in this statement. Quality is in the *doing,* and that requires work, not grandiose declarations. Further on in Nichol's article he broaches this very same issue by suggesting that, unlike OSU's most schools' vision statements are, "often meaningless because the connecting lines are seldom drawn to the educational product itself. It is easy to write glowing statements of purpose. Translating them into the everyday operations of the organization is something else. That is the hard work not being done in most institutions."[12]

Causing quality through the execution of a distinctive vision also requires a strong, synergy-building communications effort. Stuart Tave of the University of Chicago made an all-too-often forgotten statement during our conversation on quality. He said, "as for developing a program that is very attractive, any intelligent faculty member ought to be able to do that. Give me the back of an envelope. I'll write you a program and it won't be stupid—it'll be good." But he went on to add, "the problem is to find a second guy that is going to agree with me." In effect, if a vision is to become something more than a series of pages tucked into the beginning of an accreditation report, it must become a "living" thing. Everyone in the organization must understand it and must integrate it into their daily lives. It must become "philosophy in action." Accordingly, the vision needs to be shared as part of an orientation for new employees, it needs to be articulated in speeches by the president and other administrators, and it needs to be woven into an institution's public relations efforts. Everyone needs to know and agree on what makes your institution or program distinctive, and they must feel that they are an important part in achieving that vision. Everyone has to be able to answer the simple question: "In 20 words or less, what makes us distinctive?"

I need to add one last ingredient to our "choosing to be distinctive" recipe for causing quality in higher education. Strategic quality management is a crusade, and every crusade needs champions or inspired leaders who embody the vision. People like Nat Weiss of Kean College, don't just say the right words; they live them; they feel them. In 1985, Tom Kean, the governor of New Jersey, developed a series of challenge grants. Colleges and universities were asked to demonstrate how they could become "an outstanding institution" within their mission. According to Weiss, "We took the challenge. We talked about a dual vision of quality and equality and the use of assessment procedures to help us get there . . . We've worked and worked on it . . . I said I want these kids to benefit and to grow, and I'll—if the devil requires it I'll ride his back—do whatever is necessary." Weiss saw himself as leading a crusade— even aboard a devil!

The kind of effort that is required to move an organization from mediocrity to distinctiveness is heroic. It must be a shared effort and it must have, as Deming describes, constancy of purpose. Visions—those that evoke a personal meaning in people—can help foster the necessary devotion to task and commitment by painting a picture of a future worth sacrificing for.

To paraphrase an enlightening discussion of the importance of vision by Peter Senge in *The Fifth Discipline,* there are only two fundamental sources of energy that can motivate organizations: fear and aspiration.[13] The power of fear underlies negative visions—dwindling enrollments, budget deficits, a threatened loss of accreditation—that dominate many of our colleges' and universities' lists of immediate concerns. Unfortunately, the power to inspire commitment to such concerns is short-lived. People are motivated so long as the threat persists. But aspiration is decidedly different. A distinctive vision that is challenging, exhilarating, and alive in the hearts and minds of individuals is one that inspires crusades and legions of devil-defying crusaders.

5

Process, Process, and More Process

The president's office at any college or university is a magnet for problems. Large or small, complex or simple, each problem has its own unique qualities that draw it through the front door, down the hall, and across the presidential threshold. I remember one such problem from my immediate past. The president received a telephone call from a campus clergy member, a Catholic priest who was inquiring about the financial aid status of a student. The young woman, Kathy, was a nursing major, about to begin her junior year. Apparently, three weeks before classes were to begin, she received notice that part of her financial aid package would not be renewed. The notice came as a shock to Kathy—who had recently lost her father. There appeared to be no alternative except for her to take a few semesters off and attempt to earn enough money to finish out her degree program. The priest, a friend of the family for many years, became aware of Kathy's problem and decided to see if he could help.

Spending an hour or so with the director of financial aid, we found the cause of the problem. First, the qualification guidelines had changed, effectively reducing the amount of money Kathy was eligible to receive. In addition, a computer program had not been altered: even though the office had known for more than a month that the full amount would not be forthcoming, the paperwork was batch-processed along with those recipients who continued to receive the full amount. In effect, the notification came last minute and out-of-the-blue to both the student and her family. Over the next few days, working with people in financial aid, the nursing school, and development, we were able to put together a package that more than made up the difference. There was a ten-hour-per-week job in the chemistry lab, an alumni scholarship, and several small grants.

I called both Kathy and the priest to tell them the situation and can still remember their response—tears and praise for my efforts flowed with equal ease. A batch of cookies appeared the next day along with a "Thank You" card from Mom. I also received a heartfelt letter from the priest that I kept in my files. In part he said, "In the future not too distant, Kathy will be a nurse and a good one. As an alumna of URI she will dedicate important years of her life to the work of healing others. She will reach out and touch their lives, as she has touched the lives of all those lucky enough to know her. This will happen later, but only because of your help now."

Basking in the glory of "having made a difference," the thought never occurred to me that if there was one "Kathy," there probably were others as well. I was praised for the one that was caught before she slipped through the cracks, but I honestly cannot tell you whether anyone checked to see how many others were being forced into difficult, last-minute choices. The faulty notification system may still be in use today. I just don't know. I never bothered to ask—I was too busy solving a problem.

> *Solving problems is not the answer to causing quality. The solution is understanding and continuously improving the processes that give rise to problems.*

An organization has to be concerned with the day-to-day operations of getting the product through the door or delivering the service to the customer. The difficulty is that problems always get in the way. The problems are everywhere. In this regard a college or university is no different from General Motors or the Bank of America: the secretary broke her leg and a replacement is needed for at least two weeks; the copier is out of paper and someone forgot to send in a purchase order; management just got slapped with a wrongful termination lawsuit; and employee complaints over the lack of parking spaces threaten to turn into a labor dispute. All this could happen in any organization.

Of course, higher education has its own organization-specific difficulties. Colleges and universities are loosely-coupled systems of students, faculty members, administrators, accrediting agencies, and so on. They have innumerable linkages. Each person, whether dean, chairperson, or vice president, necessarily views the web of connections from her or his own perspective. Entangled by the tug and pull of these linkages, that person is often forced to react to situations seemingly beyond her or his control. For example, here are two organization-specific problems typical to higher education:

Problem: A young woman complains about a graduate teaching assistant (GTA) who is teaching her class. The GTA has pestered her about going out on a date.

> Problem: An Introduction to Sociology course is taught by a professor and three GTAs handling seminar sections. Dozens of students are shifting out of one section because of the GTA's arrogant and insensitive attitude.

It is very easy to get caught up in the immediacy, and sometimes hysteria, of solving such problems. We can spend all day long—*12 hour days*—doing an excellent job of solving problems and responding to crises. And yet like mushrooms in a warm, dark, moist place, tomorrow brings a whole new crop of problems. No matter how hard we try or how smart we are, solving problems is a ceaseless task. We are always *reacting* to singular events or responding to situations that demand our *immediate* attention. It's classic "fire truck" management. We get paid to point the nozzle at the latest hot spot. For example, a clever dean can resolve the first problem in fifteen minutes: bring the GTA in and issue a warning about the improprieties of dating students. If necessary, depending on the severity of the case or if it is a repeated offense, this problem might warrant dismissal. The second problem can be dispatched in only ten minutes—just send the GTA over to Instructional Development for some help. In spite of these decisive solutions, however, the fact remains that there is no reason to believe that the process of training GTAs will be any better tomorrow than it was yesterday. And if this is true, chances are that next semester the dean will be solving a whole new batch of GTA problems. It is easy to see how the dean's schedule can get filled with problems that occur over and over and over again. It doesn't have to be this way.

Strategic quality management considers such basic questions as whether GTA training is better than a year ago, if faculty mentorship and faculty development is more effective, whether student retention rates have improved, and so on. Solving problems will never improve the quality of anything because this usually deals with effects, not causes. Without removing the cause, in just a matter of time, the effect returns—usually to the chair outside your office door. Instead, you need to be primarily concerned with improving the process. By concentrating on the process, you are in a position to enhance the quality of your services over time. Let me beat the GTA "horse" a bit longer: the woman student who was offended may drop the class, may change her major, or may even consider transferring to another school. She may talk to her parents or to her classmates. The students who dropped out of the Introduction to Sociology seminar section have also been exposed to a lack of quality and will share their experience with others. The key terms here are "offended" and "exposed." The damage has been done. These students' perception of quality has been tainted. Problem detection, therefore, is not the same as problem prevention—no matter how efficiently the problem has been dispatched. The focus, instead, has to be on improving the quality of the service that is offered by continually improving the process that is used to deliver the service. Only thus can you prevent the problem from happening again.

FIGURE *5.1*   The Shewhart Cycle

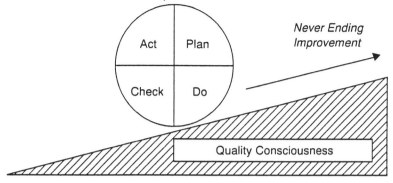

Perhaps the best way to visualize the notion of improving processes was developed over fifty years ago by W. A. Shewhart at Bell Telephone Laboratories. Shewhart was part of a group that was investigating problems of quality in manufacturing processes. In addition to his seminal work in the statistical area of quality control, Shewhart also developed a systematic approach to the problem-solving *process* as it relates to quality—the Plan, Do, Check, Act (PDCA) cycle. (see Figure 5.1).

The Shewhart Cycle consists of four steps that constitute an iterative process:

Step 1—*Plan*—This initial step is the enumeration of a plan for accomplishing some goal. It details the components involved, their interaction, and their intended result. In business it might be a sales plan. In higher education it could be a retention plan or a dormitory security plan. Regardless, it is an area that needs improvement.

Step 2—*Do*—This is the execution or implementation stage of the cycle. It involves translating the plan into action.

Step 3—*Check*—This is a data gathering step. By collecting data on our actions, we are able to compare the "do" against the "plan."

Step 4—*Act*—The final step in the cycle is to begin formalizing those things that were successful and to make changes to the "plan" in those areas where our expectations were not met.

Finally, by continuing to execute the *Plan-Do-Check-Act* cycle in iterative stages, a process-oriented way of thinking is created that results in "never-ending improvement." Too often we tend to see things in a linear fashion—with a beginning and an end. Improving processes, however, requires the kind of circular or systems thinking that is evident in the PDCA cycle.[1]

Another way to think about improving processes is described by

Masaaki Imai in his book *Kaizen*. Imai makes the case for "kaizen"—the Japanese word for continuous improvement—as being the overriding concept behind good management. He begins the book by saying, "Kaizen strategy is the single most important concept in Japanese management—the key to Japanese competitive success. In the context of this book, kaizen means ongoing improvement involving everyone—top management, managers, and workers. The message of the kaizen strategy is that not a day should go by without some kind of improvement being made somewhere in the company."[2] Within the concept of kaizen, "quality" is not meeting standards or quotas; it is the natural outcome of a process-oriented way of thinking that becomes deeply ingrained in the culture of the organization.

Do we think this way in higher education? In general, the answer is "no." You may recall my discussion from Chapter 2 where I suggest that colleges and universities do great "describing"—what courses are taught, the qualifications of the faculty, and so on. We spend much less time, however, analyzing the way we work or attempting to become better at what we do. That's not to say that campuses don't have their PDCAers. For example, when Paula Goldsmid was the dean at Scripps College, she and her faculty "did" a humanities program. And they did it better all the time:

> *A few years ago a sense of dissatisfaction arose because it was felt that in a previous change to the Humanities program we had swung too much in one direction. There was not enough of an organizing framework. In this case a group of people worked over the summer to prepare a position paper that came back to the faculty and was discussed at length and amended. We made some changes. And we continue to do so. It's tinkering. There's nothing revolutionary but there is a shared conviction that the humanities program is really important and central, and that we've got to tend it very carefully.*

"Tending" and "tinkering" improve the process. Unfortunately, we don't tend or tinker in any systematic or comprehensive manner. Why not? Efforts to cause quality in higher education by pursuing the never-ending improvement of processes are constrained in a number of ways: (1) unwillingness to change, (2) compartmentalization, (3) competition, and (4) conformance to minimum requirements.

Change does not come easily to academe.

At the heart of process-thinking, or kaizen, is a continuing challenge to the prevailing standards. This is exemplified in the story of a manufacturer who had been in business for over sixty years. As part of the manufacturing process, a large wheel attached to a furnace had to be turned in a specific way. The process was so delicate that only three men had done the job in six decades. The furnace's secrets had been handed down over time. Several years ago a new plant was built and the old furnace was torn down. It was discovered that the wheel, the wheel that had been at the heart of the process, wasn't attached to anything. Whether it's a college or university or a manufacturer's standard operating procedure, "the way we do things around here" needs to be constantly scrutinized. In fact, the rotation of the Plan-Do-Check-Act cycle is based upon the ability of the system and the people within it to change—always looking for a better way. There are some people on our campuses, like Paula Goldsmid, who is now director of the Women's Resource Center at the University of California, Irvine, and St. Francis's Bert Simon who really have made "change" an integral part of their organizational unit:

> *We are always looking at ourselves. We write a self-study that we turn in for accreditation that is now every five years—we have to produce a formal document for them. But every year we make our own long-range plan with specific objectives, tied to specific curriculum or administrative areas. We write our own self-studies—independent of our accreditation responsibilities. We really take it seriously. It's not something that we just do. That process of constantly looking and constantly saying "Let's take this apart and see how it works and see if we can put it back together so that it works better" is very healthy.*

While Simon is practicing "never-ending improvement," he and his program are a decided minority. Writing self-studies independent of accreditation responsibilities? Constantly looking at themselves? In my experience these are not standard higher education practices. College and university structures are designed to withstand change, not precipitate change. Jack Lindquist concludes in his discussion of academic innovation that "university structures and functions are intended to carry our *established* procedures by *established* means."[3] Furthermore, he suggests that change occurs in organizations that have a high proportion of individuals who are favorably oriented to change. Moreover, Robert Nordvall, in his AAHE-ERIC monograph entitled *The Process of Change in Higher Education Institutions,* bluntly concludes that "It is very difficult to institute change in an institution [colleges or universities] where little perceived need for change exists."[4] In many ways, our college campuses have institutionalized the old maxim: "If it ain't broke, don't fix it"; while at the core of never-ending improvement is another, equally venerable, maxim: "Standing still is moving backward."

Compartmentalization hinders a process perspective.

To some degree, then, change is a function of critical mass. There must be enough people who are willing to risk self-assessment, to look within a process that they are a part of to see if it can be improved. Oftentimes, however, the champions of change are difficult to assemble because of the pigeonholes we have created. We are so isolated from what's upstream and downstream that we never get to see the broader picture. The result is that we spend our time defending the status quo of our own little compartment—be it a department, a center, or an office. Our loyalties, our knowledge, and our sources of information tend to be limited to those members within our boundaries. Consequently, colleges and universities have the same shortcomings as a manufacturing firm that is organized into vertical functions such as research and development, production, engineering, finance, sales, and so on. Each unit builds intragroup loyalty and acts as a parochial domain within its own boundaries. You may recall from Chapter 3 the phenomenon described at Ford Motor Company as "tossing it over the wall"—defects and all. Without the sense of connectedness that comes from understanding the role of other members of a process, we seldom stop to dwell on the consequences of our actions. Why should we? There are few rewards for establishing such connections.

Academic units narrowly focus on their disciplines, rewarding professors for specialization. Although "learning" cuts across every departmental unit on a college campus, you'd never know it. In fact, learning takes place all over the institution but most of the activities of *student* affairs are kept strictly separated from *academic* affairs. It is very difficult to generate the kind of critical mass necessary to improve a process when the process itself has been effectively sliced and diced. Just think how we manage our main input-process-output activity. Admissions generates the raw materials, one discipline adds the doors, another is in charge of upholstery, another works on the braking system, and the career planning and placement counselors attempt to "sell the product"—again, defects and all.

Competition is a four-letter word in higher education.

Most companies, whether they are product- or service-oriented, realize that quality is a relative term and understand the concept of "positioning." Quality is something to be pursued because of its strategic implications vis-à-vis the competition. Firms know that they can never be satisfied with things as they are, especially in a new, global economy. The innovation "lead" in some industries, such as computer software, spans only three or four months. There simply is no choice other than improvement. The pursuit of perfection is a competitive necessity, realizing, of course, that as Vince Lombardi is reputed to have said: "Perfection is not attainable, but if we chase perfection, we can catch excellence."

What is the parallel in higher education? Is there a competitive edge to the mathematics department? Does the graduate program in psychology know which other schools applicants are comparing the program to? Do the administrators and professors know the relative strengths and weaknesses of those programs and where their differential advantages lie? Are they structured and motivated to improve on the quality of their services? Perhaps these are areas where the four-year institutions can learn a little something from our community colleges that realize that their customers—in this case their students—have choices: four-year schools, the military, work, trade schools, and other junior colleges. Michael Beehler, the dean of Instruction at South Puget Sound Community College suggests that, "another wrinkle of good programs is that the faculty invest continuously in doing the work." Beehler went on to describe his faculty's competitive orientation and its relationship to improving quality: "They don't sit back and assume that students will show up next semester. They don't assume that, 'Since I did a good job with the advisory committee last year, I don't have to worry about that now.' They keep the contacts going. They never rest. They get feedback. They use feedback to modify the courses." And finally, Beehler confessed, "I get frustrated with the frequency of changes that come through the curriculum committee because it's more administrative work, but on the other hand, I'm happy about it because it tells me that people are dynamic—*they're working the program* [italics added]."

> *Reliance on such mechanisms as accreditation and program review creates a "good enough" mindset.*

This is a critical point that cannot be overemphasized: *We rely much too heavily on occasional, externally-derived devices to convey the appearance of quality.* Think of the way that we approach these "quality improvement" devices. Every five years or so a manual or compendium is delivered to the appropriate administrative officer's in-basket. There are anywhere from a dozen to hundreds of relevant categories in the document—FTE Ph.D.s per FTE student credit hours, research records of the faculty, grant dollars generated, and so on. The unit is given six months to produce the evidence. Sometimes committees are formed; other times the administrator chooses to "go it alone." A memo goes out; data are submitted. Another memo; more data. A report is assembled and presented to the proper authorities. A "pass" and we have quality. Our reward? Five years of peace and quiet. A "fail" and we have to go back and look for quality again until we find it. Such exercises are often nothing more than disturbances accompanied by a flurry of paper and printouts. What California State–San Bernardino's Diane Halpern said to me is certainly more common place than it is unique:

> *We are required to report on programs every five years and every ten years for accreditation. But those reports don't get used. They get dusted off ten years later. 'Where'd you put that report?' 'I don't know; that was two secretaries ago.' Someone tries to find it and then update it. We typically ask for more money, space, equipment and secretaries. They obviously are not useful because they are not directed back to the faculty so they know what is and what is not working.*

Each disturbance results in a natural tendency to return to a period of calm—even complacency. This phenomenon, commonly referred to as "ho-

FIGURE *5.2*   "Good Enough" Quality

Quality

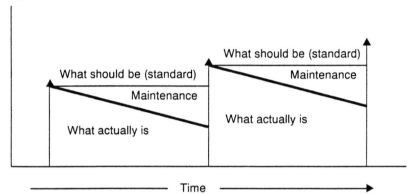

Source: Masaaki Imai, *Kaizen: The Key to Japan's Competitive Success.* © 1896 by the Kaizen Institute, Ltd. Reprinted by permission of Random House, Inc.

meostasis," is usually exemplified by the tendency of the human body to use regulatory mechanisms to maintain constancy in such physiological states as temperature or blood sugar. Exercise increases pulse rate but resistance to change presently brings the heartbeat back to a state of equilibrium. Organizations and societies exhibit similar internal processes (referred to as "balancing feedback" in systems analysis) that counteract any departure from the normal state of affairs. An adaptation of a graph used by Imai illustrates the relationship between "disturbances" and "quality." (see Figure 5.2).

Each of the spikes represents an accreditation round or program review (increased pulse rate as we sprint back and forth gathering data) and the resulting gradual diminution of attention to quality issues (the normal state of affairs) over time. The frustration of this approach to quality is real. Cal Poly–SLO's Glenn Irvin's words demonstrate this frustration:

> *We had an on-going program review that was mandated by the Chancellor's Office as head of a nineteen campus system. Every five years our faculty would have to produce a review of their program. It was standard kind of fare. I went through one cycle of those after I got here and then I called the Chancellor's Office and said, 'I want to put a moritorium on the program reviews for awhile because our faculty are working very hard at this and we are not getting any genuine result out of it.'*

This "conformance to standards" definition of quality is not sufficient for our purposes. It merely separates the worst (failure to conform) from the rest. *Improvement must become the goal, not meeting a pre-specified minimum standard.*

At the heart of any improvement process is information. We need to generate data on what goes into a process, what steps have been taken to alter those inputs, and what the outcomes are. We need to measure these variables. H. J. Harrington makes the connection in *The Improvement Process* by stating, "If you can't measure something, you can't understand it; if you can't understand it, you can't control it; if you can't control it, you can't improve it."[5] Of course, measurement is all around us—we have clocks, calendars, speedometers, blood pressure gauges, heights, and weights. So numbers are just symbols for measuring "where we stand." For instance, when the U.S. Postal Service decided it wanted to know where it stood, it hired Price Waterhouse, the accounting firm, to measure how long it would take a letter to get from Point A to Point B (certainly a measure of quality from the customers' point of view).

> "This is a very, very exciting attempt to level with the American people about how good or bad our service is," said Postmaster General Anthony M. Frank at a recent news conference. The study will involve 2,000 'reporters,' including households and small businesses, who will call a toll-free number each time they receive a piece of test mail. The Postal Service's target is to deliver a first-class letter overnight in the same city, in two days within a 'contiguous area,' and in three days from coast to coast. Internal studies have found that the Postal Service hits that first standard about 95% of the time but does worse with the other two. "It's in the 80% range, and I don't think that's good enough," Frank said.[6]

But even though measurement is a way of generating "friendly facts"— like the Postal Service who hopes to use the data to improve their service— there still remains a fear that some faceless, humorless bureaucrat will use a measuring device to label us as "too slow" or "not good enough". This fear is heightened when it comes to measuring quality. For this reason, quality needs to be measured in a different framework. First, it's necessary to substitute the term "sensors" for "measure." It is only a semantic change, but the fact is we often relate measurement to mechanical or electrical devices, or other instruments of malfeasance. But as biological organisms we are also imbued with a whole host of sensing stimuli. We have "touch," for example, enabling us to differentiate between such variables as heat and cold. Our sense of touch along with the other sensors—smell, sight, hearing, and taste—enable us to detect changes in our environment and react accordingly. Secondly, it is necessary to think of data not in isolated terms but as a "system." In any organization, information about quality can be judged on the basis of the specificity and detail of the data, the rapidity of feedback, and its relative availability to the decision maker. Taken as such, data are not sufficient without a system to deliver it. A sensory system, then, is a quality-measuring framework that connotes a comprehensive and proactive approach to organizational change.

Applying our sensory system to the notion of "never ending improvement" in the Shewhart Cycle yields the dynamic necessary to propel the PDCA circle up the incline as illustrated in Figure 5.1. We need data to help enumerate the *Plan.* Expectations must reflect an accurate sense of our competencies, resources and competition. Information is also necesary to induce action—the *Do.* The primary effect of information is to increase the confidence of decision makers and those designated to implement the *Plan.* Consequently, this also affects their willingness to accomplish the *Plan.* The *Check* stage of the cycle has to do with detecting anomalies. Sequentially, it requires sensory information that clearly signals the difference between what was expected and what was found. Finally, given what we know about organizations' inherent resistance to change, the planning gaps that have been detected will go unresolved without data to support a signal for action—an *Act.*

One more thing: Perhaps the most important function within the cycle—the kaizen—is the requirement that "sensing" occurs within a "system." Incremental adjustments (Simon's "constantly looking at ourselves," Goldsmid's "tending and tinkering," and Imai's statement that "not a day should go by without some kind of improvement") are based upon continuous refinements. One revolution of the cycle—perhaps every five years as part of an accreditation review—is not enough. "Sensing" needs to happen as part of a constantly repeating process.

This kind of data-driven thinking has become manifest throughout industry. Robert Waterman in *The Renewal Factor* has a section entitled "What Gets Measured Gets Done." In *Quality Is Free,* Philip Crosby makes "Quality Measurement" one of the fourteen steps in his quality improvement program, and says, "It is necessary to determine the status of quality throughout the company. Quality measurements for each area of activity must be established where they don't exist and reviewed where they do."[7] Harold Geneen, former chairperson of IT&T, devotes an entire chapter to "The Numbers" in his book *Managing,* and concludes: "the difference between well-managed companies and not-so-well managed companies is the degree of attention they pay to the numbers, the temperature chart of their business."[8] Finally, David Garvin, in an exhaustive analysis of the air conditioner industry, concludes that there is a relationship between a company's performance and its quality information systems:

> In this industry, quality departments at the best and better plants were not distinguished by such traditional variables as large size, a large number of inspectors, a particular organizational form, the power to issue hold orders or stop the assembly line, or the range of performance tests. Rather, they were notable for their effectiveness in managing and monitoring information about quality.[9]

Air conditioners? IT&T? What do these have to do with causing quality in higher education? The data-driven thinking of industry's Waterman, Crosby, and Geneen has been slow to come to higher education. Back in the early 1980s George Keller admonished educators on their "astonishingly meager" information in his immensely popular book *Academic Strategy:* "Improving the management information system is . . . an indispensable step in improving the everyday operation of the campus."[10] Since Keller's admonishment, colleges and universities have slowly begun to develop sensing thermometers—not just isolated clumps of data—to take the temperature of their institutions. For example, while "institutional research" (IR) has existed for years, especially at larger institutions, it has been a real boom industry in the last decade: Begun in 1966, the National Association for Institutional Research has grown from 384 members to its current number of almost 2,000. Offices of institutional research traditionally were called upon to present data in the form of projection and planning documents, position papers and department profiles to a limited audience of users. The impetus for growth in recent years, unfortunately, has been largely external. Requests for data from governing and coordinating boards, and state legislators resulted in the worker-like production of fact books specializing in the presentation of descriptive statistics—e.g., the numbers of FTE students per program or per FTE faculty member or per budget dollar.

More recently, the role of the IR professional is seen less as an accountant and more as a change agent. Stuart Terrass and Velma Pomrenke describe this orientation in an article, "The Institutional Researcher as Change Agent." Quoting Paul Dressel, they say that an "institutional research's 'ultimate success depends less on the research findings than on the promotion of action to alleviate functional weakness and to increase the effectiveness of the institution.' " Terrass and Pomrenke go on to conclude from Dressel's remarks that "What is implied is research that is accomplished and delivered so that it moves people to action, to change."[11] This shift has resulted in an institution research office at many colleges and universities that can contribute, in a forceful way, to the never-ending improvement of quality on campus.

The effective generation and use of data can overcome many of the obstacles that make a process orientation so difficult for colleges and universities. Good data can be the "red flag" that spurs action; it can enable different people to see how their actions affect others in a process; it can provide an individual with a standard of comparison (how your process compares to another one); and, it can be the impetus for a new mind-set in which "good enough" is not good enough. This is exactly what administrators in higher education need. We need a sensory system that empowers us to continuously improve the way we work.

There is a commonly quoted axiom in the Total Quality Management literature known as the 85-15 Rule. The Rule states that 85 percent of what goes wrong lies within the system, and only 15 percent lies with the individual. Everyone works within a system governed by conditions and requirements that the individual cannot control. When something goes wrong we tend to look for someone to blame or we apply our best crisis management skills to the situation. Of course, the chances are that something else will go wrong in another week or month because we haven't looked to improve the system. A vivid example of the 85-15 Rule for me was the book-ordering process at one of my previous institutions. Each semester you could plan on at least one disaster; that is, the books weren't ordered, too few were ordered, the wrong ones were ordered, and so on. The offending secretary was always given abuse and express deliveries were used to correct the error. Nothing ever changed, though. In such a situation and in countless others that occur on a college or university campus, administrators can work magic by simply taking responsibility for improving the system. But this requires tools. It is really no different than a plumber working on a plumbing system or an electrician tending to an electrical system. Each one needs the right equipment to complete the job.

All of the industry books on Total Quality Management launch a detailed discussion of statistical tools that can be used to measure, analyze, and improve a system or a process. Some of the tools are specific to industry; others are fairly complex and beyond the scope of this book. But I offer descriptions of seven basic tools that are applicable to higher education and are very straightforward in their application.[12]

TOOLS FOR PROCESS IMPROVEMENT

Flow charts or process-flow diagrams are the visual representation of the various steps involved in a process. A process cannot be improved unless everyone understands and agrees on what the process is. To that end, a flow chart describes what is going on.

Cause-and-effect or fishbone diagrams are used to depict (causes) of a specific problem (effect) and to group them according to categories. Brainstorming sessions, observation, interviewing, or survey research are often used to enumerate the causes.

Pareto charts are used to separate the most important characteristics of an event from the least important characteristics of an event. It is a way to sort out the "vital few" from the "trivial many."

Histograms are used to measure the frequency of an occurrence which is then displayed as a frequency distribution. Histograms provide valuable information concerning the variability present in a process.

Run charts show the results of a process plotted over a period of time. They are useful to see the dynamic aspects of a process and to identify cyclical patterns.

Scatter diagrams show the relationship or association (but not the cause and effect) between any two variables.

Control charts are run charts with statistically determined upper and lower limits. They are used to study the amount of variation in a process and to make judgments about the source of that variation.

Each of these tools, even the simplest ones, can go a long way to help us understand and then improve a process. In fact, by gaining command of these tools and using them, we can really begin to work on the 85 percent of what is wrong with our systems. For illustration purposes, let's examine higher education applications for the first three tools: flow charts, cause-and-effect diagrams, and Pareto charts. Larry Sherr, a statistics professor at the University of Kansas, also works as a strategic quality management consultant. One of his client institutions had a payroll process that was experiencing an extreme amount of errors and complaints. His first data-collecting task was to sit down with the key players to do some "charting." After several iterations, everyone agreed on the following description of what the process looked like (see Figure 5.3).

Doing flow charts has many advantages. First, it forces those individuals who are in a supervisory capacity and have the authority to work *on the system* to really look hard at the process under investigation. Second, it allows the others—those who work *within the system*—to get a better understanding of the notion of internal customers by being able to see "upstream" and "downstream." And finally, flow charts can reveal redundancy, inefficiency, and possible sources of misunderstanding, within any process. In this case, redundancies and inefficiencies (are four signature checks really necessary?) had slowly crept into the payroll system over a period of many years.

While flow charts attempt to describe a process, a cause-and-effect or fishbone diagram examines factors that may influence a specific situation. An "effect" is a desirable or undesirable condition or event produced by any number of "causes." Let's apply this diagramming tool to a situation that occurred at the University of California–Berkeley several years ago. According to the associate dean of the Graduate Division Joseph Duggan, the graduate school noticed that the average amount of time it took to complete a Ph.D. in history (at one of the top programs in the country with over 60 professors) was averaging 9.6 years. Of the entering cohorts from 1974 to 1976, two-thirds dropped out permanently, 17 percent earned their degrees, and if all the rest eventually graduated the total would only reach one-third. Duggan commented to me, "That's a terrible waste . . . absolutely horrendous. Let's say you have an active career of 40 years. Should you spend 25 percent of it in preparation?"

For the purpose of the diagram, then, the 9.6 years is the effect. We could begin to develop a cause-and-effect diagram based upon impressionis-

FIGURE 5.3 Payroll Flowchart

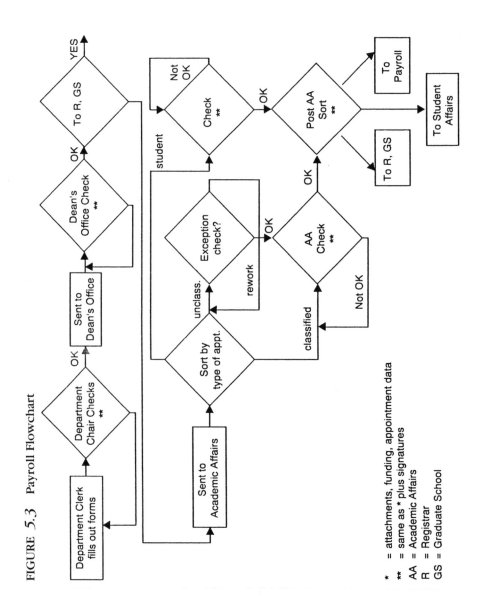

* = attachments, funding, appointment data
** = same as * plus signatures
AA = Academic Affairs
R = Registrar
GS = Graduate School

FIGURE *5.4* History Ph.D. Cause-and-Effect Diagram

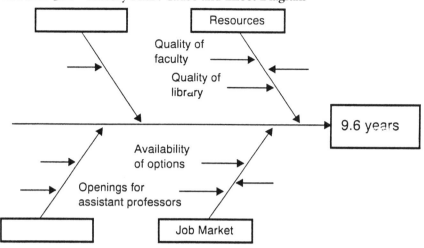

tic data derived from a brainstorming session with professors, or better yet, from "listening" sessions with Ph.D. students or recent graduates. The *beginnings* of the diagram can be constructed from Duggan's description of his talks with students (see Figure 5.4). He said, "So we started talking to students, and it became obvious that they would rather be an advanced graduate student at Berkeley, enjoying the weather, drinking good coffee, having a great library at their disposal, than being an unemployed Ph.D. in history."

While this is only a beginning, there are many benefits to be derived from a full enumeration of cause-and-effect relationships through a fishbone diagram. For example, the diagram will help a study group focus on the issue at hand, reducing ambiguous and irrelevant discussions. It results in an active search for a cause. The creation process itself is educational, for it generates discussion and people learn from one another. Finally, data must be collected. This approach can be used to scrutinize any problem situation.

Pareto analysis logically follows cause-and-effect diagramming. Once we are confident of the full range of characteristics that influence an event, we can begin to determine priorities. At Oregon State University a printing and mailing (TQM) team examined the amount of time involved in the pre-press stage of the printing process of various projects. After enumerating the causes of lost time, the team categorized the time-loss data by type. The two leading causes of time-loss were that customers held the proofs for too long and the employees were not cross-trained to deal with co-workers' absences or high work load. (see Figure 5.5).

The team attacked the vital few causes of lost time and began testing a set of countermeasures that would correct the root causes. These countermeasures included developing seminars to teach customers how to use the print-

FIGURE *5.5*   Printing Department Pareto Chart

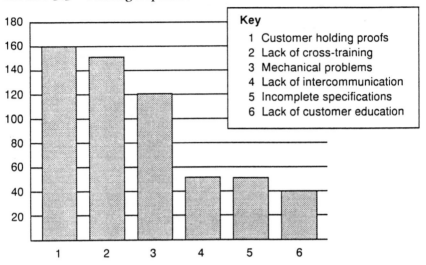

Key

1 Customer holding proofs
2 Lack of cross-training
3 Mechanical problems
4 Lack of intercommunication
5 Incomplete specifications
6 Lack of customer education

ing department's capabilities to meet their needs and implementing a new procedure for tracking proofs held by customers.

I would be remiss in closing this section without taking the opportunity to reiterate the key point of this chapter. We can't get sidetracked into seeing these tools (and data in general) as simply mechanisms to solve problems. The payroll process complaints, the 9.6 years, and the pre-press stage delays are problems. We need to avoid instinctively jumping into our red trucks, ringing the bell, dousing the flames, and then returning the truck to its normal state of quietude. Problem prevention by improving processes is still the name of our "causing quality" game. Regardless of the problem, we must not lose sight of (1) what we are trying to accomplish in the process, (2) how we can most effectively implement a process to achieve those goals, (3) how we can check "where we stand," (4) how we can ensure that the process and the people in it can change to overcome any discrepancies and take advantage of any opportunity for improvement, and (5) that we have a system in place to ensure that this process (items one through four) is repeatable. It's Plan, Do, Check, and Act. Then do it all over again.

According to Masaaki Imai, the belief that there should be unending improvement is deeply ingrained in the Japanese mentality. He offers an old Japanese saying as proof: "If a man has not been seen for three days, his friends should take a good look at him to see what changes have befallen him."[13] The implication is that he must have changed in three days, so his friends should notice the changes. The road to a "process orientation" is littered with potholes, sharp bends, and detours. It almost goes without saying that if it were so easy to pursue quality through continuous process improvement, everyone would be doing it. The theory sounds good, the logic air tight, the rewards laudable, but the implementation is flawed. In my experience the basic reason for this is that in order for us to engage in never-ending improvement, it must become the natural state of affairs. Nothing else will work. Yet it seems that the philosophy and techniques that I have described in the last few pages are anything but natural. Why? Why isn't looking at programs or institutions of higher education to see what changes have befallen them deeply ingrained in us? The following few observations may help you steer a straighter path toward quality.

Let's focus on the essential variables—those that can provoke improvement.

Too much of our time and effort is devoted to generating "safe" data. Perhaps we are burdened by the legacy of having to respond to external threats. Perhaps we suffer from selective attention—just seeing what we want to see. Whatever the cause, the effect is that a substantial portion of our data is ho-hum niceties. *We are often too busy congratulating ourselves on what we did right to see the opportunities in what we did wrong.* Tom Peters, in *Thriving on Chaos,* provides an industry example:

> "Ninety-seven percent satisfied:" An IBM executive says, "We make 300,000 components. Don't say to me, '97 percent are okay.' Say instead, '9,000 were defective.' Sounds a little different, doesn't it?" He adds: "You don't really want 9,000 angry customers, do you?" A hospital administrator concurs: "Remember, 95 percent 'happy' patients in a 600-bed hospital means that 30 are thinking about suing you for malpractice at any given point!"[14]

We need to think the same way. An administrator at a college that I recently visited told me that his college's persistence rate (graduating within five years from the time a student enrolled full-time) was about 40 percent. There was a good deal of concern about this on campus and the local media had stated on more occasions than he cared to remember that the school had a problem. So he did a little checking. According to his research, 40 percent was about "average" for his kind of institution. At that point in our conversation he developed the contented smile of someone who had just learned the answer to a perplexing puzzle. Our brief discussion ended without him mentioning the rest of the equation—the other 60 percent! The challenge that we face as managers of our colleges and universities is to dig deep (deeper than he did), to generate the uncomfortable data that shows where we need to improve, and to instill in everyone the feeling that "we can do better."

The sensory system needs to be a product of its own environment.

We noted earlier in this chapter the relationship between "fear" and "measurement." The process of stating the *Plan,* executing the *Do,* applying the *Check* and implementing an *Act* must be developed by both the people who work in the system as well as those who work on the system. It is degrading and spirit-robbing when measurements are imposed from the outside. We can show people why never-ending improvement is important, we can give them examples and success stories, and we can support them in their continuing pursuit of excellence. We not only can do these things, we *must* do them. But what we cannot do is tell them that it must be done, exactly how it is to be done, and stand over them to ensure that it is done. Unfortunately, this happens all the time. Cal State–San Bernardino's Jerrold Pritchard illustrated the point quite well when he told me:

> *The CSU system requires us to provide data to the system office and gives us a line item budget for the institutional research officer who, in effect, works for the Chancellor's office of the system rather than us. We spend all this time feeding the 'great computer monster in the sky,' but if you want special reports, if you want to know what your student/faculty ratio is in business, they can't tell you.*

This information system breeds contempt and resentment because the data are perceived to be developed solely for "accountability" purposes. Pritchard went on to say, however, that "We're having to build that system [special reports] now. We're starting to build networks internally with minicomputers that are not funded by the state, taken out of our own hide, to download data so that we can manipulate it, so that we can share it." This second system is focused on improvement. There is a big difference.

It should also be noted, quite emphatically, that the greatest roadblock in the assessment movement falls into this category as well. Assessment has struggled or flatly failed on some campuses because the legislature, the state, higher education commission, or central administration's desire to impose standardized measures. The faculty will resist such efforts and ultimately defeat them. I am reminded here of an anecdote involving the airlines' response to one of the Federal Aviation Administration's (FAA) measurement systems. The FAA decided to count and report the number of airplanes that took off "on time." Departing on time was measured from when the airplane *pushed back* from the gate, presumably to begin taxiing toward the runway and liftoff. Obviously, any problem, even small ones, resulted in lowered "on time" marks for the airline. Pilots learned rather quickly to simply "resequence" events. If they were in danger of not making the departure time, they pushed back *first* and *then* sat on the tarmac while they dealt with any loading or mechanical problems. College professors are as smart as airplane pilots, so

I have full confidence that they can also outsmart any measurement that's "done to them" as well.

A process is incomplete without closing the loop—feedback, feedback, and more feedback.

Higher education suffers from a double whammy: we are a service industry, and we are extremely decentralized. The special problem that service industries have is in measuring (or sensoring) their success—or what they promise versus what they deliver. Exactly what constitutes an educated person? We are like a hospital in that regard. Is success having the patient survive the operation? If a student passes enough classes and goes through commencement ceremonies have we delivered on our promise? Also, like doctors in a hospital, we are staffed with professionals who have widely disparate views of what the target (quality health care or quality education) is and how best to achieve it. How can never-ending improvement flourish in such an environment? When I spoke with Nat Weiss, the just-retired president of Kean College in New Jersey, he shed some light on the situation:

> *The programs that are involved in assessment on this campus start off by defining, in their own terms, what it is they think a student should be able to know and do by the time they finish the program. What should a meteorology student be able to do? What should they know, what skills, what competencies should they have? Once they've agreed on that—and that is not easy, by the way—then you have to try and diagnose how students are achieving that. Of course that is where the different modes of assessment come in. The meteorology people use a senior seminar, a project, as well as multiple choice exam. That's one way. The music department uses a performance approach with a panel of outside judges. In mathematics they use a series of snapshots at different points in their mathematical major—at the end of certain clusters. Each program, and this is critical, uses that data to feedback and make corrections and changes to improve the program itself. And that's how we move towards quality.*

A decentralized service industry, like higher education, tends to fall down on this last, vital connection. It somehow gets forgotten or simply lost in the shuffle of more important things. Yet feedback is the gestalt that provides the knowledge for fueling improvement. In a recent review of seventy-two field and laboratory studies on the effects of feedback on behavior, R. E. Kopelman found that objective, meaningful feedback affects task performance in several ways that are worth describing.[15] First, it serves as a continuous reminder of the expectation; that is, the self-correction and adjustment of behavior (the *Act* portion of the cycle). Second, specific and objective feedback promotes goal-setting behavior (the *Plan* portion). Finally, Kopelman concludes that feedback enhances motivation if it causes individuals to perceive consequences, either social or psychological, resulting from performance. Feedback is motivation-enhancing because people derive satisfaction from a sense of personal mastery or competence. They become prideful self-practitioners of the fine art of kaizen.

Grammarians wince when someone takes a perfectly adequate noun, such as "priority," and proceeds to "verb" it—that is, to "prioritize [sic]" everything in sight. So, not wishing to offend, let me offer my apologies for what I am about to advocate. Ellen Chaffee, the vice chancellor for Academic Affairs in the North Dakota University system, has suggested that one way to break out of the traditional manner in which we, in higher education, think about quality is through some simple grammatical mischief. *Specifically, let's begin to view quality as a verb rather than as a noun.*

Most people think of quality as a degree or level of excellence. It is something that *results* from our human efforts to reshape raw materials or inputs. In other words, it is an outcome of a series of linear events. The simple formula for quality in education, then, is to ensure that colleges and universities have: (1) an entering class that is soundly prepared, (2) excellent resources for facilities and salaries, and (3) an intellectually superior faculty. That is quality as a noun. In contrast, quality as a verb does not describe an outcome, it describes a reinforcing circle. To "quality" something is to target a process for continuous improvement. If we pay enough attention to quality as a verb, we will ultimately and necessarily achieve quality as a noun.

6

Involving Everyone in the Pursuit

The *Newsweek* article described a novel idea: A Minnesota school district had begun issuing three-year "warranties" guaranteeing the community and employers that its students could read and had basic math skills; if they couldn't, the schools promised to "repair" students through remedial instruction. An education with a warranty. It's an interesting concept— worry-free hiring. No fuss; no muss. Several months after having read the article, I visited Ventura College, a California community college located up the coast from Los Angeles. I spoke with Robert Long, Ventura's president, and later had the chance to chat with Robert Tholl, the director of occupational education. Many of their "quality" observations concerned the school's automotive program. Independently, they both raved about the program's instructors, students, facilities—on and on. It was late in the day but I took a chance and walked up the hill to a series of buildings that housed Automotive Technologies. Within minutes I was listening to one automotive instructor, Francis "Speed" Sattler, educate me about the world of vacuum pumps, U-joints, McPherson struts, and . . . his students. One statement struck a "warrantized" chord: "When the Ford dealer in town wants trainees he calls me up and says, 'Speed, I need another kid. Send him down.' I screen them. They don't have to. So when my students go down there, the Ford dealers know what they're getting. I do quality control all along. Why should I send a dummy out and ruin the program's and my reputation? I'd never get another guy in the door."

Of course, industry has been doing this "guaranteeing" thing for a long time. But industry went a step further. A person's name, not just an inspection number, began appearing on everything from lawn mowers to underwear— signaturing. Not too long ago I happened to look at the bag the market used for my groceries. It read: "Quality Is Our Bag . . . Personally inspected by Jeff

Gehrmann." Some companies that produce highly specialized products have gone even further than that. Full names and phones numbers are sent along in a customer information packet. These companies are putting telephones on their shop floor. If something goes wrong with your new blood chemistry analyzer, you can call the men and women who built it.

Whether we want to believe it or not, higher education has more of an assembly-line mentality than a lot of manufacturers. As a student passes us by, going from class to class, from dorm room to dining hall, each one of us adds our bell or whistle. But who is given, or assumes, the responsibility of building a quality "product?" Where are the Speed Sattler's of our first-year orientation programs, English and history departments, and our advising offices. Who is responsible for the "product" in the case of non-performance? And would we operate our colleges and universities differently if the following sci-fi scenario could actually happen:

> Ring. Ring. Ring. Hello? Is this Professor Baumann? It is; well professor, I've got a problem down here at TechnoGraph Inc. that I'd like to talk to you about. Last year we hired a fellow from your school to do software engineering—Timothy Flynn. You know his technical skills are pretty good. But last week he had to write a plan for one of our clients and I was appalled. I couldn't let it go out. There were typos, double negatives, incomplete sentences, and the structure and logic was something out of sixth grade composition. I looked on his warranty card and it says that you and Professor Newbold were responsible for 'written communications.' You know I really will have to find another supplier if this continues. This is the second one of these that I got in the last few months. That other one—Sandy Bergman—has no concept of what an introductory paragraph is and, furthermore . . .

The responsibility for quality in higher education is not something that resides in special offices or with selected persons. Causing quality requires the energy, commitment, and knowledge of everyone within the organization.

An obvious question: If, as the introduction implies, quality is not perceived as everyone's responsibility in higher education, exactly who is entrusted with the duty of creating excellence? We have historically relied on three sets of individuals to deliver us from mediocrity: (1) inspectors; (2) resource generators and allocators; and (3) protectors. First, the inspectors—regional and discipline-based accrediting agencies. By setting up minimal standards, the agencies attempt to weed out those institutions or programs that do not conform to preestablished qualifications. For example, the Policies, Procedures, and Standards of the American Assembly of Collegiate Schools of Business (AACSB) states the following:

Accreditation Standards have evolved to meet the contemporary needs of business, professions, government, and graduate and professional schools so that students who study business administration and accounting have the educational background effectively to serve modern society. Therefore, institutions meeting and maintaining the required level of quality for accreditation in professional education for business administration and accounting constitute sound choices for both prospective students and persons responsible for recruiting students with professional preparation in business administration and accounting.[1]

The quality control efforts of the AACSB and other accrediting agencies have an obvious role to play in higher education. But, as we have seen in previous chapters, this approach to quality merely *detects the defects*—those programs that don't meet minimum standards. Improvement cannot be "inspected in," especially when inspection occurs only every five or ten years.

Another set of individuals who are perceived to be responsible for quality are the "resource generators and allocators." The mindset in education has always been: "If you give me enough money, I can give you quality." Following this input approach, then, institutional quality is clearly the responsibility of the president. He or she, along with a core group of supporting central administrators, ensures quality by making an ever-increasing flow of resources available to the institution. Recently, the California higher education systems were required to absorb stiff budget cuts. Their presidential responses were indicative of their self-perceived quality roles and responsibilities: "We've been seriously damaged," said San Francisco State president Robert Corrigan, emphasizing that an expected $7.6 million revenue gap at his campus makes it impossible to conduct "business as usual." "We've been threatening quality for the last two or three years," agreed Sonoma State's president Benson, who must make up for $2 million in cuts.[2] Other resource allocators—for example, vice presidents of academic affairs and deans—are responsible for quality on campus. Every program, and every professor in every program, believes that they could do a considerably better job—if only the dean or vice president would invest more money. The same undoubtedly holds true for people in student affairs, the security office, and the physical plant. Of course while inputs are undoubtedly important, there is minimal correlation between resource size and the effectiveness of the *processes* that are employed to transform inputs into outputs. "Quantity in" does not necessarily equate to "quality out."

The final set of individuals responsible for quality, the largest and the most historically significant of the three, is the faculty. They are the "protectors." They are imbued with the traditions of the academy as artisans who impart knowledge and understanding to the students who sit before them. While it is ridiculous to argue against the central importance of professors to a college or university, professors and their departments tend to represent the vested interests of their disciplines—or craft unions—rather than the educational service that is delivered to students. As specialists in just their particular field or discipline, they cannot, by themselves, do an adequate job, of forming students into a "wholeness" that enables them to develop to their real potential according to Allan Bloom.[3] A similar thought was recently expressed by Neal Pierce, a syndicated columnist for the *Washington Post*. He referred to departments as "isolated academic bastions," and went on to say, "Many of these departments are fiercely resistant to interdisciplinary endeavors, thus obscuring for students and the world the essential oneness of wisdom."[4]

Our three sets of individuals—the inspectors, the resource generators and allocators, and the protectors—each serve an important function in causing quality in higher education. But it is not nearly enough. Strategic quality management, as we have seen, is both a philosophy and a set of tools for identifying and improving processes that lead to better service quality. This is not a task that can be accomplished by a select group of individuals. Constancy of purpose, customer orientation, process improvement, and the other mainstays of causing quality require the efforts and enthusiasm of everyone within the organization. While the inspectors, the resource generators and allocators, and the protectors may be the chosen few, in this case, they are also the insufficient few.

———◆———

Any organization that chooses to cluster the responsibility for quality with a select group of people, operates at a severe disadvantage in a competitive environment. Whether the responsibility is assumed by an autocratic president or dean on a college campus or an imperious shift supervisor at a large manufacturing firm, the effect is the same. If you free people from their direct responsibility for causing quality, they will become demoralized and disinterested in their work and "the way they work." The message should be clear: Empower the people, all of the people, or suffer the consequences. What consequences? Well, here are a few blatant ones for starters:

If you don't empower people for quality, you can lose both customers and employees

Earlier in this book, we used a phrase—"moments of truth"—that was attributed to Jan Carlzon when he ran SAS airlines. Carlzon used it to describe the following situation:

> Last year, each of our 10 million customers came in contact with approximately five SAS employees, and this contact lasted an average of 15 seconds each time. Thus, SAS is "created" 50 million times a year, 15 seconds at a time. These 50 million "moments of truth" are the moments that ultimately determine whether

SAS will succeed or fail as a company. They are the moments when we must prove to our customers that SAS is their best alternative.[5]

Carlzon goes on to describe ticket agents, flight attendants, baggage handlers, and other frontline employees as the people who are SAS during those fifteen seconds. Substituting another service industry, a college or a university, for an airline results in some obvious distinctions. One difference is the fifteen seconds. This time factor is skewed in higher education by the fact that a student spends several hours per day sitting in a classroom. Another difference is the five employees—a student routinely interacts with considerably more: the secretary in the chemistry department, the writing lab teaching assistant, the resident assistant in the dormitory, food servers in the cafeteria, the clerk in the registrar's office, her or his academic advisor, and so on. All in all, however, the comparison is strong. On a daily basis the college or university is "created" thousands of times and only a limited percentage of those creations are directly related to the actions of inspectors, resource generators and allocators, or the protectors. Numerous creations—good and bad—are *caused* by GTAs, departmental secretaries, and clerks.

Many good customers and valued employees leave an organization or unit for essentially the same reason. A student, for example, transfers because of a litany of "moment of truth" failures: having a roommate who drinks too much but being unable to break the room contract; being disgusted by rampant cheating in a lab section; being informed by the financial aid office of a cut in his or her award two weeks before the start of classes. As the student packs to leave, she or he doesn't reflect on the significant fund-raising capabilities of the president, the rigorous "library and computer services" standards of the AACSB, or the research credentials of a heralded professor who teaches in the graduate program. The student simply leaves. Similarly, the student affairs office worker has been aware of the unreasonable room contracts for years but is forced to deal with the complaints because the director sees no reason to change a policy that he or she implemented ten years ago—it's called "working in a system over which you have no control." The GTA running the lab section asked the professor to allow him to reconfigure the lab desks to reduce students' opportunity to cheat but hasn't received an answer yet (it's been three months). Finally the clerk in the Office of Financial Aid knows exactly how to improve the notification process but no one will listen. These people are frustrated because, although they have identified a key problem area, they have been stifled in their efforts to improve the situation. In all of their failed "moments of truth" the words of Harvard's Rossbeth Moss Kanter resound: "Powerlessness corrupts. Absolute powerlessness corrupts absolutely."[6] Good employees, like good customers, often have the same reaction to situations they find frustrating and humiliating. They leave.

If you don't empower people for quality, you encourage and reward slothfulness.

Let's begin with the quality movement—i.e., Deming, Juran, Crosby, et al. One of the basic axioms that is universal to the quality movement is that: mass inspection has a negative effect on quality. It doesn't work because it is essentially saying to people, "We don't trust you to do your job right." By relieving people of their quality responsibilities we merely *guarantee* sloppiness—"the inspector will catch it anyway." The result is a dangerous mindset in which our expectation for poor quality and shoddiness becomes built into the culture of the organization. As I noted in the opening chapter, accreditation procedures attempt to "inspect in" quality by setting specifications. Knowing that our program or institution will undergo accreditation in five years has virtually no positive effect on an individual's attitude or performance today. Shifting responsibility for quality away from those people who *work within the process*—developing talented students, producing research, and getting involved in service activities—to those who *inspect the process,* results in a real loss of obligation and ownership. By not expecting quality from everyone and by not giving them the tools and encouragement to pursue it (continuously), we ultimately create a tolerant environment, one in which poor quality (defective service) is acceptable. We are sending a message that is difficult to misinterpret.

If you don't empower people for quality, you will become inundated with bureaucrats and policy manuals.

If people don't leave for "responsible" positions or just slide into a state of indolence, they often attempt to find a place to exert power. This is not a healthy situation either. Empowerment allows people to exert control *over their own actions:* engineers become better engineers; teachers become better teachers; secretaries become better secretaries. Without it, people sometimes attempt to find situations in which they can—at least—control others. American industry is illustrative. In the 1960s, 1970s, and 1980s businesses became fat and increasingly noncompetitive. Like a python trying to digest a meal that weighs more than itself, Corporate America stagnated as mid-level management expanded to over capacity. Indeed, according to the Bureau of Labor Statistics, 47 percent of U.S. manufacturing employees are now in nonproduction jobs, up from 23 percent in the 1950s.[7] If you think that such bureaucracy-building is the exclusive domain of *other* organizations, you should think again. At the primary and secondary school level, the American Federation of Teachers reports that "about half of U.S. education spending goes to administration."[8] At the post-secondary level, Peter Likins, the president of Lehigh University, comments that, "Each college and university . . . should ask itself if it needs all its vice presidents, and if these vice presidents need all their managers. Over the past two decades, there has been a tremendous growth in personnel on the U.S. campuses, but it's primarily outside the faculty ranks."9

Where do these new, need-to-control-something-or-someone bureaucrats come from? Powerless people begin to feel as though the only way they can affect anything is by moving into management. Engineers don't see their career paths and rewards as coming from just being better engineers. They feel as though the only way to generate influence and control is to get an MBA and have others report to them. Some teachers and professors exhibit the same pattern of thinking. As the organizational chart of college and university administrators expands with additional layers (the provost) and solidifies (career associate deans), an ever-increasing loss of power is felt by those on the front-line. I am personally familiar with one such case. It involves a small, private college with about two thousand undergraduates. Within two years of his arrival, the new president added an assistant to the president, and a provost. Also, several of the departments in Arts and Sciences were spun-off and made into Schools—with accompanying new deans. Two thousand students and the infrastructure looked as though it were Michigan State University. Upon this scenario stumbled an unsuspecting initiate. He was the new dean of the business school, a retired CEO of a major restaurant chain. After six months he was ready to quit. Why? Because after a series of frustrations resulting from existing policies that made it difficult for him to do his job, he was rewarded with the ultimate humiliation: Needing $150 from school funds to reimburse a quest speaker's expenses, he was told by his associate dean that it exceeded the amount that the dean could sign for and his request had to be okayed by central administration. So much for personal responsibility.

If you don't empower people for quality, the organization becomes a collection of underachievers.

Perhaps the most insidious effect that results from not empowering people to be responsible for quality is also the most subtle. It is easy to identify people who don't care anymore, or good people that transfer because they want a challenge. What is not so easy is to calculate the difference between what people do and *what they are capable of doing*. According to the *Technology Review:*

> Fewer than one of four jobholders (23 percent) say that they are currently working at their full potential. Nearly half of all jobholders (44 percent) say that they do not put much effort into their jobs over and above what is required to hold onto a job. The overwhelming majority (75 percent) say that they could be significantly more effective on their jobs than they are now.10

Conduct your own mental audit. How many people—secretaries, professors, directors, deans—at your institution are working to their full potential? Name the people that you know who have special talents and skills, or bottomless energy and enthusiasm, that are being underutilized. Ultimately, there is no easier or more dramatic impact on quality than what you can achieve by simply tapping the full potential of those people who are currently working on your college or university campus. Raise the expectations and then give them the incentive to achieve those expectations. They want to be responsible for quality. They want to contribute. And they want to have the power to make things better. Give it to them. The strategic management of quality requires it.

As is the case with so many things, the theory sounds great but implementation is another matter. Even if you wanted to raise the expectations for individual quality responsibility, where would you begin? Maybe a memo. Or, better yet, a rousing speech to fire up the troops. But understand that many of the people around you have been institutionalized into thinking in terms of "it's not my job," or "you can't fight city hall," or "why bother?" So, memos and speeches won't do. Causing quality requires a more *insistent and persistent* approach to change peoples' attitudes and behaviors. By this I mean that assuming responsibility for quality should not be an option. If a person is not willing or able to assume this responsibility, find someone else who will. There is no more room for people who are content to do the minimum. Higher education cannot afford it any longer. The expectation has changed, the bar raised. And the expectation has changed for today, tomorrow, and the day after that. People should be expected to show the kind of initiative and process-improving zeal that is the signature of quality for as long as they work in the organization.

A good way to kick off this aspect of "causing quality" is to do something simple. Policy manuals are a printer's dream—nice and thick. Also, colleges and universities feel obligated to reprint them each year, distributing them to administrators, faculty, and staff. They contain organizational charts, procedures for having materials copied, policies on office hours, job descriptions, and so on. Let's assume for a moment that for legal reasons, or accreditation reasons, these manuals are a necessity. Let's also state the obvious: these manuals are rarely used for anything other than to prop open a door. It might be appropriate, therefore, to print a second policy manual—an operational one—and distribute it to everyone. I like Nordstrom's. The entire manual consists of one line: "Use your own best judgment at all times." Such a manual might be accompanied by a very short speech in which you suggest that the responsibility for producing quality service is to be assumed and shared by everyone. Indeed, anyone who sees an opportunity to create quality should assume responsibility for doing so. Quality is never "someone else's job." This speech needs to be made over and over again.

This simple advice could change the way many people do their jobs.

The "Great Stapler Incident" illustrates my point. Last year students in one of my classes started turning in their weekly case studies bound together via the historic fold-and-tear method. I had paper all over the place. At the next class session I politely requested that they use the tried and true form of binding—a staple. All agreed that this was preferable but the library, where many of them prepared the cases before class, had issued a decree in the form of a handsomely printed sign. It read—*Due to repeated thefts, staplers will no longer be provided for student use*—and was signed by the director. Most students voiced the usual complaint about how much tuition they were paying but a dozen or so decided to do something about it. They sat down and generated a list, complete with drawings in some cases, of various solutions to the problem (my personal favorite was attaching the same magnetized strips used to prevent book theft to the staplers). Following class they stuffed the library's suggestion box with their ideas. The next day the sign was gone, new staplers were out (chained to the table tops), and my case studies were back to their original, firmly fixed condition. The moral to the story is painfully obvious. The school and the library failed a "moment of truth" because no one in the library felt responsible enough to take the initiative—they had to be embarrassed into doing something. A silly example, no doubt, but how many times does the same lack of spontaneous initiative-taking, with small problems and large, occur in your college or university every single day? "Your own best judgment" should have suggested to someone, "Why penalize the students who need the service for the irresponsible actions of a few?" It should have occurred to someone that, "We have people in this library with advanced degrees, certainly we should be able to out-fox a few light-fingered nineteen-year olds." Or more simply: "These students pay too much tuition not to get the best service we can possibly provide."

Liberating all people to pursue quality has another angle as well. The "Great Stapler Incident," and other examples that spring to mind, have to do with *responding* to a situation. The creation of quality implies that pro-action is needed. The process of improvement requires that we seek out new ways to do things—not because the old ways are bad, or problematic, but simply because there might be a better way. The wellspring of these new ways is "ideas." A great example of idea-generation in action is provided by Carnegie-Mellon's Dick Cyert. First he told me that, "It's ideas, more than anything else, and the ability to implement those ideas, that determine quality." Then came the example:

> *We went along with a mediocre to poor English department for a while until we brought in an outside visiting committee and we mulled the thing over ourselves and decided to move into the rhetoric field, hired a new department head, put some resources in, and developed an idea which now has made us, by outside observers' views, one of the two best writing programs in the country. So without a hell of a lot of money, with a lot of sweat and some outside grants—*

which you don't ordinarily think of in English—but with an idea, we've built something grand. The other thing that we were able to do that made it great was that we did it with an interdisciplinary slant. We said that we were going in the rhetoric direction but we got cognitive psychologists together with the rhetoricians, and they developed a new discipline in "how to teach writing." Now that came from ideas, from pushing hard on ideas.

Ideas for improving a process simply do not come easily to people who have been conditioned to think that their sole responsibility is to respond to problems via a narrowly-defined set of administrative policies and procedures. Problem prevention is at the very soul of strategic quality management, and it requires a pro-active, empowering mindset.

Let's move on to another implementation issue. If you want to have a house built, you hire a contractor. You assume that in order for the contractor to do a good job, he or she needs to assemble a team of competent people who have the experience and training to complete the work. This includes an electrician who is educated on matters concerning wiring and voltage, a person to lay the foundation trained in reading blueprints, and skilled carpenters who have specific knowledge of joists and miters. Education's "house of quality" is built in much the same way. It requires a broad team of people, working together, who have the tools and the skills to construct a learning environment of the first order. So it follows that colleges and universities, who are in the business of educating others, must do a superior job of educating themselves. Right? Wrong. In a recent address to the Association of Institutional Research, Larry Sherr of the University of Kansas spoke on the subject of quality in higher education. In Sherr's written manuscript there is only one sentence in the entire paper that is bold-faced. It reads: "I know of no institution in our society that does a poorer job of educating its own employees than higher education."[11]

This is a brutal indictment. And your immediate reaction is probably a strong denial to Sherr's accusation. After all, many of you have a Ph.D. or Ed.D.—terminal degrees. You can't get any more education than that. Granted. But beyond having our professors educated in the intricacies of their discipline, what education do we provide? The following matrix may help order your thinking (see Table 6.1).

Beginning with the first category under "Education Types," you should ask yourself how you educate your new employees. Each year a college or university hires dozens, perhaps hundreds, of people for each of the employee categories listed. There are new secretaries, electricians, computer programmers, admission counselors, department chairpersons, graduate teaching assistants, and professors—all with their own separate set of expectations. Many of them, for example, have the kind of narrow views that Diane Halpern at Cal State–San Bernardino suggests, "Every faculty member, I believe, thinks that he or she has been hired to teach two or three courses." It follows that an admis-

TABLE *6.1* Education and Training in Higher Education

	Employee Categories				
Education Types	Professors	Instructors, GTAs, and GRAs	Administrators	Professional staff	Clerical-Technical
New employee					
On-the-job					
Formal development					

sions counselor sees him or herself as being hired to recruit students, a secretary to type letters and to answer the telephone, and a librarian to catalog books. But what about our thoughts on customer orientation and vision? Remember the admonition: "I suggest that you consider getting up from behind the desk, opening the door, walking down the hallway, grabbing the first person that you see, and asking 'In 20 words or less, what makes us distinctive?' " What better place to *begin* building and reinforcing a distinctive vision than at the *beginning?* Pat Ewers had some thoughts about beginnings, visions, and quality from her experiences at DePaul University:

> *Some institutions do a great job of selling the idea, the purpose. They get young faculty to buy into the vision—into the excitement of what they are about as an enterprise. And they also convice them, from the beginning, that building their own career is more appropriately done when they are building something else as well. You've got to be willing to build the institution at the same time that you're building your career. Excellence really comes when there's that click between the institutional agenda, the programmatic vision, and the person who comes into achieve it. One thing that I have worked very hard to do is provide a kind of orientation for new faculty where we talk about what the mission of the school is and what our values are. We welcome them, sit them down, and have dinner with them the first week they are here. It's all part of a recognition of the commitment that you are inviting people to share.*

Scanning across the employee categories, it should become evident that this "indoctrination into the vision" is important for everyone because each person—the secretary, the GTA, the clerk—has a role in making the vision come alive.

On-the-job education, the second category, is the informal process of encouraging people to better themselves in the performance of their jobs. The following are a few examples. We spoke in an earlier chapter about understanding who our internal customers are—upstream and downstream.

This "broadening"of our field of vision might entail encouraging an admissions counselor to spend more time with the department chairs so as to learn about program strengths. Such first-hand, downstream knowledge would help the counselor do a better job of articulating the comparative advantages of a program to a would-be first-year student. There is also "deepening." Is it totally unreasonable, for example, to have department secretaries sit in on faculty meetings for some other reason than to take the minutes? Would they be better able to "use their own best judgement" if they had a better understanding of the business of the department? Obviously these kinds of learning situation— enabling people to understand the extended process and assume responsibility for it—don't just happen. Early in his tenure at Carnegie-Mellon, Dick Cyert developed an on-the-job education mechanism for department chairs:

> *I believe that the most critical people in building strength are the department heads. So I started a series of meetings with just the department heads, twice a semester on Saturday mornings, and have been doing it for many, many years. It was important for them to educate each other on how they recruited faculty, on how they upgraded their curricula, on how they did strategic planning—so that there was an education process for department heads on very critical points and at the same time I was able to give them my views and my desires for the school.*

There are numerous, similar ways to enhance job performance and there are also many common practices that should be reconsidered. One of the most detrimental, for example, is the cost-containment exercise of leaving positions open for months in order to save money. If you can do without the position for that long you should consider eliminating it entirely. If the position is essential to your operations, then there are significant advantages to be gained from overlapping a five- or six-year, street-wise incumbent with a new hire.

Finally, we should consider the obvious usefulness of professional development programs. It never ceases to amaze me that we teach our students (and industry employees through training programs) such skills as public speaking and media management, but the dean of Arts and Sciences will make a statement to the press that is ill-conceived, insensitive, or incorrect. A little closer to home, the American Assembly of Colleges and Schools of Business (AACSB) devoted its recent annual meeting to Total Quality Management. Sessions were devoted to "Integrating Quality Into the Classroom," "Total Quality Management: A Research Agenda," "Total Quality Topics in Executive Education," and many other topics. Of notable absence was a session entitled "Business School's Role in Facilitating TQM as a Management Philosophy and Practice on My Campus." We research it, we teach it to students, but we apparently don't see the need to educate ourselves in it.

In a 1990 edition of *Change* magazine, James Bess of New York University states, "Newly minted faculty presently have practically no idea *how* to teach, rarely having received any instruction in graduate school," and yet the only time most faculty members are encouraged to develop their instructional skills is when their student evaluations become a source of embarrassment.[12] Indeed, a 1985 study found that at over three-quarters of the institutions surveyed, only a small minority of "faculty who really need to improve" were involved in any type of development program.[13] Additionally, of those professional development programs that are in existence, most of them focus narrowly on professors and teaching, to the exclusion of research and service, and the non-academic staff. In an ideal world, wouldn't a secretary in the romance language department be able to speak French and a chemistry secretary have 101-level chemistry knowledge? The courses are being taught right down the hall.

Whether through orientation sessions, on-the-job training, or formal development programs, people know when you are investing in them. It's not just a matter of "here's your desk and here's your job description." They will pay you back in loyalty and dedication to duty a thousand times over. Informed and educated people also work smarter. They don't make as many mistakes and when they do, they know how to fix them. Ideas for improvement bubble to the surface when people understand the extended process, the expectations, the connections, and their responsibility for causing quality. Underachievers become overachievers when they consider themselves to be a meaningful, necessary part of a distinctive vision. Empowering people to cause quality through education is an investment, not an expense.

The implementation of involving everyone in the pursuit of quality, then, necessitates both incentive (through continually communicating a new standard of excellence or degree of responsibility) and investment (through education). But perhaps the most effective way of involving everyone in the pursuit of quality is through a conscious effort to foster teamwork. People are social; they want to be part of a group. We form automobile and bridge clubs, we join fraternities and sororities, and we compete on bowling and badminton teams. We spend a great deal of time doing things in groups. Strategic quality management practitioners work hard to influence how groups are formed in organizations and how teamwork can help improve the quality of products and services. How teams form is of particular concern to W. Edwards Deming. He suggests that one of management's primary responsibilities is to break down the organizational barriers that inhibit teamwork. In industry this means the barriers between departments (manufacturing versus sales), between organizational levels (us versus them), and between the organization, its suppliers, and its customers. He emphasizes that by reducing differences, jealousies, competition, and "turfship," individuals can begin to shift their attention to more important issues—like improving quality. General Electric's CEO, John F. Welch, Jr., has stated the matter in corporate survival terms:

The winners of the nineties will be those firms who can develop a [corporate] culture that allows [organizations] to move faster, communicate more clearly, and involve everyone in a focused effort to serve more demanding customers. To move toward that winning [corporate] culture we have to create what we call a 'boundaryless' company. We no longer have the time to climb over barriers between functions like engineering and marketing or between people—hourly, salary, management and the like.[14]

Quality emerges in these kinds of organizations when everyone is given a chance to work on improving processes. A team of people working together for a common purpose creates a learning laboratory; that is, by engaging in hand-to-hand combat with quality improvement as a group, they begin to reach a common understanding of the dynamics of a process. Creative energy is generated as people bounce ideas off of each other and explore new ways of "doings things around here." Confidence, pride, and satisfaction increase. There is an acceptance of change because team members themselves inspire the innovations. Implementation is a snap for the very same reason. Thus the organization as a whole benefits as the improvements help the organization realize its distinctive vision.

The practice of teamwork may take many different forms. The form that has gained the most notoriety is the quality control circle (QC). QC circles burst upon the American industrial scene in the early 1980s after being labelled "Japan's productivity tour de force." Of course, like so many things, QC circles didn't travel so well. The greatest problem seems to have been one of their key characteristics—"voluntary participation." Circles in this country can, and often did, quickly dissolve into an elitist schism of "us" versus "them." Some U.S. companies then began using a variation of QC circles called "quality teams." The critical distinction between the two is that teams are mandatory. The idea is that if everyone is *capable* of contributing to quality improvement, they shouldn't have the option of sitting on the sidelines—"everybody is in" with quality teams. Finally, the latest twist, self-managed teams, goes one step further by reducing the power of mid-level management and by giving teams increased responsibilities to arrange their own schedules, buy equipment, have a say in hiring and firing, and so on. A recent survey of *Fortune* 1,000 companies published by the American Productivity & Quality Center in Houston shows that while only 7 percent of the work force is organized into self-managed teams, half the companies questioned say they will be relying significantly more on such teams in the years ahead.[15] One of the best examples of "everybody is in" teamwork is Baldrige-Prize-winning Cadillac's notion of "simultaneous engineering." Since 1985, Cadillac has been conducting formalized training to help break down barriers, thereby effecting a cultural change that fosters teamwork, communication, and group decision-making. The result is an organizational structure held together by teams such as Vehicle Teams, Vehicle System Management Teams, and Product Development and Improvement Teams.

How are we organized for strategic quality management teamwork in higher education? First, back in the early 1980s, several authors suggested that "teamwork" might be useful on our college campuses. Some colleges—Des Moines Area Community College, Lane Community College, University of Cincinnati to name a few—have had some success adapting the Quality Circle concept to their schools.[16] Successful adaptations, however, have been extremely few. There are probably several reasons why QC circles have not found higher education to be fertile ground. First they were never implemented as part of a management system that involved a major shift in how an institution would be administered. They were an add-on with no cultural base. That is, while QC circles had the added advantage of using specific problem-solving tools, they were never perceived as part of a broader management philosophy. Also, successful adaptations were limited to non-faculty areas such as the physical plant, the finance office, the registar's office, and the bookstore. Further, perhaps QC circles never made it because we just didn't need them. After all, if there's one thing we've got, it's teams. A college or university campus is thickly populated with departments, committees, subcommittees and task forces. Some of them display great teamwork, and in many of my campus interviews the discussion of quality revolved around a team of people. Here is just a sample:

> *"Biochemistry has a very good record of quality of getting students [PhD] through in five or six years. So, we asked them what they did in a systematic way to ensure that kind of record. One of the things they do is to get together once a year and discuss all the students. They take their folders out and look at what courses they took, what their grades were, how their research is going—all the faculty talk about all the students. This way they get all the faculty involved in all the problems of the department."* (Joseph Duggan, Associate Dean of the Graduate School, University of California–Berkeley.)

> *"The Chem E program works extremely hard as teachers. For example, they don't use graduate students as TAs. The Chem E professors TA for each other in their junior level "intro" courses. They come to each others' lectures. You can imagine the difference that makes in the culture of the department. Normally, I can't discuss the course you're teaching with you because I know little if anything about the way you're approaching it. If I'm coming to your course, however, we have a lot to talk about."* (John Wallace, Dean, University of Minnesota).

These are wonderful examples of how departments *can* work together. But most departments don't work this way. Academic departments tend to represent the vested interests of faculty disciplines rather than the educational service delivered to their customers. As such, they operate as competing interests rather than as advocates for quality. Committees are just groups of people, not functioning teams. Many of them are temporary (e.g., recruiting) or have a narrowly-defined charge (such as the calendar committee or the academic appeals committee). They certainly aren't trained in problem-solving techniques; many meet only once or twice a year, and they aren't charged with improving anything. There is one exception to these generalized criticisms of departments and committees, and that is committees or teams that have been organized for purposes of student assessment. They are unique in that they focus on process (i.e., student talent development) improvement and often require the kind of barrier-busting that Deming refers to in his work. Pat Hutchings' quote from a recent AAHE Forum illustrates the unique teamwork required to implement a successful assessment program:

> A broader conception of the tasks of assessment means a broader involvement by people from across the institution. Assessment for improvement is not a one-office, data gathering operation but a total institutional responsibility, an ultimate interdisciplinary challenge. Assessment issues are cross-cutting: in class and out, student effort and faculty teaching, student preparation, and institutional expectations. To get the picture in view we need teams of people representing diverse perspectives and expertise—faculty from various academic disciplines, student development staff, advisors, administrators, students, and alumni. The goal of assessment is a mindset: that quality improvement is everybody's business.[17]

Teams and teamwork are at the heart of strategic quality management; indeed, they are an essential part of the delivery system. A college or university committed to pursuing quality needs to understand what its critical processes are. The administration must bring the people who work both in and on those processes together, breaking down the barriers between individuals and pigeonholed groups as Deming in industry and Hutchings in higher education would have us do. The next step is to empower the team by giving up top-down administrative control. Leadership in the new management paradigm *coordinates* the actions of people to help them pursue quality, it doesn't try to *control* quality in through policies and procedures. Teams are further empowered through education. The problem-solving methodologies and the tools described in Chapter 5 used at Cadillac, the Hospital Corporation of America, and Oregon State University need to be taught to everyone. Finally, the revolution of teamwork must be allowed to infect the institution by implementing solutions, bragging about successes, and rewarding improvement wherever it happens. The result will be "quality in action" as teams seek to improve the registration process, reduce the drop-out rate, minimize the errors in the payroll system, ensure that graduates have the kinds of skills needed to perform in their chosen careers, and hold the line on the increasing costs of periodical subscriptions in the library.

In other chapters of this book I discuss quality in visionary terms, statistical terms, customer terms, and cost terms. In this chapter I have urged you to think about quality in still another way—in personal terms. The responsibility for quality should be freely given to everyone. This is not a simple request; in fact, for some of you this will be a nearly impossible request because it asks you to give up control. Also, the responsibility for quality must be passionately assumed by everyone. Again, this is not easy. Most secretaries, residence assistants, adjunct instructors, and admissions counselors have never been asked to do anything but what fits within the narrow confines of their task-driven job descriptions. Both giving and assuming needs to happen if you are to cause quality in your college and university.

Peter Seuge captures the essence of this individual responsibility with his notion of "personal mastery" in *The Fifth Discipline:* " 'Personal mastery' is the phrase my colleagues and I use for the discipline of personal growth and learning. People with high levels of personal mastery are continually expanding their ability to create the results in life they truly seek. From their quest for continual learning comes the spirit of the learning organization."[18] For this fundamental reason, the passion, the spirit for quality cannot simply trickle down from the top; it must be a fountain from which everything flows.

7

Pride: The Engine of Success

When we speak we tend to sputter and stammer a bit, trying to say the words at the same time the thoughts are being formulated. So, without the benefit of a real-time, word processing unit attached to our vocal chords, we often muddle our way through a conversation. But there are also times when we are so sure about an issue that the words just flow—easy and true. Many faculty members and administrators in my "quality" interviews touched on issues relating to pride and self-esteem. Glenn Irvin, associate vice president of Cal Poly–San Luis Obispo spoke with the clarity and conviction of someone who has come to a certain realization. In the course of our conversation Glenn said to me: "People would tell you here that 'We teach better than anyone else teaches.' Now I can say candidly that the quality of teaching here is very, very good. There are places where the teaching is better. But when you have people who are convinced that they are the best, *you are going to get there.*"

Sounds simple. But the fact remains that colleges and universities are filled with faculty, staff, and administrators who have serious doubts about their own ability. They want to do a good job. They want to contribute in a meaningful way. Circumstances, however, keep them from reaching their full potential. What kind of circumstances? Well, here's a simple one: Not too long ago I had lunch with a friend from a nearby college. This particular day it was obvious that something wasn't right with him. He choked out the words "Look at what these @*∞¿≤!!! said to me," while tossing me a letter that he had yanked from his briefcase. It was a one-page, four-paragraph letter from the school's faculty review committee. The "committee" stated that they had looked at his student evaluations and concluded that he needed to address a deficiency. His rating on the "stimulated my interest in the subject" question was below the mean score for the college. Matters pertaining to this deficiency (i.e., trying harder to make the class more interesting) occupied the bulk of the letter. The final paragraph acknowledged, almost grudgingly it seemed, that his overall evaluations were acceptable. So, why was he so upset? He was, first of all, angry because he taught *Introduction to Statistics,* a required course that innumerates find anything but stimulating; second, his evaluations on other, more important attributes such as "planned each class session well" and "provided helpful feedback," were outstanding; third, he knew he was a good teacher and prided himself on it; and finally, the "committee" had a couple of "less than stellar" professors who had no right to judge anyone else's teaching performance.

Jan Carlzon ends his book, *Moments of Truth,* with a story about two stone cutters who were chipping square blocks out of granite. A visitor to the quarry asked what they were doing.

> The first stone cutter, looking rather sour, grumbled, "I'm cutting this damned stone into a block."
> The second, who looked pleased with his work, replied proudly, "I'm on this team that's building a cathedral."[1]

Apparently, many members of the faculty at Cal Poly–SLO and the second stone cutter have something in common—they feel good about themselves and the contributions they are making. *They are going to get there.* My friend and the first stone cutter have a common bond as well. The hurt that I heard in his voice that day reflected the initial traces of bitterness and detachment so deeply inscribed in the words: "I'm cutting this damned stone into a block."

> *Causing quality in higher education involves the process of creating and maintaining an "unshakeably" prideful administration, faculty, and staff.*

If a quality product or service is rooted in people's enthusiasm for excellence, the obvious management task is to hire motivated, prideful employees. Any organization—a manufacturer, a hospital, or a college—that is loaded with these inspired people who will strive for quality and be intolerant of mediocrity. People who are passionate about their endeavors don't compromise. They want to do their very best. And their fervor is contagious. As the saying goes, "A rising tide lifts all boats." One obvious way to cause quality, then is to fire everyone who displays "stone cutter" attitudes and replace her or him with a "cathedral builder." Eliminate the disgruntled employee, create a more positive environment, and prideful work will become the company standard. The more "cathedral builders" the better. But let me expand on

Carlzon's story: the "stone cutter" had been employed for three years while the "cathedral builder" had only been working for three weeks. Does that change things? It may. In fact, it could very well explain their contrasting views of their jobs and their lives. If you think about it, motivation, pride, and passion are common characteristics. I remember my first teaching position. There was some nervousness, of course, but the more dominant feeling was a sense of enthusiasm, a sense of excitement. I wanted to be the best at what I did. Everything was fresh and new. Few people begin their professional lives with a firm commitment to do the very *least* they can do to get by. They don't start off saying, "I'm really interested in doing a lousy job." And yet there is no denying the abundance of sub-par performers working in our colleges an universities. How can this be?

Well, we often fail to realize that everyone works within a system. The chancellor of the University of California at Los Angeles works within a system—the UC System, headquartered in Berkeley. The dean of Architecture at Cooper Union works within the institution's academic affairs system. A cook in the Stonehill College cafeteria works within a system that is administered by the vice president for Business Affairs. Each of these systems has a direct effect on the way in which the work is done. The cook's performance, for instance, depends upon the kind of equipment she or he has, the quality of food available from suppliers, the number of people that need to be fed, and so on. This is the 85-15 Rule that was discussed in Chapter 5. The Rule, as you recall, states that 85 percent of what goes wrong is the fault of the system, and only 15 percent lies with particular individuals who work in the system. Unfortunately instead of analyzing and improving the processes within the system, we tend to look around for someone to blame. The fact is that people enjoy taking pride in their work, they want to do a good job, but very few are able to do so because of poor management practices. The standard systems used in most organizations debase the human spirit and rob individuals of their own self-worth. We do it in a hundred different ways. In fact, "demotivation" is viewed to be so prevalent in industry that Philip Crosby devotes an entire chapter to it in *Quality Without Tears*. Here are some of his thoughts on the matter:

> Employees are turned off to the company through the normal operating practices of the organization. The thoughtless, irritating, unconcerned way they are dealt with is what does it . . . What sort of indignities are we talking about? We don't need to reach back to Charles Laughton mismanaging the "Bounty" for our example. Certainly there hasn't been a case of "keelhauling" in American industry for decades. The indignities that cause problems are much more subtle than that.[2]

If the indignities that cause demotivation and disenfranchisement in industry are subtle, they are even more so in higher education. Nonetheless, I believe that demotivation on a college campus is accomplished in three distinct ways: we degrade, we hassle, and we ignore.

How do we degrade people? Let's take, as an example, performance reviews. If a college or university states in its recruiting material—as every institution does—that it has great teachers on its faculty, then it makes sense that it should develop a standard of excellence to measure its professors' performance against the standard. Such a review should be based upon valid and reliable data, should provide the incentives and means to correct any discrepancies between "ideal" and "real," and should be timely. More often than not, however, performance reviews are not based upon good data. We don't have experts "sit in" on professors' classes. We don't have peer professors at other institutions review professors' syllabi. We take the expedient route. We ask students to answer fourteen multiple-choice questions, toss the data into a computer, grind out some averages, and then slip the results back into the professors' mailbox. At some point in time a committee, or an associate dean, reviews the accumulated numbers and passes judgment.

How about incentives to improve? Do most performance reviews provide the incentive and the means to correct deficiencies? In any performance review or assessment it is critical that its intellectual foundation be based upon improvement—continuous quality improvement—and not merely accountability. As such, the procedure should be to locate shortcomings, scrutinize them, trace the sources of the problem, and make corrections. Criticism, by its very nature, doesn't tell an individual what should be done, but rather what shouldn't be. Although we're quick to use the stick—as with my friend—we seldom seem to be able to find the carrot. We're fault-finders, not praise-givers.

Then there is the issue of timeliness. At many institutions once professors have tenure they are routinely reviewed every two or three years. The resulting data are anything but timely. Indeed, *if one of the mechanisms of "causing quality" is problem prevention rather than problem detection, it is inconceivable that you could prevent anything by measuring it every three years.* And even if you do detect a problem, the chances are the professors are not going to view it as constructive criticism because they are being put in the uncomfortable position of defending something they have probably been doing for three years. Most teaching performance reviews, therefore, are dishonest to those who are "labeled" as poor teachers, and degrading to those who are good teachers but are subjected to the vagaries of an inherently ego-destroying system. Don't assume that the academic side of the house is anything special in this regard. Several years ago, one of the directors at a university I am quite familiar with was fired. His job performance was lousy and everyone knew it. Nonetheless, his union cried "foul" and threatened a lawsuit. The union's contention was that there was no basis for dismissal, and upon reviewing the director's personnel file and interviewing his supervising vice president, they were found to be absolutely correct: Over a five-year period, not one job performance discussion was conducted, nor the mention of approval or disapproval placed in his file. It is degrading to work in a system that can't find the time to provide people with the means and the motivation to alter their behavior.

While colleges and universities have many degrading practices, they have even more ways of hassling. What's hassling? Perhaps the best description is offered by Crosby: " 'Hassle' means that the people inside the company spend more time working on each other than they do making something happen."[3] The actions that hassle people and create a negative atmosphere are usually not big items—but they make up in sheer numbers what they lack in size. In one of my few system or board interviews, Ed Goldberg, the chancellor of the New Jersey Department of Higher Education, made the observation:

> *Out of the faculty members in New Jersey, maybe we have 1 percent, maybe we have 10 percent, I have no idea of the numbers, who would fit my definition of nationally recognized scholars in their discipline. But for the others, whose scholarship, in terms of cutting-edge, refereed journals, is less than our stars, who get their satisfaction out of some writing, curriculum revision, and helping students learn, it is easy for the structure that they find themselves in to turn those people off and block their attempts to improve. We do it in a thousand and one ways.*

"Hassling" illustrations abound and I (and probably most people) could fill a book on the subject. Here are a few typical examples from my past: a four-part form, six-month process to get "thick" overhead transparencies stocked along with the "thin" ones; a library policy stating that bound periodicals could not be checked out (even by faculty members on a twenty-four hour basis); a department that did not allow student files to leave the department office (forcing advisors to take notes under the watchful eye of the file-guarding secretary) and; a campus parking policy that required *all* permits to be renewed *every* semester. In a conversation with Jonathan Fife, director of the ERIC Clearinghouse on Higher Education, at an AAHE national conference, he said, "I believe that in an organization that has as its primary employees people who are protected from being fired and protected to a certain extent from responding to direct orders, that the management of those institutions is often frustrated at not being able to exert control. They cannot impact on these sacred cows, but they can affect something else—like where the xerox machine is located." It's a sad, but undoubtedly true, commentary. Organizations are loaded with people who add little steps to a process, who make small details into bureaucratic mountains, and who enjoy the power and control of enforcing standard operating procedures.

Finally, if our first two demotivators haven't adequately sapped your energy to do a good job, the place where colleges and universities often excel is by simply ignoring people. A small child will break a glass, finger paint the wall, or tease the cat in order to provoke a response from a parent. Why? Because the opposite of love is not hate. Love and hate are closely related. The opposite of love is abandonment. It's being ignored. And colleges and universities have ignoring down to a science. As I have noted before, when we first hire people into a college or university, how often do we use the opportunity to indoctrinate them with the vision of what makes our institution or our program special? Do we sit down and tell them "This is what we are most proud of and this is how you can contribute?" Do we take the time to show them, in detail, how they fit in? Do the secretaries and other staff people know what's upstream and downstream from them? With professors, our approach is often particularly dispiriting. We hire individuals as assistant professors, show them their offices, assign them their classes, and then forget them. Unless they're obviously deficient, the next time we closely scrutinize their work is five, six or seven years later when they are up for promotion or tenure—"up or out." If they are sharp, they will figure out, as best they can, what the expectations are and what criteria will be applied to measure their accomplishments. The whole process smacks of some mystery novel in which the reader desperately searches for clues along the way so as not to be surprised by the final page's "whodunnit." Father Charles Beirne, the former vice president of Academic Affairs at the University of Santa Clara, addressed this concern well when he said, "If someone gets hired, you have to show that you are not indifferent as to whether they will succeed or not."

Ultimately, a college or university's greatest opportunity to "demotivate by ignoring" occurs with post-tenure faculty members. Christine Licata wrote an enlightening ASHE-ERIC Higher Education Report in 1986 entitled *Post-tenure Faculty Evaluation: Threat or Opportunity?*[24] Perhaps unpredictably, her main point in the piece did not deal with hiring, firing, or accountability. Rather, the key conclusion was that because of benign neglect, individuals, like flowers that are not watered regularly, wither and die. Without someone saying "Now, what do you want to do and how can I support you?," how are they going to grow? They aren't. They're going to drift. It's not love, it's not hate—just abandonment. And by abandoning them and their hopes and dreams as we often do, we encourage them to become mediocre.

There are two consistent responses that individuals exhibit while in a demotivating environment. Both have a direct and pernicious impact on quality. The first response is a slow but steady disengagement from their work. As professional rewards diminish, as the enthusiasm for "making a difference" declines, the individual retreats from the challenges of work. You know the type. In previous years they were considered to be among the best and the brightest. They were always involved in something interesting, always excited about a new course or research project. But as the years went by their zeal waned and they "settled" into a survival mode—in by 10:00 A.M. out by 2:00 P.M., teach, office hours, and home for a late lunch. They continue on because they need the paycheck, not because they are convinced that they can make a difference.

And that's just the ones who stay! How about the ones who leave? Employee turnover has been the subject of hundreds of studies in organizational behavior. One fairly consistent finding is that there is a positive relationship between performance and turnover: Better performers are more likely to resign.[5] Indeed, Steers and Mowday, the leading researchers on turnover, predict that high performance leads to increased expectations, which lead to increased turnover if those expectations aren't met.[6] Survey after survey shows that people leave to accept "a *better* position." What's better? Studies reveal that as many employees quit for intangible reasons as do for money. Maybe more. These intangible reasons encompass lack of respect or recognition, an unfriendly work environment, little opportunity for personal development, inconsiderate treatment, and an inability to get along with a superior—all spirit-stealing reasons. Add one simple fact to this—good performers have choices—and you have an instant recipe for a low quality institution or program as *the good people leave and the others, the disengaged, seem to stay forever.*

◆

W. Edwards Deming feels so strongly about this subject that he has made it one of his key points—*remove the barriers that rob people of pride in their work.* In fact, he states that failure to act on this point "may be the single most important contribution of managment to poor quality and loss of market, save for failure to act on Point 1 (Create constancy of purpose toward improvement of product and service)."[7] There is simply no substitute for providing individuals with the conditions, incentives, and equipment for doing a good job. The next few pages focus on precisely the kinds of barrier-smashing activities that can be performed by academic administrators to transform a *demotivating* environment into a *motivating* one.

It is necessary to provide visible, unwavering, and challenging expectations.

Pride is a natural by-product of past successes. Accomplishments generate pride, and pride generates quality in the services we provide. Take a look at an example from the classroom. Bert Simon of St. Francis College narrates: "It shouldn't be a mystery what we want the students to do. And many times we find out when we tell the students what it is that we want them to do, and how we want them to do it, that they are able to accomplish it. But when students have to try and figure it out—'What does he want?' 'What is he getting at?'—it creates lots of frustration, confusion, and poor performances." It makes sense in the classroom and, it turns out, it also makes sense in an administrative setting. Ev Fleischer, the executive vice president at the University of California–Riverside also spoke to me about expectations:

My view of management is making sure the expectations are clear: every single faculty member should be striving to be at the top of his or her field—publishing books, generating grants, outstanding teaching, and doing service work as well. It's the model of the ideal faculty member. And I think that if you push that, and make sure those units or persons who strive to do that, and to some degree achieve it, get resources and are rewarded, you are creating a positive work environment.

This is a challenging and unwavering expectation. The danger, however, is that such expectations can easily descend into meaningless hyperbole. But Fleischer continued: "You don't stand up in front of people and say, 'We're going to be wonderful and we're going to do this and that.' My view is that the way you really get faculty and deans and the university behind you is that, somehow, every single action you take is speaking towards your expectations—what quality and productivity mean to you." In effect, the expectation must become tangible and ubiquitous. We are not talking about grand, superlative-laced speeches or memoranda that are suitable for framing. An earthly illustration of the kind of expectation Fleischer is describing was artfully conceived and communicated by Edward Eddy, the president of The University of Rhode Island. Soon after his arrival at Rhode Island, he began conducting a series of "state of the university" meetings with students, faculty members, and alumni. One of the concerns that was voiced was the appearance of the campus—soda cans and paper littered the grounds. In the weeks and months that followed, I often walked with him across the campus (I was Ted's assistant at the time) and it didn't take me, or anyone else, very long to get a clear indication of what the new expectation was. No trash escaped his watchful eye. He would dive into a bush to snare a Coke can or a candy wrapper and then carry it, like a prize, to a trash receptacle. No task force was formed, no circulating memos. Indeed, the "visible expectation" was complete when a picture of one of Ted's little treasure hunts was captured by a student with a camera and printed on the front page of the campus newspaper. The appearance of the campus began to improve rather dramatically as the expectation led to an obvious conclusion for most people: if the president can pick up trash, so can I. Strategic quality managment requires such well-defined expectations.

It's impossible to feel ignored if someone is paying attention.

During the 1930s a small group of Harvard researchers conducted a series of experiments in Western Electric's Hawthorne plants. The goal was to measure the impact of work conditions on productivity. In a classic experimental design, the researchers proceeded to change something in the environment—holding all other variables constant—and then observe the effect. The decade-long experiments produced seemingly contradictory results. For instance, they'd improve the lighting and productivity would increase. Then they'd turn the lights down, anticipating a drop in productivity. But productivity would go up . . . again. While there have been many interpretations over the years, the prevalent one is that work conditions were not the primary factor in productivity. Prior to a group of Harvard researchers showing up, the workforce at the Hawthorne plants was ignored. To some extent, the research variables—turn the lights up, turn them down—were less relevant than the mere fact that someone was paying attention. Many of the people that I talked to in my campus wanderings were, in effect, practitioners of this same scenario. They instinctively looked for opportunities to show others that they were paying attention, that they were concerned, that they were watching. They immersed themselves in the actions of those around them. Perhaps no one said the words with more conviction than the dean of Arts and Sciences at the University of Wisconsin at Eau Claire, Lee Grugel, "I think it's very important for administrators to be around faculty. I go to music events because I like music and also because I want to keep sending a gentle message—I care a lot about these people." It should be obvious that many of the tools and techniques in strategic quality management, such as an emphasis on training and understanding processes, create Hawthorne-type effects.

Involvement spreads responsibility and makes everyone part of improving quality.

As we noted in the previous chapter, one of the mainstays of strategic quality management in industry has been the Quality Circle or, its descendant, the quality team. Again, a "circle or team" is a group of people whose responsibility is to identify areas in need of improvement and to devise solutions. While the mechanics of quality teams (and their degree of success) differ significantly from one organization to another, the underlying assumption is universal. Everybody in an organization is capable of contributing; everybody knows something about his or her job or the work of his or her unit that can be improved; and everybody wants to be part of the decision process. Unfortunately, most college campuses have evolved into a series of isolated departments that are, in turn, occupied by an array of independent specialists. Problem solving within such an environment is often limited to mundane, territorial issues or becomes the occasional, ordained right or an *ex officio* agent—the dean, the vice president of academic affairs or "program review." The result is predictable. Take, for example, this description of an expanded program review process at the University of Kansas:

> A . . . problem . . . has to do with departments who unilaterally decide that they are "too busy" to enter into the program review process, or that they have too many problems at the moment to undergo review, [or] that a concurrent accreditation is taking too much of their time, or the like. Several departments in

[the] university have in effect refused to cooperate in the review process. In the face of their collective stubbornness, the process has broken down. What can be done about that problem is unclear. When an academic department refuses to admit the review committee and announces its intention to subvert the process, the response tends to be one of bafflement and confusion. The resolution of this recalcitrance awaits a more ingenious mind.[8]

The more ingenious minds are all around us. Recall Bert Simon's description of his "brainstorming sessions" from Chapter 3. While he noted that the process of involving everyone was time consuming, he also concluded that, "it makes the individuals feel as though they have responsibility for the 'whole' program, not just the courses they teach." Another example? I nominate Martin Krivin of William Patterson College. Krivin, the coordinator of the Jazz Studies and Performance Program, easily filled a two-hour audio tape with his "quality" beliefs. Here's one: "You have to let the faculty, especially the adjunct, know that they are an integral part of the entire program—and that their recommendations and suggestions are not just important for you to hear but that *they are necessary for the program to evolve.*"

> *Solving problems in such a way that they don't continue to occur and exploiting opportunities is prideful; reacting to a crisis is not.*

Since I have broached the subject of both program reviews and performance reviews in this chapter, let me take a moment to expand on how they can relate to "spirit robbing." If one of the ways that we can "cause quality" is through continuous improvement, it necessarily suggests an *incremental* building process. But most program and performance reviews are judgmental and reactive. Opportunities have long since passed, and problems, left to fester alone, ultimately develop into full-scale health hazards: a program that loses its accreditation; a professor lecturing to a classroom full of empty chairs. I like the description tendered by Pace's Pat Ewers: "Where people are constantly engaged in a critical self-examination of how effectively they are doing things, improving and changing—that is an exciting place to be." The key to the statement, and the one that distinguishes it from most examinations or reviews, is the word "constantly." A sharpshooting example from a *Harvard Business Review* article entitled "Robust Quality" is illustrative (see Figure 7.1).

Improvement, according to the illustration above, is a series of modest, incremental course corrections. Ewers went on to discuss what she termed, "tough-minded" programs: "They won't suffer a person going on very far. Because this is hurting the program. They give the kind of feedback that says this is how you have to improve [a small adjustment in the sights]. Are you willing to do it? Give it a try. And if that doesn't work, the person is gone. Because just letting it drift for six years and then making a decision allows six years of ineffectiveness to operate within the system." Bull's eye!

FIGURE *7.1*   Incremental Course Correction

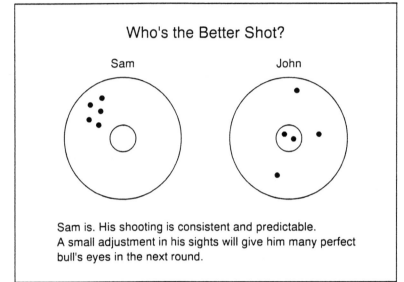

Who's the Better Shot?

Sam is. His shooting is consistent and predictable.
A small adjustment in his sights will give him many perfect
bull's eyes in the next round.

Pride is not a stationary concept. It moves.

The problem of disengagement that we touched upon earlier has received a smattering of attention in the higher education press. One recent *Chronicle of Higher Education* article, "Faculty Generation Gap Brings Campus Tension, Debates Over Rating of Professors," details the difficulty that a shifting expectation of scholarship brings to college campuses. It notes that it is not uncommon at many institutions to have a group of faculty members known as "terminal" associate professors—people who have been on the faculty fifteen or twenty years but are never likely to satisfy the scholarly requirements for full professor.[9] The potential problem of "senior deadwood," as some have called it, faced by every college or university can only increase as we head into the maturing years of professorial baby boomers. But the fact remains that human relations issues get short shrift on most college campuses. They are steeped in "touchy-feely" notions and beyond the understanding, or perhaps caring, of most administrators who are consumed with budgets, FTE counts, research grants, and the like. Indeed, another *Chronicle* article concludes that, "although higher education institutions may understand the problems facing senior professors, they provide little help beyond a few traditional faculty-development programs."[10]

We need to understand that the target Sam and John are shooting at is not stationary over a forty-year professional career. What motivates someone at thirty-five does not necessarily provide the same thrill-of-the-chase at fifty-five. Smith Holt, the dean of Arts and Sciences at Oklahoma State University, explains it well:

> *It's important to realize that there are different phases in a faculty member's life. Some faculty members really do prefer, as time goes on, to no longer run the grant "rat race," and are excellent teachers and want to involve themselves more in the teaching—and it's not a cop out. In order to have a quality program you have to use your resources in the best way possible. And as long as every faculty member is contributing to their fullest, it is going to be a good program. When the time comes when people begin to shift, you've got to be able to recognize it and reward them and praise them for it.*

It will take a unique blend of creativity and caring for our institutions to significantly impact this barrier to pride. But every college or university that expects professors to make a commitment to spend a significant portion of their lives in service to the academy owes them a wide range of understandings, options, and possibilities. It may also take a certain amount of "tough-love." I can't leave this section without sharing the "tough-love" ideas of John White, the president of Nebraska Wesleyan University. NWU has instituted a system of "required" sabbaticals. At least every ten years, faculty members *must* take a semester off at full pay or a year at three-quarters pay after the Faculty Development Committee approves their plans. According to White, "We have almost had to kick several faculty members, including one long-term department head, out of the nest—'I don't need to go,' 'I don't want to go.' We're doing things to cause people to get out of a rut and re-evaluate their goals." People should not be seen as an expense item, like the physical plant and equipment, on an institutional balance sheet. A college or university needs to see each of its quality-causing employees as an investment, as an *appreciating* asset. And by the way, professors have no particular lock on the notion of "deadwood." The pride of professional growth and achievement can, and indeed must, be stimulated in the development, admissions, accounting, and alumni affairs offices.

A little praise goes a long, long way for a lot of people.

There are some absolutely great bricklayers and a few that missed class the day the teacher talked about straight lines. Most bricklayers are pretty average. The same is true, whether we want to believe it or not, of medical doctors, airplane pilots and college professors. In any group of ten people, one will be in the bottom 10 percent, one will be in the top 10 percent while the remaining eight will tend to cluster about the mean. As such, there are only three possibilities: outside low, outside high, or what might be called "in the system" of a normal distribution (see Figure 7.2).

FIGURE *7.2* A Normal Distribution (Bell-Shaped Curve)

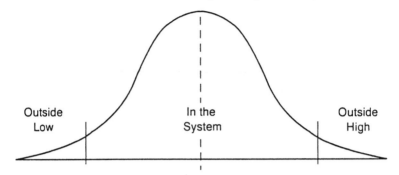

We tend to do a lot of management-by-exception in higher education; that is, attending to "outside low" and "outside high" while ignoring all those who are "in the system." Bryan and Tucker in *The Academic Dean* suggest that there are perhaps "only two times when a dean needs to communicate and interact directly with faculty members of one or more specific departments."[11] The first involves those events or occasions that come under the rubric of normal relations—e.g., a monthly faculty meeting or the operation of various committees. Then, according to the authors, "there are unfortunately those times of crisis when a dean must sit down and *deal* directly either with all of the department's faculty members or with at least the leaders among them. Such crises are almost always brought on by a lazy or incompetent—or sometimes psychotic—department chairperson."[12] These are the laggards— the bottom 10 percent. At the other end of the distribution are the one or two people—the top 10 percent—who bring in the $2 million National Science Foundation grants. The stars get stroked all the time. But what about the 70-80 percent of the people who cluster about the mean? Earlier I quoted Ed Goldberg. He spoke of the "others": those professors who weren't the nationally recognized scholars and how we "turned them off." He went on to say, "They hunger for change, for stimulation, provided that the framework, leadership, real caring, and small amounts of incentive are there. They are hungry for ways of further developing. They are hungry for encouragement."

We cannot assume that someone with a Ph.D. is self-motivated. We didn't receive a lifetime's supply of self-esteem along with our diplomas. We are all susceptible, wonderfully so, to positive feedback: atta' boys and atta' girls, winks, back-slapping, and "one minute praising" (as Kenneth Blanchard points out in *The One Minute Manager;* most organizations spend their time trying to catch people doing something *wrong.* He suggests trying to catch them doing something *right* and then praising them for it). The real gains in quality, then, do not necessarily come from managing the exceptions— outside high and outside low. The real gains come from shifting the entire distribution, *including* the 70-80 percent of professors, painters, secretaries, clerks, associate deans, or granite workers "in the system," to the right. Tom Peters, author of *Thriving on Chaos* says:

> Consider this: A new owner of Fletcher Granite Company in Westford, Massachusetts, observed a record-breaking productivity effort by one of his employees. On impulse, he grabbed a two-way radio and publicly lauded this prodigious feat, with everyone listening in. A colleague of the worker later reported to the president: 'Lou is walking on cloud nine. He's been here thirty-five years, and it's the first time the boss has recognized his work.' What a sad story! Want to hear another 200 to 300 like it?[13]

Does pride cause quality or does quality cause pride? As academics we are always interested in questions of causation versus association and trying to separate out effects. We intuitively know that the association is strong. In industry a hastily-designed product, along with inadequate testing of prototypes, translates into the production of low quality merchandise. Everyone in the company suffers a loss of pride because everyone is associated with the making of "junk." Is there any reason to believe that things are different in higher education? Given the chance, every professor, every security officer, every budget analyst would love to be associated with something special in her or his professional life. No one really wants to be associated with a college or university that is considered to be a joke by the students and an embarrassment by the board. As far as this book is concerned, the answer to the question should be obvious: We are interested in developing a systematic approach to "causing quality." Pride helps do that. Why? Because people on the college campus that have it, and are encouraged to use it to improve their performance, will ultimately settle for nothing less than quality.

8

It's All in the Attitude

We are all familiar with the struggles that a parent has with an indifferent youth. We see them in the grocery market and at the mall. The mother or father is clearly upset with something and the child is standing off to one side—detached from the fuss. Reaching across the void, the parent snatches the youngster by the shirtsleeve and, with all the authority that adulthood can offer, declares: "You better change your attitude right now young lady, or else." Fast forward ten or twelve years. Our indifferent youth, now a college sophomore, is in the office of her faculty advisor having received grades that threaten to make her a distant campus memory. The professor attempts to make an impression: "Suppose that by paying a modest sum, you could get a permit to go into the largest store and help yourself to everything— diamonds, watches, expensive clothing—the only limit being what you could carry away. Only a fool would say, 'Guess I'll take some paper clips and chewing gum.' And yet consider what you're doing. You and your parents are paying for a college education that entitles you, to the limit of your capacity, to absorb the accumulated wisdom of the ages, to intimate acquaintance with the geniuses of all time, to a knowledge of the universe and the wonderful possibilities of tommorow; and your attitude is, 'Guess I'll take a few snap courses, ride a pony over the hard places, and be content to keep an eyelash above the flunking point.' "

Regardless of where we are in life or what we are doing, attitudes and expectations establish what gets done and what doesn't get done. All the "snatching" or "lecturing" in the world will not make this any different. Our attention and effort is channeled into those things that strike an emotional chord. And if that chord rings loud and true it can create extraordinary devotion to the task at hand. The attitude I am describing was expressed over and over again on the various campuses that I visited. I especially enjoyed one afternoon's discussion with Paula Goldsmid, formerly the dean at Scripps College. Scripps has a three-part humanities internship program that includes placement within an organization (e.g., museum, shelter, publishing company), a seminar that connects the humanities with issues pertaining to the work, and an independent project. It's a very selective program with high visibility. But there's a problem. "It's tremendously expensive per student," according to Goldsmid. "Money isn't thrown at it but there's a full-time person who directs the program and several faculty members who co-teach the seminar and that is all for fifteen students a year. We certainly couldn't manage if all of our programs were that expensive. But there is a commitment to doing it." She went on to say that, "We talk from time to time about doing it both semesters or expanding it in some way, but people always come to a concern that it would change the character of the program—it would not give the director the time to work with the students and the organizations." Finally she concluded, "The faculty and administration are pretty comfortable with it being a special program that's especially expensive. It's one of the things we do that we really like and that we are really proud of." It's all in the attitude.

> *The ability to cause quality depends upon an attitude that makes "do-it-right-the-first-time service" an integral part of the everyday lives of administrators, staff persons, and faculty members.*

An "attitude" is one of those wispy concepts that theoreticians love and practitioners hate. It's easy to think in terms of managing a budget or administering a program review. Attitudes, in contrast, don't have such concrete manifestations. Of course, describing attitudes as opposed to behaviors is bad enough, but if a concept like an "attitude" is combined with an equally difficult-to-define concept such as "quality," you have the makings of a zen-like conundrum.

Attitudes influence how we respond to certain situations, propel our actions, and fuel our emotions. They're not black and white or clearly definable. But they do exist and we all have them—attitudes about democracy, television, authority, race, and religion—even about such insipid things as lemonade and the color blue. Changing attitudes requires a new vision and a commitment to it. Something (or someone) has to give us new information or insights to change our minds about any of the above.

Much of what we do on a college campus involves attitude change. Certainly that applies to our classrooms and other talent development situations. It also applies to how we administer our colleges and universities. In today's world, reality involves budget cuts, diminished enrollments, forced retrenchments, and continued calls for accountability. We can take these pains with our heads down and shoulders languid. We can react, cry foul. Or we can stand up straight and redirect our energies in a positive, forceful direction. It's our choice. I repeat: it's all in the attitude.

The first and most important attitude we need to change is that we are somehow exempt from the conventions that generally apply to service industries. In any college or university we (administrators, staff, and professors) provide a service to other groups (students, employers, society), as well as to each other. This is still difficult for many within the campus walls to accept. And even if we accept the notion that we provide a service, that service is often perceived to be so unique, so special, that none of the standard rules and practices of the service industry apply. We believe ourselves to be apart from other institutions in our society. We need an attitude change. Derek Bok is one person whose attitude about higher education's role in society is on the right track. In an interview on the occasion of the Harvard president's impending retirement, Bok commented:

> Whether you are looking at entire schools, like schools of education, or schools of public administration or social work, whether you look within schools at what is really going on . . . you are struck by what an inverse correlation there is between what society needs from these institutions and what we are taking most seriously. If you take some of the basic problems facing our society . . . and then make a list of all the things that a university could contribute . . . and ask yourself how do all these things rank in the list of priorities of the modern university, one is struck by how low they rank.[1]

Our colleges and universities, as Bok implies, are in *service* for society. Indeed, the kind of service we provide is at the very core of a democratic society. We can no longer continue to isolate ourselves from all other institutions in this society by lamely declaring that we are different, too complex. No matter how common and degrading it may seem to some, higher education has the same operating characteristics as a bank, an airline, or a restaurant. The fact is that we do have customers. We provide them with a service and an exchange takes place—a *quid pro quo*. We serve our students: We teach them about Shakespeare, Euclidian space, gene splicing, and debits and credits. They pay us money. We serve our alumni: We keep them informed about their alma mater and their classmates. They give us goodwill and money. We serve industry: We send them educated men and women, and basic research from our laboratories and clinics. They support us with their tax dollars and research grants. We serve. *And we need to have a "service" attitude because the quality that we cause, or don't cause, is largely "service quality."*

Let me begin by noting rather quickly the obvious ways that a service is distinguished from a product. First, services are intangible. They are performances rather than objects and, consequently, cannot be seen, tasted, or touched. An art history lecture is a performance, a Buick is not. Second, services involve simultaneous production and consumption. At the same time that the service is being produced it is also being consumed; in this case, while the art history professor is speaking, the student is, hopefully, listening and learning. An automobile, in contrast, is designed, manufactured, sold, and *then* consumed. Third, services are heterogeneous. No two art history professors cover the Impressionists in exactly the same way. The parts that go into an automobile must be exactly the same so as to ensure their being interchangeable. Finally, services are perishable. The lecture is a performance that doesn't inventory well. If the Buick isn't sold this week it can be put on the back lot and brought out again next week.

It follows from this brief overview that the nature of quality in services is probably different from quality in products. In fact, there is one very basic difference. A product, let's say the automobile, has a high proportion of search attributes as opposed to experience attributes. That means that you don't have to "experience" or drive an automobile to make numerous quality judgments about it. Brochures will tell you such "quality in fact" information as the kind of braking system, turning radius, and acceleration rate. Data are also available (e.g., J.D. Power's Customer Satisfaction Index) on the average number of complaints from new owners. A service, in contrast, requires greater experience. You experience an airplane flight or an art history course. There is far less "quality in fact" data that can be generated prior to the service actually being produced and consumed.

The next logical question is: How is the quality of an "experienced" service judged? Again, with a Buick we can measure legroom and headroom just by sitting in the automobile. We can jam the accelerator to the floor in order to judge "pick up." But what criteria do we used to evaluate a service? A. Parasuraman, Valarie A. Zeithaml, and Leonard L. Berry, a group of researchers affiliated with the Marketing Science Institute, have generated ten "service quality dimensions" through their research with a wide variety of service organizations.[2] A brief description is provided below along with a number of higher education applications (see Table 8.1).

Divided this way, it is easy to see the "reasonableness" of the service quality notion. "Access," for example, includes a number of basic higher education issues. Are the department and its professors easily accessible by telephone? Are there convenient office hours for the professors and for the students? Are the offices themselves in a convenient location? "Communications" is also an obvious source of perceived service quality. A college that continuously attempts to inform the community as to its purpose and distinctive ability to serve will have an effect on its customers' perception of service quality. "Competence" is clearly an important dimension. Are the professors, teaching assistants, secretaries, and administrators knowledgeable and skillful? Do they demonstrate that knowledge in their interactions with students, parents, community leaders, and board members? Then there is the "tangibles" dimension. Are the art department studios adequate (i.e., layout and light)? How about the equipment available for use in each of the studios? All of these dimensions, and the other seven as well, obviously influence a customer's perception of the quality of service that is offered. And these examples just focus on students and external customers. The dimensions of service

TABLE *8.1*   Dimensions of Service Quality

Dimensions	Higher Education Applications
ACCESS involves approachability and ease of contact	• maintaining customer-driven office hours • providing an efficient telephone system
COMMUNICATION means keeping customers informed	• explaining services/costs, and vision • assuring the customer of intentions
COMPETENCE means possession of the required skills/knowledge	• demonstrating teaching excellence • developing research capabilities
COURTESY involves politeness respect, consideration	• treating students with dignity • insisting on equal treatment for all
CREDIBILITY includes honesty, trustworthiness, believability	• delivering on recruiting promises • having fair and reasonable policies
RELIABILITY involves consistency of performance and dependability	• getting rid of incompetent employees • reducing registration/billing errors
RESPONSIVENESS concerns the readiness to provide the service	• returning telephone calls promptly • providing timely resolution of complaints
SECURITY is the freedom from danger, risk, or doubt	• assuring physical safety • protecting individuals' privacy
TANGIBLES include the physical evidence of the service	• maintaining campus grounds • acquiring appropriate technology
KNOWING THE CUSTOMER means making the effort to understand	• providing individualized attention • developing the means to "listen"

Source: A. Parasuraman, Valerie A. Zeithaml, and Leonard L. Berry, *A Conceptual Model of Service Quality and its Implications for Future Research,* The Marketing Science Institute Working Paper No. 84-106 (Cambridge, MA: The Institute, 1984), 13–14. Reprinted by permission.

quality affect our internal customers as well. "Knowing the customer" is important to the computer services staff. Are professors able to conduct their research using the hardware and software that is provided?

The strategic benefit of understanding the dimensions of service quality, and their application to an individual professor, program, office, or college, can be extended even further. There is strong empirical evidence available in the services marketing literature to suggest that perceived service quality is not so much a function of absolute ratings on these dimensions, but rather the relative difference between "expected" service and the "perceived" service.[3] That is, satisfaction with a service is related to the confirmation or disconfirma-

FIGURE *8.1*   Service Satisfaction

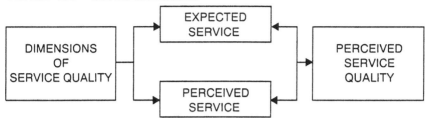

tion of expectations. *To cause "perceived service" quality it is necessary to meet or, hopefully, exceed the expectations that customers have concerning quality across as many dimensions as possible* (see Figure 8.1).

This would seem to be a fairly straightforward task—identify the service quality expectations and then work to meet or exceed them. Certainly this would appear to be a healthy attitude for anyone in a service industry—and one we need to adopt in higher education. Unfortunately, customer expectations are often disconfirmed by a gap that exists between what is expected and what is perceived to be delivered. There are four basic reasons for such gaps in higher education. First, there can be a difference between a customer's expectations and what others perceive that customer's expectations to be. This is usually the result of our misunderstanding the dimensions and what levels of performance connote high quality to customers—i.e., poor listening habits on our part. One professor I know consistently gets only fair student evaluations because she underestimates the abilities of her students. She doesn't challenge the students (she doesn't "know" their expectations) and, consequently, they resent the way that she conducts her classes. A college can make a similar "gap" error. John Slaughter, the president of Occidental College, made the following observation about his institution: "Occidental considers itself to be a quality, liberal arts college, but that has been known primarily by people here—people who are close to it. When you get outside of Eagle Rock, it isn't all that obvious." The gap, in this case, is a lack of "communication."

While the first gap error is largely based upon poor listening habits, the second is more of a constraint problem. It is possible to know what customers' expectations are and still not be able to deliver them. In this case the administration may face resource or allocation constraints, or may find it difficult to respond to market conditions, or may simply be indifferent to the situation. A number of colleges are facing a problem here, especially as it relates to "tangibles" and "access." Increasingly, students are entering college with computer skills. They *expect* to use PCs for word processing, graphics, and to run statistical programs. But the cost of staying ahead of the obsolescence curve with both hardware and software can be staggering. It is not uncommon for a college student to be asked to use an older version of software than he or she used the year before in high school. In a slightly different fashion, the term "flexibility" was one that came up often in my conversation with Frank Ellsworth, the president of Pitzer College. At a small college, the tenure system can make it very difficult to be "responsive" to new ideas, opportunities, shifting expectations, and market conditions. And so Ellsworth is continually looking to develop a "wide range of options and possibilities" so that both he and his faculty members are not limited to doing tomorrow what they did today.

It is possible for the administration, faculty, and staff to be well aware of service expectations and to have the resources, commitment, and flexibility to meet those expectations—and *still* not satisfy a customer. Sometimes the service provider does not perform at the level expected—a service performance gap. The case of Professor Grimm that was described in Chapter 3 is a good example. The hypothetical professor taught one course in a three-course sequence on American economic institutions. The gap resulted from the professor continually straying from the course's syllabus, leaving the students unprepared for the next course in the sequence. Tony Branch, the vice president of Academic Affairs at Golden Gate University, has a similar challenge when it comes to Golden Gate's School of Taxation. The program has high expectations and a solid reputation but must rely on industry professionals as part-time instructors. This is a service performance gap waiting to happen. But Branch let me in on his gap-reducing system:

> *When it comes to our adjuncts, we have rigorous requirements. They have got to have the appropriate tax degree, usually from NYU which is the Harvard of the tax schools. They have to be with a Big Six accounting firm and at least an associate, junior partner, or tax lawyer. So we are very selective. We have a curriculum for each course that is devised here on the main campus, and in devising that curriculum, we have local faculty from the off-campus sites in Seattle and Los Angeles select one person from the three or four that teach a course to come to San Francisco for a central confab to update and refine the course. We do insist, at the price of academic freedom, that the instructors stick pretty close to this ideal course model.*

And finally, discrepancies between service delivery and communications—whether in the form of exaggerated promises or misinformation about the service—can affect perceptions of service quality. According to Cal State–San Bernardino's Jerrold Pritchard, the university adopted the Dartmouth Plan as its organizing framework years ago. The idea was to keep general class size small while at the same time identifying those places in the curriculum where large lectures, taught by Ph.D.s using the didactic mode, were most appropriate. It sounded good on paper because the large classes paid the bills and allowed professors to protect the average class size in their majors and other targeted courses. But what's on paper and what gets practiced are often two different things. According to Pritchard, "Our goal was to have 20 percent of our classes large, have no intermediate size in the forty to sixty range, and have everything else small. It hasn't worked out because we haven't got enough large classrooms to do it so we have been drifting toward more and more forty to sixty size classes." The university's inability to construct the classrooms is a clear example of the second service quality gap—resource constraints that make it difficult to deliver the service as expected. However, the problem would be severely compounded if the university continued to promote itself to prospective students, parents, and community members according to the Plan instead of reality.

Colleges and universities have a unique challenge. That challenge is to change our attitude about the safe, island-like environments in which we work, and face up to the reality of the new world in which we exist. Within the last decade a different lexicon has evolved on college campuses—"productivity," "assessment," and "cost containment" are some of the more stark terms. We can now add "service quality" to that list. Whether we like it or not, we are in a service industry and our customers define quality in "service quality" terms; that is, meeting or exceeding their expectations. Not delivering on service quality expectations—the expectation/reality gaps of the 1990s—is a certain recipe for mediocrity at best, severe fiscal and morale problems at worst.

◆

Once we begin to change our attitudes about being part of the broader service industry, we need to work on another attitude change as well. Many people within our campus walls have a "we can't afford it" attitude about quality. Throw the idea away. Quality does cost, it's true. But the cost of "unquality" pales in comparison.

What should be painfully obvious from our discussion of the last few pages is that the cost of service quality is expensive. The act of "listening" to customers is time consuming, energy depleting, and can require a certain amount of cold hard cash. Setting up an advisory board in a school of nursing or education, and operating it in such a manner as to generate a better understanding of the dimensions of quality, should not be considered a nice little diversion from everyday problems. Such boards can be tremendous vehicles for "educating" our colleges and universities about the needs of industry, society, and local communities and for understanding their perceptions of our services. But such knowledge does not come easily—nor cheaply. It requires hard work to move beyond a token group of people who sit around a conference table twice a year dining on cold cuts and listening to *your* plans for an expanded computer lab.

Other listening opportunities are costly as well. Surveying your alumni requires a budget of some size and the expertise to construct, compile, analyze, and communicate the results. Attending local Kiwanis Club, Rotary Club, and town council meetings can take a chunk out of your day. Conducting interviews with first-year students to extend your knowledge of their expectations is an enlightening but exhausting foray into the unknown. Setting up a Customer Service Center in the physical plant to respond to concerns across the campus requires the reallocation of scarce personnel resources. Then you must react to what you've heard. The services that are provided, from the security in the dorms and the greeting by the telephone operator to the mix of courses and majors that are offered, need to be adjusted to meet the expectations. This requires strong leadership, resource allocation choices, and effective communication efforts. Again, none of this comes cheaply. The cost of meeting or exceeding service quality expectations is an expensive proposition for any college or university to consider—but it may well be the most highly leveraged investment your college or university can make.

Expenses that we accumulate to cause quality in any organization are starkly apparent. Our postage costs for doing mail surveys sky rockets. The bill for new computer software sits on your desk until it gets paid. Recruiting top notch professors is an obvious debit to the institution's balance sheet. The costs are overt and so we skimp where we think we can. Tom Maher, the vice president of Academic Affairs at St. Francis College, put it best when he told me, "We are so cost-conscious that our first, knee-jerk move is that when we lose a faculty member, or a high quality staff member, we go out and try to find the least expensive replacement. And then we pat ourselves on the back if we are able to do it." Unfortunately, while the costs of quality hold our attention, we seldom attempt to calculate the cost of *not* conducting the survey or *not* hiring the better, more expensive faculty member. The price of *not* attending to quality is a cost that organizations become accustomed to, because it is invisible to the naked eye. The cost of "un-quality," never seems to see the light of day and, consequently, tends to be easily dismissed. Being aware of such costs, however, is central to the task of "managing in" quality.

There is another type of "un-quality" cost: any expenditure in excess of those that would have been incurred if the service had been performed correctly *the first time*. Of course we all know that "to err is human," so it is unreasonable to expect perfection. Right? Well, thirty years ago Philip Crosby suggested something different.[4] He argued that we are conditioned throughout our lives to accept the fact that people make mistakes. That's just the way it is. Mistakes are inevitable. But the question Crosby raised was, "Do we always make the same percentage of errors in each thing we do?" Take cashing a paycheck, for instance. Can it be assumed that people who err in ten percent of their work activities will be shortchanged on the same ten percent of checks they cash? Will they forget to pick their kids up from the babysitters' house one in ten times. Will their car run out of gas the same percentage of time every month? If these assumptions are wrong then errors must be a function of the importance we place on certain tasks and our own willingness to accept mistakes. An extraordinarily pithy example of this kind of expectation was provided by the *Toronto Sun* newspaper a few years ago:

> They're still laughing about this at IBM. Apparently the computer giant decided to have some parts manufactured in Japan as a trial project. In the specifications they set out that the limit of defective parts would be acceptable at three units per 10,000. When delivery came in there was an accompanying letter. 'We Japanese have hard time understanding North American business practices. But the three defective parts per 10,000 have been included and are wrapped separately. Hope this pleases.'[5]

We have been conditioned to accept errors and, consequently, we spend much of our time finding mistakes and then either throwing them out (the three units) or fixing them. Crosby labeled the reverse process "Zero Defects" based upon his reasoning that if errors are not inevitable we can and should work to prevent them from happening in the first place.

Within the last year or so industry and government have graciously provided two dramatic, impossible-to-dismiss illustrations of the *cost of doing things wrong.* While you are probably familiar with the Perrier recall debacle, you might not be aware of the specific costs involved.

LOSING ITS FIZZ

For Perrier, the decade of the 1980s was a bonanza. Sales in the U.S. alone rose from $40 million to more than $800 million as the bottled water became a symbol for the status- and health-conscious. Then, in early February of 1990, reality struck a cruel blow. Perrier, the purest of the pure, was contaminated. The headline—Perrier Loses Its Fizz—and an opening paragraph of the *Newsweek* article gave the overview:

> 'It's perfect. It's Perrier," was its advertising slogan. Its chic green bottle became a status symbol for an entire generation of Yuppies. Then came the bitter chaser: Source Perrier, the mineral water's manufacturer, announced that traces of benzene, a toxic chemical, had been found in some of its products. After first pulling only its exports to the United States and Canada, the French company announced it would extend the recall to every bottle of Perrier, everywhere in the world."[6]

It turned out that Perrier, straight from the source, contains traces of benzene that occur naturally in the gases that give Perrier its fizz. Filters are routinely used to extract the chemical. Apparently, the cause of the problem was that the filters had become saturated—*someone had forgotten to replace them.*

The recall itself was impressive—160 million bottles from 120 countries. Then, four months later, there was the relaunch. A new label marked with the words "Nouvelle Production" was unveiled to go along with a $25 million marketing campaign. The new slogan—"Perrier, Worth Waiting For." The estimates are that if everything proceeds according to plan January 1991 sales will be back to 85 percent of January 1990 sales.

Not to be outdone, the National Aeronautics Space Administration in conjunction with private industry, recently upped the ante of Perrier's multimillion dollar cost of "un-quality" to a new stellar level—apparently to run into the billions.

OUT OF FOCUS

In August, 1990 the Hubble Space Telescope was launched by the space shuttle Discovery into a 330-mile-high Earth orbit, placing it above the interference from Earth's atmosphere and enabling it to scan the farthest, faintest corners of the universe for new planets, black holes and quasars. The telescope's images were supposed to be seven to ten times clearer than images obtained by ground-based telescopes. Unfortunately, from the very beginning the images that Hubble sent back to Earth have been blurred—out of focus.

The problem apparently was in the making almost ten years ago when the telescope was being manufactured by Danbury Optical, a division of Perkin-Elmer. At the heart of the telescope are two finely ground mirrors that are designed to gather, magnify, and focus starlight at a tiny spot at the back of the telescope. An optic device used to guide the making of the main, ninety-four-inch mirror was believed to contain a spacing error of about one millimeter—the diameter of the tip of a ball-point pen. But further investigation of the error by a federal panel of research scientists found that the real culprit was not the specifications of the optic device itself but that the fact it had been used *upside down*.

The resulting misshaped mirror does not sufficiently concentrate light on its surface leaving the entire $2.6 billion project in jeopardy. NASA officials have begun to plan a 1993 shuttle mission to install a set of corrective lenses.

The costs associated with doing things wrong fall into two categories: scrap and rework. In the case of Perrier, scrap is the 160 million bottles that were recalled and then destroyed. Rework is the cost of fixing a defect. The 1993 shuttle mission to the Hubble can be billed to rework. Obviously, these are extreme illustrations of the scrap and rework costs of "un-quality." The

TABLE *8.2* The Condition of the Professoriate

	Two-year Colleges	Four-Year Colleges
The undergraduates with whom I have close contact are seriously underprepared in basic skills	85%	70%
This institution spends too much time and money teaching students what they should have learned in high school	73	65

*percentage of professors agreeing with the statement

Source: *The Condition of the Professoriate: Attitudes and Trends* (Princeton, NJ: Carnegie Foundation for the Advancement of Teaching, 1989), 19. Reprinted with permission of the Carnegie Foundation for the Advancement of Teaching.

millions of dollars involved are not everyday occurrences for Perrier or NASA, or they would both be out of business. These were aberrations that turned into public relations nightmares. But while Perrier and NASA would contend that their recent problems are asymptomatic of the way they conduct their business, according to Philip Crosby, product companies spend 20 percent or more of their sales dollars doing things wrong and then having to fix the problems.[7] Most of the 20 percent that individual organizations experience are not headline-grabbing flubs. The vast majority of the costs of "un-quality," as we noted earlier, goes unnoticed . . . quietly and indifferently dismissed as the normal and accepted costs of doing business.

Products provide the most dramatic examples of the cost of "un-quality." Interestingly enough however, service organizations may have the greater problem. Crosby goes on to comment that "Service companies spend 35 percent or more of their operating costs doing things wrong and doing them over."[8] The reason for this is that service "un-quality" is even more unobtrusive, and consequently more tolerated, than product "un-quality." If the service organization does not meet the customer's service quality expectation, the problem is often either ignored, trivialized, or passed along. Our educational system is illustrative of the amount of time we spend "doings things over again." In a recent study by the Carnegie Foundation for the Advancement of Teaching, the issue of faculty attitudes toward undergraduate preparedness was explored (see Table 8.2).

These are *extreme* numbers. As downstream customers of high schools our service quality expectations are clearly not being met. So what do we do about it? Do we return the defective product? Most high school students don't come with a money-back guarantee, so returning them is not an option. Often we ignore the problem and reduce our own expectations. Other times we don't perceive we have a choice and attempt to perform expensive, Hubble-like rework. All of this, of course, is in contrast with the notion of helping to ensure that things are done right the first time, or reducing the cost of rework and scrap by "protecting our supply." Ted Sizer, a leading advocate of high school/college collaborations, in responding to the question "Why should colleges and high schools bother to form partnerships?" stated:

> There are a wide variety of reasons. The most obvious is to be neighborly; institutions, like individuals, should support each other in the community. A second reason, for colleges, is self-interest. The stronger the high schools, the stronger will be the students coming into college. Furthermore, the better the relationships between a particular college and high school, the more likely that the high school teachers will recommend that their students go to that college. A third reason is that schools are an enormously important social institution, universities should be more concerned with the shape of society. Both to understand and to improve it, our universities should understand schools very well. And if they find the schools wanting in certain ways, they should help to improve them, insofar as they can.[9]

Sizer, in effect, is an advocate of Crosby's "Zero Defect" concept—we should be concentrating on preventing problems rather than finding them and fixing them.

How about another rework example? Remember the convoluted payroll process that was flow charted in Chapter 5? The process was not working well; errors and complaints were commonplace. After collecting data, it was discovered that 50 percent of the payroll forms were either not completely filled out or were filled out incorrectly. The solution? People in the payroll office spent hours on the telephone at the end of every two-week period tracking down the correct information. Rework. And that wasn't the half of it. The flow chart revealed that, depending upon where the transaction began, there were between three and seven inspections (approval and signature) in the process—before the forms got to the payroll office. Also rework. And they still got it wrong!

Turning to the notion of scrap, let's take the example of a highly qualified first-year student. From the material that we covered earlier in this chapter, we know that this young woman or man has certain expectations. She or he has "access" expectations, "competence" expectations, "security" expectations, and so on. The expectations may have been influenced by friends, parents, or guidance counselors. The institution may have contributed to the formation of the student's expectations through its catalogs or admissions officers. The expectations exist. They are real. For the sake of our example, let's assume that one of the major reasons why this student chose to attend a specific college is because of "access." The student, right or wrong, believes that small class size is a mark of quality and the chosen college markets itself as having an *average* student faculty ratio of fourteen to one. Our young friend proceeds to pay the tuition, moves into the dormitories, and eagerly awaits the first day of classes. Unfortunately, not quite understanding the true meaning of "average," the student is startled to have three out of five classes with more than thirty students. Expected service equals fourteen; perceived service equals thirty. The resulting perceived service quality gap may or may not provoke an action. Understanding how a student trades off the various dimensions of service quality can be a complex undertaking. But simplifying the scenario for a moment, let's assume that the student is disenchanted enough to leave (either dropping out to work or transferring to another institution). So what? So a few leave. Unfortunately, on some campuses those who leave outnumber those who stay. Nationwide, almost one in five college students fail to "persist" beyond their third semester.[10] Few of these students volunteer their reasons for not returning. More than likely, the students—like our disenchanted one—simply disappear. No complaints, no excuses. They just walk away.

And how does the institution respond? With quiet indifference. In fact, as long as the aggregate numbers hold up—enough newcomers to replace the ones who left—the loss usually goes virtually unnoticed. No one takes the time to calculate the cost of scrap. No one seems to care. Undoubtedly, if they had taken the time they would be shocked by the numbers. First there is the foregone income stream. Take tuition, room, and board and multipy their sum by three more years. Don't forget the books, snacks, and T-shirt purchases at the book store each year. Multiply by three again. Add in the occasional parents' visit. Then you might want to also include the long run. What's your average annual alumni gift? Multiply by 50. Now let's start calculating replacement costs. If instead of losing half of your first-year class before graduation you only lost 25 percent, how would that affect your operations? Well, you would have to recruit one-third less students with a concomitant decrease in admissions officers, catalogs, and so on. According to an Admissions Marketing Group survey it costs about $1,700 to recruit a single student.[11] For some, the costs are considerably greater. A recent *Fortune* article on education stated: "Case Western Reserve, which like many major universities now actively recruits not just athletes but the unathletic as well, spends an average of $2,400 per student on mailings, promotional videos, and other courting efforts."[12] Add in the replacement cost.

And finally there is the incalculable loss of goodwill. While the student won't announce his or her reason for leaving to you, he or she will announce it to parents, younger brothers and sisters, friends, neighbors, and impressionable high school seniors. A *Journal of Higher Education* article entitled "Student Perceptions of College Quality" is illustrative. One of the conclusions made by the two Colgate University economics professors who conducted the study was, "Of particular interest to Colgate's recruitment efforts is the way the people connected with the college influence perceptions. Current Colgate students appear to have a significant influence on prospective students' perceptions of academic, social, and athletic qualities."[13] Can you imagine the impression produced by a disgruntled former student? Whatever you calculate the cost of losing a customer to be—whether it is a student, a taxpayer, a legislator, or an employer—in actuality it is probably a lot worse. The cost of scrap in higher education is enormous.

A final thought on the subject of scrap: Tom Peters has a little section in *Thriving On Chaos* entitled "Treat the Customer as an Appreciating Asset." One of the people that he quotes is a grocery store owner who said, "When I see a frown on a customer's face, I see $50,000 about to walk out the door."[14] His good customers buy about $100 worth of groceries a week. Over ten years, that adds up to roughly $50,000. For some reason, those of us in higher education miss the point. When students frown we ignore them because they are mere students, and we assume there's more where they came from. When legislators frown we dismiss them as not understanding the complexities of our institutions. When society frowns, as Derek Bok suggests it is doing, we just go about our business as we damn well please.

$$\blacklozenge$$

We are in a service industry, and our charge is to provide the best possible service at a reasonable cost. Was the payroll process described in this chapter providing good service? Not with the number of complaints it received. Okay, so it wasn't great service but at least it was cheap. Wrong again. Any process with that many inspectors and that amount of rework is hardly a bargain. How about service to the student? Tuition increases continue to outpace inflation and yet a quick glance at *Money Guide's* "America's Best College Buys" shows that the graduation rates (percentages of students who graduate in five years) of many colleges are 40 percent or less. If any business converted only 40 percent of its input into output, it would be filing for bankruptcy! Yet an article in the *Chronicle of Higher Education* described the reaction of higher education officials to new legislation that Congress approved requiring colleges to release the graduation rates of all students. The title of the article says it all: "Colleges Fear Data on Graduation Rates Could Be Used Against Them by Congress." Unfortunately, our response to these and other service quality problems is typically reactive. Larry Sherr, the consultant on the payroll snafu, told me: "People blamed everyone but themselves. The payroll office blamed the people who initiated the forms; the people in the departments blamed those that filled out the forms."

As institutions, we can continue to ignore our problems or engage in the finger-pointing that we seem to do so well. We can grab onto short-term solutions such as "Forty ways to contain your costs." But my gut-feeling is that many of the problems our institutions are dealing with would be greatly reduced by a change of attitude. We need to shift gears from denying that we are in a service industry to becoming service fanatics. We need to go from doing the minimum for our customers—internal and external—to exceeding their expectations. We need to become less accepting of things as they are and more willing to improve them, continuously. We need a change from doing things wrong and then doing them over to doing them right—the first time. We need to discard our mantle of arrogance and get busy at nurturing a competitive attitude—on the basis of a distinctive vision and service to our customers—in an environment in which scarce resources, calls for accountability, and demands for quality are not an occasional inconvenience but an implacable condition.

9

A Culture of Quality

Assessment is a core element of causing quality in higher education for no other reason than it stresses improvement. Specifically, assessment activities focus on a handful of thoughtful questions: What knowledge or abilities do we intend our students to acquire? Are they successful? What is the institution's contribution to student learning? What do we know about that contribution? Such questions provoke data-gathering efforts that, in turn, can be used to alter teaching methods, curriculum development, administrative policies, and so on. Assessment has all the attributes of a process that yields never-ending improvement.

It is hard to imagine a college and university that isn't pro-improvement, especially one that has a tradition of excellence. So why has there been such a battle at a school like the University of Virginia? In a recent issue of *Change,* Pat Hutchings and Ted Marchese took the pulse of the assessment movement by visiting several campuses where "assessment has recently arrived." In the case of the University of Virginia (UVa), the assessment initiative can be traced to a legislative resolution passed in 1985 directing the State Council of Higher Education of Virginia (SCHEV) "to investigate means by which student achievement may be measured to assure the citizens of Virginia of continuing high quality of higher education in the Commonwealth." An abbreviated chronology of the ensuing events as detailed by Hutchings and Marchese includes the following:

- April, 1987—The SCHEV approves "Guidelines for Student Assessment." The guidelines leave wide latitude for institutions to devise their own approach; urge the use of existing data; ask for attention to general education, remediation, the major, and alumni follow-up. Each institution is required to develop a plan and then report yearly on its progress.
- June, 1987—UVa submits its first plan. It calls for the use of interviews to track the "university experience" and student progress in general educa-

tion; outcomes studies are to be tested in five majors; an alumni follow-up study is to be developed; and a proposal is to be sent to the faculty for assessment-oriented senior projects for all students.

- April, 1988—The chair of UVa's Assessment Steering Committee writes a condemnation of SCHEV's having mandated assessment without specifying *why* it was doing so; that is, for failing to point to "some problem." He concludes: "The Assessment Steering Committee rejects the idea that outcomes of education can be agreed upon by educators—at UVa or anywhere."

- June, 1988—In response to UVa's annual report, SCHEV expresses serious concern over the stretched-out time tables, scaled-back plans, and claims of insufficient funds. It also raises questions about the research design.

- July, 1989—UVa submits its required report. It includes the results of a fifteen-page questionnaire administered to a portion of the freshman class; an update on the progress made in the assessment of the five majors; and a preliminary discussion of the future (now 1992-1993) alumni follow-up study.

- August, 1989—SCHEV rejects the report. The review (conducted by SCHEV staff and a national consultant) expresses "disappointment with the general progress" of the university, which to the reviewers suggests "a lack of commitment to the overall ... process and an absence of effective leadership."

- August, 1990—Provost Paul Gross responds: "I find myself at odds with your ideas ... on what assessments are worth doing in a place like this, how much it is worth spending on the activity, and what relationship they can be expected to have to improved learning for *our* students."[1]

There is nothing to suggest that this "Marquis of Queensbury" exchange is unique. Indeed, similar tête-à-têtes have been occurring and will continue to occur between most institutions and their governing or coordinating boards. It is a clash of cultures—a test of wills. The campus community values a set of beliefs: academic freedom (i.e., the responsibility for education is that of the individual professor), and the notion that each institution is uniquely complex. Such a culture finds it difficult to interpret any external mandate as a selfless mechanism to help it improve. Instead, "improvement" is perceived as a blatant intrusion on the right of the institution to manage its own affairs. The other culture, the board, is seen to be driven by an insatiable need for "accountability" and a furtive desire to conduct "inter-institutional comparisons." Therefore, the results of an American Council on Education campus survey on assessment are understandable—almost three-fourths of the respondents express "fears about misuse of effectiveness measures by external agencies."[2] Campus culture has spoken.

The changes that are part of causing quality in higher education are so fundamental that they must take root in an institution's very essence, in its culture.

Perhaps the most succinct way to think about culture is that of a social or normative glue that enables an organization to solve problems. The shared meanings of a group allow it to develop commonly understood ways of conducting daily activities. For better or worse, every organization has a culture—"how we do things around here"—and because culture is context-bound, every organization's culture is different.

The study of organizational culture has its primary intellectual roots in two disciplines: anthropology and sociology. The elements that comprise a culture for an anthropologist include language, ritual, and custom while sociologists tend to view culture from the perspective of social structures and the exercise of power and influence in interpersonal relationships. Both anthropology and sociology, and allied disciplines such as communications and social psychology, have produced a wide and deep tradition of work that has formed a solid foundation of scholarship and a host of insightful review articles.[3] But a recent surge of interest in organizational culture has less to do with its scholarly traditions than it does with two major factors affecting contemporary U.S. business: (1) economic turbulence that has led to major changes in organizations and (2) recent writings about Japanese industry and management. Beginning with Ouchi's *Theory Z* (1981), Pascale and Athos' *The Art of Japanese Management* (1981), and *In Search of Excellence* (1982) by Peters and Waterman, a wave of research and writing has lead to one inescapable conclusion—a strong culture is a powerful driving force behind the success of business organizations. Indeed, Deal and Kennedy conclude their book, *Corporate Cultures* (1982) with this statement:

> In sum, the future holds promise for strong culture companies. Strong cultures are not only able to respond to an environment, but they also adapt to diverse and changing circumstances. When times are tough, these companies can reach deeply into their shared values and beliefs for the truth and courage to see them through. When new challenges arise, they can adjust. This is exactly what companies are going to have to do as we begin to experience a revolution in the structure of modern organizations.[4]

Interest in organizational culture as it applies to higher education has at least three areas of departure from the management literature. First, while the research tradition in anthropology and sociology found fertile ground among management audiences and management scholars, the same cannot be said for higher education. Certainly there have been notable exceptions such as Burton Clark's *The Distinctive College: Reed, Antioch, and Swarthmore* (1970), and Karl Weick's classic article "Educational Organizations as Loosely Coupled Systems" in *Administrative Science Quarterly* (1976). But none have had the impact on higher education that the *In Search of Excellence* rubric had on management. In fact, a recent review of culture in American colleges and universities by George Kuh and Elizabeth Whitt, in their *Invisible Tapestry* (1988), devoted almost half of its pages to non-higher education topics.

Second, differences in organizational structure and the nature of the profession of higher education have resulted in a much greater emphasis on sub-cultures rather than on an overarching campus culture. For example, Burton Clark describes four types of "academic" cultures that result in a series of nested groupings: the culture of the discipline (e.g., chemistry or political science); the culture of the profession (i.e., professorship); the culture of the enterprise (i.e., a college or university); and the culture of the system (i.e., higher education).[5] Kuh and Whitt also describe in detail the literature that pertains to two additional campus sub-cultures: student cultures and administrative cultures.[6]

Finally, and perhaps most importantly for this book, organizational culture can be studied as either an independent or dependent variable. Higher education has taken the anthropological line that suggests that institutional culture is immutable, or as one researcher states: "Culture, when viewed as an independent variable, is a complex, continually evolving web of assumptions, beliefs, symbols, and interactions carried by faculty, students, and other culture bearers that cannot be directly purposefully controlled by any person or group."[7] In contrast to this largely descriptive approach to culture is the more prescriptive sociological orientation favored by the behavioral scientists. The title of a recent *Fortune* magazine article, "Creating a New Company Culture," illustrates the more causative orientation of management's view of culture.

But how does organizational culture, whether it *exists* in a college or university or is *managed* in a business enterprise, relate to causing quality in higher education? Well, quality, as we have seen throughout this book, is not a classy hood ornament that you affix to a car as it is rolled off the end of the production line. It is not a set of resource measures such as the size of the institution's library holdings or its endowment. Furthermore, quality is not merely a set of tools such as student outcomes assessment or pareto charts. Instead, it is a philosophy that is manifested in people's words and actions, how they think and feel about themselves and their jobs. As such, the only way that causing quality can become the norm in a college or university is when it becomes a part of the culture of the place, part of "how we do things around here." In fact, before we look at some specific properties of culture, I need to describe in greater detail the link between some of the quality-causing actions from previous chapters and the culture of a college or university.

Making quality "everyone's job" is impossible when a campus has a weak culture.

There are three levels of control in an organization: first-order controls refer to direct supervision or control by direct orders (or rules); second-order controls are the more remote "standard operating procedures" or policies; and third-order controls are found in the assumptions or "givens" that are part of the organizational culture.[8] Shared or taken-for-granted assumptions can be viewed as a kind of automatic pilot that provides a decision-making framework for people's actions. Without such a normative, third-order framework people would tend to rely on someone else to *tell them* what to do (first-order) or they would apply the old "that's our policy" incantation (second-order). Let me offer a simple example.

Some time ago I called a colleague of mine at a small private college. I had lost her direct telephone number and so I called her department number. No answer. I called the main number, asked for my colleague's office number and was given the department number by the campus operator. After repeating that I wanted the direct line, I was told that professors' office numbers were not given out to anyone—*policy*. I put myself in the place of a college student, paying $15,000 a year for "personal" treatment, wanting to talk to my professor and having to butt heads with a "you can't have her number" policy. Several days later I had my friend inquire as to the source of the policy. It turns out that the company that sold the telephone system to the college had suggested it, and no one had questioned it in five years. Some smart person in the system, over that length of time, must have realized that the policy was suspect. But the culture said "shut up, sit down, follow the rules." The strong culture of a high quality organization relies on third-level understandings—questioning the wisdom of any practice that has a detrimental impact on the customer—to *coordinate* activities. Meanwhile, the "un-quality" organization relies on orders or policies to *regulate* activities.

Continuous improvement, a fundamental element in causing quality, is easier to accomplish in strong cultures than in weak cultures.

Organizational cultures tend to be inherently conservative in that they celebrate and diffuse shared meanings based upon past experiences. Colleges and universities are, in that regard, uniquely celebratory and diffuse. Such quips as "It's easier to move a cemetery than a college," or "Change in higher education occurs over the bodies of 10,000 dead professors" have become standard one-liners over the years. In my campus wanderings, however, I became keenly aware of the accepted norm of both revolutions and evolutionary change among quality programs and institutions. For example, at the University of Chicago, Stuart Tave talked to me about the university's humanities program. The professors in the program would meet once a week to discuss the topics that would be addressed the following week:

> *The sense of politeness was sometimes awful. People were insulting one another—'Goddammit you do not understand the function of the messenger of Oedipus.' And we'd go on like that. I found I was hearing things, learning things in this kind of process. Now these were like-minded people in the sense that they really had a commitment to the discipline, the institution, and its mission.*

Tave went on to say that, "According to Richard McKeon, a great philosopher and scholar at Chicago, the secret of improving the humanities college was to have a revolution every five years—a Jeffersonian principle." Without the security and sense of purpose provided by a strong culture, organizational members feel powerless and unable to act decisively. Thus, a college or university needs to have a strong culture in order to affect the change that is a necessary part of never-ending improvement.

A strong culture enables people to feel better about what they do.

Do professors, secretaries, or students from Harvard University "feel" any different about themselves than their counterparts at Central County College? If we can believe Deal and Kennedy, the answer is *yes:* "When a sales representative can say 'I'm with IBM,' rather than 'I peddle typewriters for a living,' he will probably hear in response, 'Oh, IBM is a great company isn't it?' He quickly figures out that he belongs to an outstanding company with a strong identity. For most people, that means a great deal."[9]

On our college campuses such "feelings" are important as well. Outstanding professors, sharp secretaries, and talented students have choices. If they don't feel comfortable in the culture of the institution, if they don't feel empowered by the values of the organization, they exercise their options—the professors move on to other schools, the secretaries transfer to other departments, and the students transfer to the college down the street. It's the cost of "un-quality." Pure scrap. In contrast, if they feel good about the basic beliefs of the organization and if they adopt the values of a strong organizational culture, they will ultimately become part of the glue that creates a feeling of distinctiveness. I remember LeRoy Greason, the president of Bowdoin College, talking about his biology department. Perhaps not so strangely, he didn't recite the faculty's credentials or the SAT scores of the entering class of biology majors. First he talked music: "The biology department can give you a string quartet. Two or three play the violin and another plays the spinet. They have not only their scholarship as a bond but also their music." He then talked about newsletters: "They have their own newsletter that is sent out to all of the majors and alumni. John Holland, the chair, has been writing it for years. It's very funny and. . . ." The strength of the biology department at

Bowdoin is a function of how its members feel about themselves and each other.

These examples illustrate the close connection that exists between quality and culture. And perhaps even saying "close connection" is not a sufficient description. Having a customer orientation, working to understand and improve processes, developing measurement systems, and cultivating a service attitude in everyone, are necessary parts of a strategic quality management effort. But they, and the other prescriptions that have been advocated in this book, are still not enough to cause quality in any meaningful, comprehensive, or enduring fashion. Jonathan Fife put it extremely well: "With quality, it's a matter of constantly reinforcing the priorities, goals, and values. In fact, quality exists over a long period of time because it is value-laden and then those values become institutionalized." We are foolish to think of quality in terms of the numbers of Ph.D.s on the faculty or the status of one's accreditation standing. Quality runs deeper than that, much deeper. Quality must be embedded in the institution's heroes, it must be manifested in the way that the buildings are maintained, it must be evident in how people treat each other, and it must be at the very essence of what the organization and its members hold most dear.

A culture of quality is one in which members develop, share, and continually reinforce a common understanding of what quality is and how to pursue it. That's nice—a polite, tightly-wrapped statement. Unfortunately, *describing* a culture of quality and *causing* one are light-years apart. If we are to infect the organization with a passion for excellence, we need to go several steps beyond a well-meaning description. The first step is to generate a more detailed enumeration of culture. Let's begin at the most "invisible" level. At the core of an organization's culture is a set of basic assumptions and beliefs. These assumptions and beliefs are *learned* responses that stem from espoused values; that is, as a value produces a behavior, and as a behavior begins to function successfully as a problem solver, the value slowly is transformed into an underlying assumption about how things are done. And as the assumption is increasingly taken for granted, it drops out of awareness becoming a powerful and unchallengeable "given."

While there are many quality-related beliefs on college campuses, let's look at one that hinders quality. In industry, companies regularly review their product lines to assess the profitability of individual products and to evaluate issues of compatibility and overlap. There is an assumption that unless the product is contributing to the bottom line, its continued existence is in jeopardy. It is an understanding based upon the fact that the company must make intelligent decisions about scarce resources to remain a viable enterprise. Of course, in higher education we don't manufacture products nor do we issue quarterly reports to stockholders. But we are in a service industry and we do make daily resource allocation decisions designed (supposedly) to enhance the quality of our operations. In spite of this, at many institutions there is a bone-deep belief that academic programs are *now and forever*. When we add programs we are being innovative, forward thinking, on the leading edge. It is a basic assumption that institutions of higher education should be looking for new academic endeavors. But there does not appear to be a similarly held belief on most campuses that programs need to continue to demonstrate their value. The story told by Lee Grugel, dean of Arts and Sciences at the University of Wisconsin–Eau Claire, is hardly unique:

> *We have a program, a minor program, in Scandinavian Area Studies. Students have to take some language, some history, and so on. There were two retirements and initially the department said, 'Gee, it would be nice if we could hire someone to replace these people who are leaving.' But at the same time we, as a university, need to consider whether we should be offering Russian and Japanese as opposed to Swedish and Norwegian because they are more important languages. And we need to offer more courses in black studies and women's history. So we took a proposal to the curriculum committee to abolish the minor. It failed. Certainly there was sincere concern expressed from the local community but there was also an unstated agenda as well on the part of some faculty members—we're going to exercise our faculty rights to tell the administration that they can't abolish a program.*

The Scandinavian Area Studies example illustrates why values, beliefs, and basic assumptions are so powerful in either creating or hindering a culture of quality. People don't speak of assumptions directly—they must be inferred from behaviors—and some basic assumptions contradict overtly stated norms, so people are reluctant to admit to them. Certainly, no one at the University of Wisconsin–Eau Claire would state for the record: "Each of our academic programs has an inalienable right to exist." But the fact is that the administration would probably have to show extreme fiscal exigency and then trot out a "retrenchment" plan to accomplish what should be an ongoing process of strategic management and quality-causing resource reallocation.

On a more visible level, basic assumptions, beliefs, and values reveal themselves in many different ways. An organization exists as a system of shared meanings and, through the development of shared meanings, members achieve a sense of commonality of experience that facilitates their coordinated view of what is most important within their organization. One way in which shared meanings are formed is through people's interpretation of actions. *Symbolic actions* are any act or event that serves as a vehicle for conveying meaning, usually by representing something else. Such actions can be as incidental as The University of Rhode Island's president, Ted Eddy, picking up trash while walking across campus or as purposeful as Oregon State University's physical plant setting up a Customer Service Center. Each action represents something else—that everyone should take responsibility for the way the campus looks, or that we are looking for ways to improve the quality of our service operation. Here is a short collection of actions, from industry and higher education, and their probable "quality" meanings:

- At the Paul Revere Insurance Company they have "Meetless Friday's," a day each week in which everyone is encouraged *not* to schedule any meetings: *Don't get bogged down in bureaucracy. Get out there and make things happen because quality is something we do, not something we talk about.*

- John White at Nebraska Wesleyan embarked on a deliberate effort to bring speakers of "national" reputation to campus: *We shouldn't see ourselves as a good Midwest institution but as a national-class university. The standard of quality has been raised.*

- At Hyatt hotels, senior executives—including its president—put time in as bellhops: *We define quality in terms of customer satisfaction. The customer is king and you can't understand a customer's view of the world if you're hiding behind some desk on the 33rd floor.*

- Cal Tech's administrators, including the president, provost and, vice provost teach on a regular basis: *The "practice" of teaching and research is first, the "administration" of it is a distant second. We need to be primarily concerned with quality as it occurs in the classroom and in the lab.*

Another way in which meanings are shared is through *rites and ceremonials*. Harrison Trice and Janice Beyer in an article entitled "Studying Organizational Cultures Through Rites and Ceremonials," define a rite as "planned sets of activities that consolidate various forms of cultural expressions into one event, which is carried out through social interactions, usually for the benefit of an audience." A ceremonial, in turn, is a "system of several rites connected with a single occasion or event."[10] Rites and ceremonials, therefore, act to heighten the expression of shared meanings. Table 9.1 is adapted from Trice and Beyer, illustrating the types of rites in a college or university and their manifest or latent social consequences.[11]

There is a flip side to the notion of rites and ceremonials as "shared meaning." Please understand that individuals within your organization will *infer* meaning even if it isn't intended. For example, if your rites of passage are weak, you are saying something about how much you value membership to the organization. If your rites of degradation fail to differentiate between levels of quality, you are sending a message as well—"incompetence (or the idea that errors are inevitable as Philip Crosby argued against in the last chapter) will be tolerated." Ceremonials also convey meaning regardless of what is intended. One school I am familiar with, has a ceremony as part of a convocation in which awards are given out for excellence in research, teaching, and administration. While each person receives an identical amount of money, *only the research winner is asked to address the assemblage.* Intended

TABLE *9.1*   College or University Rites

Types of Rites	Example	Manifest and Latent Social Consequences
Rites of passage	Interviewing, orientation	Challenges the institution to articulate its values and to facilitate the transition of persons into social roles and situations that are new for them
Rites of degradation	Non-renewal of contracts	Defends group boundaries and value systems by redefining who belongs and who doesn't
Rites of enhancement	Awards and promotions	Provides public recognition of individuals for their accomplishments; motivates others to similar efforts
Rites of renewal	Professional development	Focuses attention on those issues that the institution deems to be important
Rites of integration	Social gatherings	Encourages and revives common feelings that bind members together and commit them to the group

Source: Harrison Trice and Janice Beyer, "Studying Organiation Cultures Through Rites and Ceremonials." *Academy of Management Review* (October 1984): 655. Reprinted with permission.

or not, the ceremony reinforces what quality accomplishments are deemed to be most important at that school.

Another culture-bearing form is the *hero*. If values are the soul of the organizational culture, then heroes personify those values and provide tangible role models for others to follow. There are two basic types of heroes: one is the leader who embodies the vision of the institution and the other is the situational hero. Leaders are human symbols of both quality accomplishments and quality aspirations. Both industry and higher education have their heroes—Lee Iacocca and Derek Bok, Steven Jobs and Robert McCabe. But it is particularly important within the context of causing quality that we don't neglect the situational heroes. These are the people that are mentioned throughout Jan Carlzon's *Moments of Truth*. They could be baggage handlers, ticket agents, or flight attendants at Scandinavian Airlines. It didn't matter to Carlzon what their job description was. What mattered was that during that fifteen-second "moment of truth" when the airline was "created," an individual needed to display heroic efforts, if necessary, to satisfy the customer. Indeed, if quality is "everyone's responsibility," then heroes should literally blossom throughout the fertile fields of an organization—in the registrar's office, in physical maintenance, in security, or, for example, in UCLA's sociology department. According to Howard Freeman, the sociology chair, the department had experienced a "rollercoaster ride of quality" for years. Recently, however, a turnaround could be traced to a single person's entrepreneurship. According to Freeman:

> *Our new director of graduate studies, Jeff Alexander, went out and recruited the best graduate students that there are in the country. He is the author of dozens*

of books and has an international reputation. So he decided he would call up the chair of the sociology department at good undergraduate institutions, and say, "Look, if you let me talk to your best graduates, I'll come and give a free lecture." And he started going out on a circuit. He hit fifteen or twenty good schools, first-rate, Haverford, Reed, as well as some of the major schools. All you need is ten bright graduate students a year and you'll have a terrific program.

A hero, like UCLA's Jeff Alexander, provides a lasting influence within the organization—a living, breathing symbol that sets a standard of performance while making success both attainable and human.

The culture of quality is also embedded in the *stories, sagas, and myths* that circulate within an organization. Stories are narratives that are based upon true events often containing plots, leading and supporting characters, and symbolic meanings. Sagas and myths are historical narratives that describe the accomplishments of a leader in heroic terms or fictional events that are used to explain the origins or transformations of something. Storytelling is essential to causing quality in higher education or in any other type of institutional setting. For instance, I have repeatedly suggested that high quality organizations empower people to make decisions on the spot—without dutifully checking with a superior, without thumbing through a policy manual. Sounds like anarchy. And it could be anarchic if attention is not paid to hiring good people, training them properly, *and telling them stories*. With stories, an individual has only to place a problem into the framework of a well-known story about how such a problem was handled in the past to know what should be done. Shared scripts, therefore, convey a set of assumptions and implied values that guide and limit decision making.

In addition to their specific impact on decision making, stories, sagas, and myths also have more general roles as third-order controls. Alan Wilkins, in his article "Organizational Stories as Symbols Which Control the Organization," speaks directly to these roles.[12] First, stories facilitate recall. According to the data cited by Wilkins, a concrete story is more easily and accurately recalled than a chart or statistics that document the same event. At the University of Rhode Island we spent two years putting together and then implementing a new admissions plan. One spring day when it became apparent that we had exceeded even our own most optimistic goals, Ted Eddy, the president, managed to acquire the resplendent helmet worn by the marching band's drum major. Helmet in place, he proceeded to march across the campus, with vice presidents and deans in tow, to the admissions office. We spent an hour toasting our successes with champagne, soda, and "kudos" all around. No one remembers the admissions statistics. Everyone remembers the day the president donned the plumage to salute the admissions office's efforts.

Additionally, stories, sagas, and myths generate strong beliefs by being used as historical "evidence." My conversation with John Shay, the president of Marygrove College demonstrates my point. He spoke of his struggles to upgrade the quality of his institution through some very difficult times. He believed that in the last few years Marygrove had really turned the corner, and then he launched into a wonderfully passionate speech about the music program and the choral—"You've got to believe me that when you hear our choral they are, by any objective standard, absolutely fantastic. Our choral is like another place's football team." To support this belief he then proceeded to tell the story of the choral's five-city tour of the Soviet Union.

Finally, stories and the other narrative forms of culture encourage commitment. Wilkins tested this proposition by obtaining transcripts of organizational stories through interviews with employees of different companies, and measuring levels of employee commitment with a survey instrument.[13] In the organizations in which commitment was stronger, a larger number of stories were told, and their content was more positive. One only has to read through Burton Clark's classic article, "The Organizational Saga in Higher Education," to conclude that a similar association exists between the stories and sagas of a strong culture and a commitment to quality on college campuses. As Clark eloquently states:

> In an organization defined by a strong saga, there is a feeling that there is the small world of the lucky few and the large routine one of the rest of the world. Such an emotional bond turns the membership into a community, even a cult . . . The organization possessing a saga is a place in which participants for a time at least happily accept their bond.[14]

It should, by now, be obvious how important story telling is to strategic quality management. Above all else, an institution that commits to a new management paradigm must produce winners; that is, success stories like the ones that were used to introduce the profile of Oregon State University's TQM efforts in Chapter 2 (e.g., reducing the time taken to complete remodeling jobs or decreasing the number of journal vouchers returned to departments for error correction). In Mary Walton's book, *Deming Management at Work*, she specifically talks about "bragging" at the Hospital Corporation of America. In effect, the more stories that emerge from our quality-causing efforts, the more bragging we do about our successes, the greater the likelihood that the philosophy (and the application of its tools and techniques in a systematic way) will become accepted throughout an organization as the way we work, "the way we do things around here."

I began this section by describing the beliefs and values that are the basic assumptions of an organizational culture. These assumptions are the most fundamental threads in the "visible tapestry" of culture. At a more manifest level are the rites, stories, and heroes that embody those beliefs and values. In addition to these levels, it is also important to realize that culture also reveals itself in *visible* artifacts—Stanford's ubiquitous sandstone archways or the sunken gardens and the Chistopher Wren building at the College of William and Mary. If one can assume that the physical environment of a campus is a series of premeditated choices designed to fulfill a specific academic or social mission, then the existing buildings and grounds reflect a legacy. One can almost feel the richness of that legacy in a passage from an article entitled "Walk through History on Campus:"

> Whether a revered landmark, a quiet oak-lined quadrangle, or the historic disarray of fraternity row, the images evoke lives lived and years past. We want them to remain, and, indeed, college campuses have been good repositories of memory . . . Whatever the age or setting or spread, college campuses tell the history and settlement of the region, a sequence of distinctive places with buildings that can be read like books. An autumn stroll through a campus—especially with a good guide—can be suffused with history as light through coloring leaves, as stirring to the spirit as it is to the senses.[15]

In a unique way, a college campus projects the distinctive values and hopeful aspirations of those individuals who live and work at the institution. It is important, therefore, in our rush to develop a good measurement system, a strong service orientation, and a distinctive vision, that we don't neglect the mundane details of a fresh coat of paint, neatly manicured lawns and well-maintained buildings. Paint, lawns, and buildings send messages as well.

◆

I would like to return to the beginning of the previous section for a moment. I stated that the first step in moving from a description of culture to actively managing culture was to disaggregate the concept into its component parts—rites and ceremonies, heroes, beliefs, and so on. Our lives would be simple, indeed, if we could stop with that. But it should be obvious that we are not just talking about management when it comes to causing quality in higher education. Many, if not most, of the issues that I have discussed call for a clear departure from the beliefs that are found on college campuses today. The strategies and concepts of "kaizen," "the cost of un-quality," "stuck in the middle," "quality as a verb," and "between the ears quality," are not consistent with the current academic administration rhetoric. So, we are not really talking about *managing* culture, we are talking about *changing* culture. And once we begin to talk about changing culture, we really take the discussion onto another level. As any psychologist will tell you, it is difficult enough to change a single person. With a culture, a set of assumptions evolves into an interrelated pattern that has shared meaning for many, many persons.

Culture, as we have noted, reflects what has worked in the past. Consequently, if substantive change is to occur it must give people an improved framework or paradigm for living their work lives. Even that is not sufficient. The sacred cows of an entrenched culture are notoriously tough. What has to happen is that a new paradigm must manifest itself in people or processes that will, over time, be consistent *deliverers of change*. I have chosen to discuss three culture-changing delivery systems: leadership style, recruiting practices, and intraorganizational communications.

There can be no culture of quality without consistent and persistent leadership throughout the organization.

It is difficult to think of a topic that has generated any more attention in the study and management of organizations than "leadership." There are the authored gurus of leadership—Warren Bennis, John Gardner, John Kotter. There are the myriad articles in *Reader's Digest, Chronicle of Higher Education,* and *Fortune* with titles such as "How to Be a Leader," "Educating Leaders: When Did You Last See a Budding Thomas Jefferson on Campus?," and "Wanted: Leaders Who Can Make a Difference." The leadership seminar business is booming. And finally, there are the "numbers" offered by leadership researchers—the six behavioral dimensions of leadership, the seven skills to leadership, the fifty recommendations for leadership and, my personal favorite, the 1,400 discrete skills that Lin Bothwell has suggested positively correlate with leadership.[16]

In spite of all this, leadership's role as a "deliverer of change" is uncommonly simple. Leadership involves just two elements: (1) movement and (2) followers. So, the key question in causing quality is, "How can leaders create movement in the culture of a college or university campus?" One of the most effective ways that movement can be generated is through the personal behavior of leaders. For example, the existence of a culture of quality is decidedly a function of what campus leaders say it is. As we have seen, the concept of quality throws most people for a loop. They all want it. They think it's a damn good idea. They are even willing to work hard to get it. The problem is that they aren't quite certain exactly what it is. Leadership can create movement by articulating a distinctive vision of what quality means to the institution—clearly, concisely, and concretely. Charles Glassick, the retired president of Gettysburg College and now the director of the Robert Woodruff Art Center in Florida, spoke to me about visionary leadership and painted a picture that was part watchdog, part cheerleader, and all visionary: "My sense of leadership is a person who keeps a focus on the vision for the institution—always aspiring, always reaching and keeps everyone moving." Such leaders, whether a president, a dean, or a respected professor, facilitate movement through their communication of the vision which infuses energy and synergy into the organization.

The existence of a culture of quality will also be the direct result of how leaders spend their time—what they do. Yes, a leader must promulgate a vision, but the most awe-inspiring words won't budge a culture unless it is supported by actions. I can offer two culture-budging stories: one from industry and one from higher education. When Roger Millikin, president of Millikin Corporation, became distressed with late deliveries, he announced a policy under which customers receiving late shipments from Millikin would get a 50 percent price reduction. There was a clear meaning in the action—a commitment to on-time delivery. And according to the story, the problem began to diminish quickly. Another leader, Robert McCabe of Miami–Dade, was faced with disastrous academic standards in the early 1980s. On one of the campuses the modal grade awarded by instructors was an 'A'. At another campus a not completely atypical student had registered for over one hundred credits and had completed only six. The decision to impose standards as part of a more comprehensive reform effort had significant risks—both financial and political. Nonetheless, McCabe and the administration at Miami–Dade proceeded with their plan and in the first term suspended 3,200 students. A new standard of quality had been set. In both of these instances a leader reinforced a vision by providing organizational members with tangible proof of her or his personal commitment to quality. And in both instances the effect was dramatic. Millikin Corporation has since received the U.S. Department of Commerce's highly prestigious Malcomb Baldrige National Quality Award and Miami–Dade is now regarded by many as one of the very best community colleges in this country.

A culture, strong or weak, is a learned behavior. People don't stumble upon the notion of "this is how we do things around here." The assumptions that are developed and carried forward are the result of a subtle educational program that is produced and directed by old organizational members for the benefit of new members. A paradigm shift, therefore, asks people to disregard what they have learned. In the case of strategic quality management many of the topics that we have covered describe a new order—a very different way in which a college or university should operate. So, the leadership delivery system must not only include what is said about quality and what is done about it, but also *how* it is said and done. Let me paraphrase the words of Edgar Schein, an organizational researcher from MIT on this point. One of the functions of leadership, one that is especially crucial to our discussion, is to provide guidance at precisely those times when habitual ways of doing things no longer work, or when an environmental change requires new responses. At those times, and this is where Schein's thoughts are most compelling, leadership must not only insure the wisdom of new and better methods, but must also provide some security to help people tolerate the anxiety of giving up old, stable responses, while new ones are being introduced.[17] It is not a coincidence that each of our profiled organizations (or in one case, a system) from Chapter 2 enjoyed the firm commitment and steadying influence of their respective presidents.

In addition to the personal behaviors of the leader, there is another way in which leaders needs to assert assumptions about quality—*through the formal and informal systems it creates.* In Deming's *Out of the Crisis,* he makes "institute leadership" one of his fourteen points. The notion of leadership that is espoused, however, is not your garden-variety charismatic hero. In fact, my interpretation of Deming is that he is speaking of a kind of "enabling" leadership. A Deming-type leader is someone who helps others do their jobs better. Such a leader is not appointed because he or she knows everything but because he or she has the ability to create the prerequisites for the work that must be done. You may recall from an earlier chapter my discussions with Nat Weiss of Kean College in New Jersey. Weiss is a true believer in the talent development notion of quality: "What happens between the time that the student enters the college and the time that student leaves—intellectually, culturally, and socially—is really what makes a good college or program." But while Weiss was preaching his vision of education and assessment, he was also working hard to alter some very fundamental relationships:

> *I had to sell the vision [of assessment] to the faculty. I had to bring them in and I have a unionized faculty—a very powerful AFT [American Federation of Teachers] union. And I mean they're strong. The senate was controlled by the union. What I did was to pull out some of the best union people who are really talented, but strong union people, and bring them into the process. We worked and worked and we destroyed the whole adversarial relationship myth. We replaced it with essentially a trusting, cooperative relationship and each year they became more deeply involved.*

This is the kind of systemic change that can lead to a culture of quality. By eliminating a barrier to causing quality, Weiss "enabled" the vision to become deeply embedded in the basic beliefs of the institution. Thus, he ensured that the changes would become part of the fabric of Kean long after he was gone.

> *A culture of quality can be profoundly reinforced and amplified through an institution's recruiting practices.*

We have a tendency to think of recruiting or hiring as the act of plugging up organizational holes. In higher education, don't we speak of "filling that position" in the housing office or computer services? Don't we also talk about "replacing" professor so-and-so in the English department and the number of "openings" we have in the business program? Whenever I hear these terms I can't help but visualize reserve troops being rushed into a breach in an army's front line. What happens when we change the focus on the recruiting picture? Instead of "replacing" or "filling" a position, we could begin to think in terms of "improving" the institution or the college or the department. Every new vacancy, then, from a cook's helper to a chancellor, becomes an opportunity to hire someone who may become a hero, someone who could empower others to achieve better results, someone who might find a better way to serve the students or the alumni. Since every person in an organization is eventually succeeded by someone else, the institution can be transformed

FIGURE *9.1* Recruiting for Change

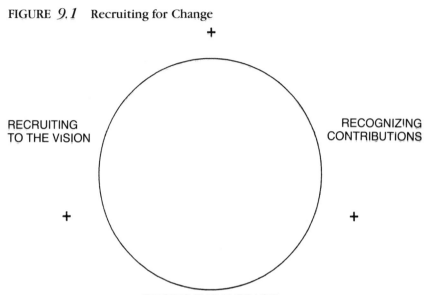

over time—bit by bit, day by day, one appointment after another. Given this, perhaps a good way to see recruiting is from a systems thinking perspective that reinforces and amplifies change (see Figure 9.1).

The circle in Figure 9.1 suggests that a cultural transformation could occur through personnel practices that enable the institution to move from a static notion of replacement to an invigorating belief in improvement. Beginning at the bottom of the circle is the practice of recruiting to "raise the average." I think, and apparently others do as well, that colleges and universities are either improving or losing ground. There are simply no other options. I can say this so confidently because it was one of the most common points of demarcation between quality and un-quality that I heard in my campus interviews. I offer two samples: Arnold Speert, president of William Patterson College says, "I think the key to building star programs is that the people who hire are not afraid of hiring somebody who has a greater reputation or potential than they are or will have;" Jerry Kissler of the University of Oregon says, "The best programs that I am aware of have a standard for hiring people that are better than they are. The general feeling is that if this appointment doesn't raise the average of the department, we shouldn't make it." The implication is that a person is not merely being hired to teach the "19th Century Authors" sequence but, rather, is being sought to improve the current standard of quality in the English department. Such a divine discontent for the status quo is the basis for "raising the average."

Further, the idea of improvement through recruiting has a significantly greater effect when the hiring reinforces and enhances the distinctiveness of the institution. In any institution there are a certain number of core positions in academic affairs, students affairs, and other areas that are required. You need English composition professors, a chief executive officer, a registrar, and a person to lock up at night. But 'beyond a surprisingly limited number of core personnel, there is tremendous discretion in where an organization invests its human resources. If this is true, then significant changes can occur by focusing our "raising the average" efforts on certain visions, rather than simply filling current vacancies with above-average replacements. In fact, think back to Deming's notion of "constancy of purpose" or White's statements about "synergy" and couple them with the words of Duquesne University's Michael Weber:

> *The leaders of really good institutions or programs present a vision of where he or she wants to go and then hires to that vision. They do not try to fill in every single void in the discipline but, in fact, have taken a good look at their programs and said, 'Look it, we can't do everything because we're not going to have forty-two faculty members but we can do certain things and do them very, very well. And we are going to hire to strengths.' You really need to identify what it is that you want to do well and then try to avoid dissipating your energy and resources in a whole variety of other areas.*

By carefully combining these powerful dynamics you can create tremendous energy, the kind of synergy that is capable of delivering change to a culture.

There is one final element in this amplifying loop. "Raising the average" and "growing the vision" amount to pure organizational rhetoric if you don't "recognize contributions." As I have suggested, culture is a learned behavior. We can make all the grand visionary statements we want, and we can pepper the institution with endowed chairs and inviting job descriptions, but none of that will have any staying power unless things are institutionalized. That means that heroes must emerge from this circle, and the rites of enhancement and renewal need to reward and celebrate their deeds. If that happens, the good people—those that are raising the average and growing the vision—will stay. And if they stay, their shared experiences will create an increasingly strong culture—one that emphasizes third-order controls and exhibits stability and purposefulness. Such a culture, a strong one, is best able to encourage change and to ultimately institutionalize the prescription of strategic quality management.

> *A culture of quality requires open, honest, efficient, effective, barrier-breaking, and fault-free lines of communications.*

We cannot "control in" quality. This didn't work in industry and it hasn't been successful in higher education. The accountability route, whether it is an accreditation team or a legislative committee, is never going to be able to mandate quality. The only real quality, the only lasting quality, comes from the hearts and minds of the administrators, faculty, and staff on campus. This requires a culture in which communication plays a much different role than it does at most colleges and universities today. Let me present a set of specific changes that I believe need to occur in order for communication to be most effective. First, we need to have a cultural transformation from one that dwells on data that is being reported to external agencies to one that encourages the sharing of information throughout the institution. Remember the results of the American Council on Education's assessment survey at the beginning of this chapter? Three-fourths of the respondents expressed fears about the misuse of effectiveness measures by external agencies. In a previous chapter I cited new Congressional legislation that requires colleges and universities to release the graduation rates of its students. The *Chronicle of Higher Education* article that reported the legislation begins, "Beware of lawmakers with new data."[18] That's not where our energy needs to be expended—defending our turf from the evil data-manipulators.

We need to be concerned with two things: converting data into information, and then sharing it. Data are stimuli with the potential to become information if they can be used to reduce uncertainty. Campus administrators have not done an adequate job of working *with* faculty and staff members to develop and share appropriate measures that yield *information* about important quality-causing processes. Instead, we have historically worked *on* faculty and staff members to generate *data*. Past lessons have shown these people that such data-generation efforts yield either the mindless type of data dumps that crowd the pages of program reviews or data that are used for the limited purposes of accountability. In an article that appeared in *Change*, R. Eugene Rice and Ann E. Austin reported their findings from the Taskforce of the Academic Workplace in Liberal Arts College (appointed by the Council of Independent Colleges). After a national survey and site visits, the authors described the operating characteristics of ten "excellent" colleges. One key discriminating characteristic was described in the following way:

> *Willingness to Share Information.* The respect for faculty, and the sense of trust that permeates these institutions, is fostered by the sharing of important information. Detailed data and the complexities of institutional decisions are communicated in open forums. Faculty are heard on critical issues and know the details when they debate with administrators or among themselves. This depth of faculty understanding mitigates against polarization.[19]

At such institutions people are convinced that sharing information improves the ability of the institution, and its component parts, to achieve a stated goal—in our case, the strategic management of quality.

A second aspect of the communications delivery system is improved feedback. Throughout this book I emphasize the importance of feedback mechanisms in "causing quality." From a communications standpoint, every formal action that is taken, every policy that is implemented, and every process that is charted should be replete with dotted-line feedback loops. Feedback is at the very core of "kaizen" and the implementation of never-ending improvement. But we don't do it. Here's an example: almost a year ago I was asked to be the outside reviewer for a college's business administration program. It was part of a mandated five-year program review cycle. I took my work seriously. I read their collected "data" and interviewed the faculty members. The resulting report was an honest look at the program's strengths and weaknesses, and some recommended courses of action. Several weeks later I turned in the report to the dean, was thanked, and received compensation for the services rendered. It just so happens that one of the program's professors is an acquaintance of mine. According to his account, the professors were given the opportunity to look over the original draft that came from the data generation exercise, but the final program review document, including my report, went straight to academic affairs and has not been heard of since. By solely directing information flow upward, instead of upward, downward, and round and round, we reinforce a belief that quality needs to be "controlled in." The existence of feedback loops throughout an organization can dramatically change the culture because the symbolic meaning attached to feedback is clear—you are empowered and you are responsible for improving your own performance. In sum, we need to direct the communication flow, as St. Francis College's Tom Maher showed me, to those people who are in the best position to cause quality:

> *Program reviews are not used by me to identify who's doing the job and who isn't. I want it, rather, to be the basis for reflection. The other day we had a Biology review and the review team presented its findings to the faculty. They laid it out flat for us. There were a lot of good things that we were doing and I think that was great for our people's self-esteem. We also have some professors who are decent teachers but who have become disengaged professionally and we need to think about ways to support them in a process of rejuvenation. Faculty members need and deserve that kind of reflection.*

A third change that is needed is one that gets center-stage attention from W. Edwards Deming—breaking down organizational barriers. Organizations are not created with barriers. Barriers evolve over a period of time as problems arise with communication, competition, and jealousy. The resulting barriers make it difficult for people to see their role in various processes, scrap and rework costs increase, and there is a noticeable decrement in quality-causing synergy. I noted at the beginning of this chapter that most of the research on the subject of culture in higher education focuses on sub-cultures—students, disciplines, the profession—and not on the culture of the institution. This is not just an unfortunate occurrence. The problem is real and

TABLE *9.2* The Condition of the Professoriate

	VERY IMPORTANT	FAIRLY IMPORTANT	FAIRLY UNIMPORTANT	NOT AT ALL IMPORTANT
How Important to You Is Your College or University?	40%	45%	12%	2%
How Important to You Is Your Academic Discipline?	77	20	2	0
		A LOT	SOME	NONE
How Much Opportunity Do You Have to Influence the Policies of Your Institution?		20%	49%	30%
How Much Opportunity Do You Have to Influence the Policies of Your Department?		73	23	4
	NEVER	RARELY	SOMETIMES	OFTEN
Indicate the Extent to Which You Participate in Departmental Meetings?	1%	3%	8%	88%
Indicate the Extent to Which You Participate in Campus-Wide Meetings?	17	19	31	33

Source: *The Condition of the Professoriate: Attitudes and Trends,* (Princeton, NJ: Carnegie Foundation for the Advancement of Teaching, 1989), 19. Reprinted with permission of the Carnegie Foundation for the Advancement of Teaching.

severe, as should be plainly evident from The Carnegie Foundation for the Advancement of Teaching's technical report—*The Condition of the Professoriate* (see Table 9.2).

These numbers should be downright frightening. A culture of quality? Shared meanings? Improving processes? A distinctive vision? All of these things become virtually impossible goals to achieve in such a fragmented, isolated environment. Barrier-breaking is needed —lots of it. We need more cross-functional teams in higher education. We need to pursue those questions and processes that extend beyond the departmental boundaries or pigeonholes we protect so well. Specialization cannot come at the expense of integration. As Carl Naegele, who has just returned to the faculty after serving as the dean of Arts and Sciences at the University of San Francisco said to me, "Integration, overlap, connectedness, and symbiosis are all necessary parts of being a university."

Leadership, recruiting, and communications, then, are the delivery systems by which the values, beliefs and assumptions of quality can become institutionalized. These are hardly the ingredients for a quick fix. Indeed, culture-changing systems require one specific personal characteristic in those of us who are interested in causing quality in higher education—a great deal of patience.

Thomas Hardy wrote in his book *The Dynasts* in 1908 the following: "My argument is that War makes rattling good history; but Peace is poor reading." Evidently the same thing can be said for quality—it makes good history. In my discussions of "a culture of quality" I have emphasized the present and the future. I wanted to speak about culture from the perspective of change and the mechanisms needed to *implement and institutionalize* a causing-quality philosophy. But not too long ago, after having wrapped up my campus interviews for this book, I was discussing my ideas with Alexander Astin at UCLA (where I was a visiting scholar at the time). While much of our talk was around the relationship between assessment and strategic quality management, we sidetracked at one point. The details are sketchy in my mind but his closing remark is not. He said, "Daniel, never underestimate the importance of momentum in higher education." I decided to review the notes from my campus interviews, to rethink whether the philosophy of strategic quality management and the culture of a college campus really were compatible.

In several instances, the individual I was interviewing literally began with a history lesson. Rosemary Schraer, chancellor of the University of California–Riverside, took me back to 1905 and the citrus experiment station that was later to become UC–Riverside. Harry Smith, the president of Austin College, told me that he was lucky enough to become president just after a retiring trustee finished writing a book, *Wholeness and Renewal in Education: A Learning Experience at Austin College,* about each program of the college and how it had been put in place: "It helped me to understand how we had gotten where we were." Another group of people spoke more directly to the management of the history. St. Francis College's Tom Maher showed concern because, "I don't think that a lot of deans, provosts, presidents, and the like think ecologically about how programs develop over time." And Nancy Avakian, associate vice president at Virginia Commonwealth, spoke to a plus: "A sense of history adds to the swagger with which one approaches things, it adds to the ability to negotiate."

I also realized that a few people had thoughts that specifically reflected Astin's sense of dynamics. Victoria Fromkin, the dean of UCLA's Graduate Division said, "Good departments get better and bad departments get worse." Then there was Michael Beehler at South Puget Sound Community College who described programs that were on the downslide as carrying "sea anchors." Howard Freeman at UCLA put it well: "It takes a long time for bad things to happen in a university. It's like a chronic disease that you have for many years before it gets you." And finally there were the words of Norman Bradburn, then provost of the University of Chicago: "What impresses me the most is the degree to which there is a continuity in the culture of excellent programs and institutions. There's a self-sustaining aspect to quality when the culture gets transmitted from generation to generation. When you find places where things have declined it's usually because there has been some break in the culture."

My conclusion is that strategic quality management will not be accepted at those institutions that could probably use it the most—those that are clearly struggling. Their reaction to their circumstances will be to "dig the same hole, only deeper." The culture is not strong enough, the people don't have enough self-confidence, to risk the "thought revolution" that strategic quality management entails. There is also good reason to believe that our very best institutions will be unwilling to depart from their current administrative philosophy. In this case the logic of "if it ain't broke, don't fix it" probably applies. That leaves the rest—and there are hundreds and hundreds—in which the invigorating precepts of strategic quality management could create the momentum for a new paradigm. An approach in which quality really does make "rattling good history."

Telling the
Quality Story

The headline of a recent *Los Angeles Times* article read: "LeSabre's Success Proved Point for GM: Quality Sells." The story begins with a retrospective on the tough times in Flint, Michigan—the aging birthplace of General Motors, a town that has come to symbolize everything that went wrong with the U.S. auto industry. Yet, according to the story, amid Flint's industrial rubble, one GM factory has been transformed into a showcase of quality, building cars that are nearly as trouble-free as the best from Japan. According to the J.D. Powers & Associates survey on automotive quality, the 1989 LeSabre turned in the highest quality score ever posted by a domestic car. The announcement had an immediate effect:

> [T]he LeSabre has proven once and for all to GM executives that if they build quality cars, people will respond; the LeSabre took off like a rocket on the sales charts after last June's release of the Powers survey. In July, LeSabre sales rose more than 91% compared to those of July, 1988; in August, nearly 99%. The public perception of quality made LeSabre the hottest domestic car on the market. "The dealers told us that people started coming in with newspaper clippings about the quality ranking and would say, 'I want one of these cars,' without even knowing what a LeSabre was," said George Gurnsey, Buick's product satisfaction manager.[1]

Is there a similar "quality" undercurrent in higher education? Well, among the numerous customers that a college or university has, there is at least one who has expressed a consistent concern for quality. One national survey explored the criteria first-year students used to choose the college in which they were currently enrolled. The most important factor in the choice process was "academic quality."[2] This response does not vary from those students enrolled at Stanford or at a small, local college; nor has it changed in the eight years since the study was initially done. Furthermore, *The American Freshman* survey sponsored by the American Council on Education and UCLA has been tracking the attitudes and behaviors of first-year students since 1966. One of the questions that has been asked over the years is, "What are the most important reasons for selecting this college?" The most oft-cited response, for twenty years, has been "good academic reputation." It consistently and convincingly beats "graduates get good jobs," and "offered financial assistance" for the top spot.[3] Quality, perceived or otherwise, sells. And it doesn't appear to matter if it's cars or colleges, LeSabres or liberal arts.

In responding to a market or a public, those of us who are interested in causing quality need to follow a straightforward formula—(1) define what quality means to the market, (2) match market needs with organizational resources, vision, and competitive position, (3) strive to improve quality in areas that create a "quality" advantage, and (4) communicate our accomplishments and aspirations to the market. The first three elements of the formula refer to the strategic management of quality—the subject of this book (so far nine chapters and hundreds of examples and quotes on the topic). The final element would appear to be the easy part. Just tell the story. All we need to do is provide the information and, as with the LeSabre, people will respond.

Well, that might be true, but the fact remains that *colleges and universities have a long way to go in their story telling abilities.* The student/parent market is a perfect example. In his book *College: The Undergraduate Experience in America,* Ernest Boyer uses the results of a national survey of college professors, students, and parents to formulate his ideas about the current state of affairs on our college campuses. In the opening chapter he writes, "one of the most disturbing findings of our study is that the path from school to higher education is poorly marked. Almost half the prospective college students we surveyed (47 percent) said that 'trying to select a college is confusing because there is no sound basis for making a decision.' " Boyer goes on to suggest that without adequate information, many students choose a college almost blindly with, understandably, predictable results: He says that "once enrolled, they often are not satisfied with their decision [perhaps due to the gap between service quality expectation and reality] and far too many, for the wrong reasons, transfer or drop out [scrap]."[4]

Continuing with this example a bit further, Boyer notes that during the course of the study he examined the viewbooks used by colleges during the recruitment of prospective students. He concludes that while the material is attractive and well written, "promotional booklets and brochures are more visually appealing than informative and, if we judge from the pictures, it would be easy to conclude that about half of all college classes in America are held outside, on a sunny day, by a tree, often close to water."[5] Wouldn't it be nice if we could easily dismiss Boyer's mordant observations? Unfortunately, his criticism is closer to reality than most of us would care to admit.

George Kuh and Michael Coomes confirm in an article entitled "What

Prospective Students Really Need to Know About Institutional Quality" the point that differentiating between institutions on the basis of substantive "quality" criteria is a difficult task. They offer the following recruiting material descriptions from different kinds of institutions as an illustration:

> The College seeks young men and women of intellectual promise who share a strong commitment to Readmore's educational philosophy, for in its collegiate community, students and faculty together carry important responsibilities for the quality of education. (A private college in the Northeast)

> To offer to all students a quality education consisting of specific elements of a liberal education and of professional training as well as the opportunity for community service. To provide each student with the opportunity for self development proportionate to his/her particular abilities and adapted to his/her special needs. (A small university in the West)

> Quality and diversity have been what set the University apart: contributing to its special character, providing its strength, reflected in its teaching, research, and public service activities. Quality programs tend to attract qualified and committed students. (A major state supported research university in the Midwest)

> Ivy Covered is distinctive in being both a university dedicated to scholarship and research of the highest quality and an undergraduate college committed to highly personalized teaching. (An Ivy Institution)

> Educational vitality has been part of our four-year liberal arts college since 1870. In every program individual attention is important. With our [fifteen to one] student-faculty ratio, you'll get the help you need, when you need it. Quality education at a reasonable cost. (A liberal arts college in the Midwest)

> Source: Reprinted with permission from George D. Kuh and Michael D. Coomes, "What Prospective Students Really Need to Know about Quality," *College and University* (Winter 1984): 167–68.

Their conclusion? Kuh and Coomes write: "On the surface, these descriptions seem very similar. Therefore, prospective students and parents no doubt encounter considerable difficulty in distinguishing between institutions of high quality and of marginal quality."[6] My conclusion? My views have been reaffirmed by the battle for MBA candidates that is contested on a daily basis in the newspapers throughout the country. One that has appeared regularly in the *Los Angeles Times* has a catchy headline—"Quality to the Highest Degree." If such cleverness is not, by itself, enough to make you rush to register, you could read the text that begins: "With the proliferation of graduate degree programs available to working adults, you have to consider the quality of the curriculum [at this point, I could not agree more]." Reading further: "By choosing the University of _____ MBA program, you can be assured that you're receiving the highest quality education available [really, how can I be assured?]." Well, here comes the assurance: "Our academic standards guarantee that a degree from the University of _____ is held in the highest regard." That's it. Quality is defined in terms of having academic standards. Apparently this particular institution has them, while others do not. Quality does sell but not like this. It sells when the institution is willing to take the time and effort to follow the formula of defining, matching, creating, and communicating quality. Quality sells if colleges or universities can speak in their customers' "language of quality." Without that language, customers are literally forced to compare innocuous advertisements or pore through inane recruiting materials.

Now, vigilant defenders of higher education might rationalize that colleges' written conveyances with prospective students are just one small slice of an entire communications effort that institutions manage. Such a narrow, isolated view does not do justice to their more comprehensive endeavors. A broadened panorama of customers, in contrast, includes the general population, local community leaders, industry executives, and politicians who are also concerned with various aspects of quality. Indeed, these publics have begun to, as I have noted throughout this book, voice their quality demands with more and more conviction. Local community leaders are not taking for granted the enhanced "quality of life" argument that colleges and universities have made for decades. Effective "town and gown" relationships are becoming increasingly dependent upon a *quid pro quo* in which the benefits of having a college or university in the community are being weighed against the costs (e.g., the cost of services such as fire and police). Industry continues to spend an increasingly large portion of its revenues on training programs (American corporations budgeted more than $44 billion for training expenses in 1989, an increase over the previous year of more than 12 percent). While some of the spending reflects pro-active enlightened management, another portion of the training is directed toward rework; that is, teaching employees, including college graduates, skills that industry should reasonably expect their new hires to have acquired in our colleges. Politicians—national, state, and local—have all joined in the quality crusade as well by establishing blue ribbon committees and task forces to investigate and report on quality. It would appear that with all of these constituencies clamoring in unison, communicating quality would be uppermost in the minds of higher education professors, administrators, and staff. Regretably, it is not.

Since many colleges and universities appear to be turning a deaf ear to the calls for a better articulation of quality, a recent national task force had some pointed remarks for higher education leaders. In 1988 the Council for

the Advancement and Support of Education (CASE) issued a document entitled the "Special Advisory for College & University Presidents." It was the
product of the collective wisdom of the National Task Force on Higher Education and the Public Interest which studied the adequacy of communications
between higher education and its many publics. The introductory statement is
an eye-opener:

> We write the nation's 3,400 college and university presidents to ask for your
> help in addressing two urgent tasks—improving higher education's perfor-
> mance in areas of abiding concern to the American public and communicating
> to the public that improvements are, in fact, being made. Presidents know only
> too well that criticism of higher education is becoming more strident and more
> widespread. Some of it has been fueled by specific people or incidents. Much of
> it, however, is deep-seated: a growing public perception that higher education is
> faltering in the delivery of its services to our citizens and its promise for the
> nation's betterment.[7]

The advisory goes on to note that the Task Force found the polarization
of views between on- and off-campus constituencies most clearly drawn
around five major issues, one of which is the "quality of higher education."
The ensuing "quality" discussion covers items relating to the proper balance
among research, scholarship, teaching, the nature of the curriculum, and the
public demand for assessment. The final paragraph on quality reads: "We do
not expect that significant, overnight change will occur in building public
understanding that educational quality exists in a variety of institutions. Understanding that quality is the important, inherent element of higher education
will grow as institutions communicate how they are addressing public concerns and taking action on them."[8]

The weight of evidence is overwhelming. From our befuddled high
school student to our demanding state legislator, each is *trying* to make judgments regarding the quality of an individual college, university, or the quality of
a higher education system. In both cases the customer is stymied. Why? Why is
defining, measuring, strategically managing and, especially, communicating
quality so difficult? One reason is that many in higher education are seemingly
incapable of understanding the need to communicate. In Chapter 3 I told the
story of both professors and administrators who have attended my "managing
for quality" workshops. To quote from earlier in the book: "I have yet to make it
through one of these workshops without having a dean or professor stand up
and, in a bit of a huff, proceed to query, 'What does this have to do with me?'
Their point is that they do a good job in the classroom. They know their
material; they make their classes interesting; they are available during office
hours and beyond, and they just completed a draft of a book. That's quality.
Period. End of discussion." This, as you recall, is a transcendent view of
quality—innate excellence is, or should be, universally recognized. And it is

not the responsibility of any professor or administrator or staff member to interpret it. It exists and that should suffice.

In a slightly different vein academics have historically felt that the academy must be appropriately insulated from society in order to be effective. The honored tenet of "academic freedom" has been used to maintain a distance from a whole host of evils, both real and imagined. But the act of constructing barriers to protect our institutions also tends to leave them unable to respond to legitimate inquiries. One obvious example of this kind of barrier is tuition. Quality, as we know, can be defined in value-based terms as well as in transcendent terms; that is, a degree of excellence at an acceptable price. Consequently, a legitimate concern is the cost of the services provided measured against the worth of the services provided. The concern escalates each year in direct proportion to the amount of our colleges' and universities' announced tuition increases. The topic has been the subject of television news programs (e.g., an October, 1990, NBC news story entitled "The Coming Crunch," noted that in ten years the cost of a four-year state college education would be $33,000), recently published books, and numerous magazine and newspaper articles. One particularly rancorous skeptic in a *Los Angeles Times* article entitled "Increases in Cost of College Again Outstrips Inflation" wrote, "As long as I'm seeing people paying $20,000 a year and people sitting in large lecture classes and being taught by teaching assistants who don't speak English well, I don't see any way to justify these tuition increases."[9] Coincidentally, in the same week, the *Chronicle of Higher Education* ran an article in which education leaders congratulated themselves on their restraint. A president of a major higher education association, for example, commented that he was pleased that the average increase in tuition at private colleges had fallen from 9 percent last year to 8 percent this year.[10] While insulation has its benefits, its major weakness lies in a concomitant detachment that leaves colleges and universities unable to respond empathetically to legitimate concerns.

Another reason for our ineffective communication efforts can be traced to a belief that selling, or having to tell the quality story, is somehow inappropriate for a college or university. Almost thirty years ago Donald Faulkner began an article in the *Journal of Higher Education* with the statement that, "College public relations is the sum of all the efforts that are made to give the constituency a full understanding of the institution. This understanding is basic to the good will which is needed by the college to fulfill its objectives— to recruit teachers, research men [*sic* and women,] administrators, and students, and to secure financial support." But Faulkner also went on to say, "The methods used by modern business to create an atmosphere conducive to public acceptance of its products and services are often considered incompatible with the ideals, and beneath the dignity, of the educational institution."[11] In some ways, we really haven't changed that much since Faulkner wrote this piece. Certainly colleges and universities have invested heavily in marketing and public relations efforts. But most of what could be construed as "communicating quality" comes from offices on campus that are far removed from where quality actually occurs—in the classroom, in labs, in advising sessions. Without the ability or encouragement to connect customer-driven definitions of quality to specific campus activities or accomplishments, these offices often produce the kind of homogenized marketing jargon that equates quality to, say, "academic standards" as our MBA advertisement exemplified.

A final important observation: The most stubborn impediment to telling the quality story is simply our inability to define, measure, and strategically manage quality. In order for us to get beyond "innate excellence"—and the knee-jerk response "We know quality when we (the educators) see it"—we must be committed to the philosophy and practice of "managing in" quality that has been discussed in previous pages. Quality involves the never-ending improvement of systems or processes. It is clearly impossible to talk about quality outcomes, especially in user-based or value-based terms, if we don't study and work on systems or processes.

> *The truly effective communication of quality can only come after we have developed an intimate understanding of our institution's day-to-day efforts to improve quality in all of its operations.*

◆

The preceding section was a narrowly-crafted description of the market-driven demand for quality, the ineffectiveness that colleges and universities exhibit in communicating quality to its publics, and a brief (and admittedly intuitive) explanation as to why we don't perform this function as well as we could. It may be useful to take a step backward and examine the broader nature of colleges and universities as social systems with distinct communication needs. For example, higher education institutions, like all systems, use boundaries to describe the line of demarcation between one system and another. Such boundaries can be physical (e.g., campus walls and gates), others psychological (e.g., mode of dress and various initiation rites). In addition to physical and psychological differentiation, boundaries are also defined by the relative number of interactions involved; that is, professors at a specific institution interact more often with each other than they do with the professors at another institution or the employees at a local manufacturing firm and so on. All organizations need to be concerned with how they manage these boundaries. Indeed, Robert Miles, *Macro Organizational Behavior,* specifies a series of boundary-spanning activities that require close attention:

- Representing: This is the presentation of information about an organization to its publics for the purpose of shaping the opinions and behaviors of other organizations, groups, and individuals.

- Scanning and monitoring: An organization needs to generate information on the key trends and environmental events that impact its operations.

- Processing information and gatekeeping: The meaning of environmental information must be interpreted in terms of opportunities, constraints, and contingencies it poses for the organization.

- Transacting: Every organization needs to be concerned with the efficient acquisition of inputs and the effective disposal of its outputs.

- Linking and coordinating: There are a whole host of possible inter-organizational connections and alliances that are a natural outgrowth of operating in a dynamic environment.

- Protecting: Boundary-spanning activities need to occur in such a way that they enhance organizational effectiveness while at the same time they do not hinder the autonomy necessary to do what is in its own best interest.[12]

The communication of quality across institutional boundaries is at the very core of our efforts to move from a transcendent view of quality (as it may or may not occur in isolated areas of a college or university) to one that is user-based and includes an understanding of quality in terms of value. All of these boundary-spanning activities contain communication elements that are necessary to colleges and universities as quality-causing social institutions. For example, we have always accused board members and legislators of not understanding the complexities of higher education. At the same time, we expend minimal "representational" effort attempting to educate these customers about what we do and how well we are doing it. Our "monitoring" is questionable in that we seem to significantly lag behind societal needs in many areas. Teacher education programs, for example, continue to come under fire for spending a disproportionate amount of time on pedagogy while school districts are calling for discipline-based skills. We spend inordinate amounts of time complaining about the quality of high school students (and doing the requisite amount of rework) but spend little time "transacting" with schools in a way that would result in an improvement in their output or our input.

All boundary-spanning activities expose the institution to judgments regarding the effectiveness of its transactions and linkages. So, in every instance quality is being communicated over, under, and through our campus walls—whether we like it or not. In a competitive environment the management of such communications is not an interesting option. It is a strategic necessity. With this in mind, we need to explore a number of do's and don'ts in the fine art of story telling.

Telling the quality story is not a series of four-color pictures in our recruiting view book.

By and large, colleges and universities have looked for the quick fix. While the president is out raising funds, and deans are busily responding to program reviews or generating accreditation data, and professors are preparing their lectures, the responsibility for telling the quality story has befallen public relations and admissions officers. This is story telling by default. You may recall that in Chapter 4 I reported the results of a survey of higher education administrators. According to the survey, the most important challenges facing higher education institutions over the next five years were (1) maintaining enrollment, (2) facilities and technology, and (3) adequate resources. Maintaining quality was a distant fourth. "Improving" quality didn't make the list. The effect of this mind-set is utterly predictable. The strategic management of quality is a comprehensive approach that requires the contributions of everyone in the organization to improve continuously our ability to meet or exceed customer expectations. This is hardly a band-aid. I am talking about a commitment to a philosophy that represents a major change in the values that exist on a college campus—a paradigm shift.

But rather than reshape the culture of a college or university to cause quality, the easier alternative is to reshoot the viewbook, contract a company to produce a video, double the advertising budget or, as several *Chronicle of Higher Education* articles suggest is happening, fire the admissions director. One of these articles begins, "As competition for new students grows tougher, college presidents are treating admission directors like football coaches, firing those who can't put the numbers on the board."[13] Two weeks after that article appeared one admissions officer penned a rejoinder in which he suggested that many admissions offices had probably reached the limit of what marketing could do for their institutions and that, "the dismissal of a chief admissions officer for 'not bringing in the class' is too often a knee-jerk reaction that masks deeper management problems."[14] The deeper management problem is simply not giving the admissions officer something of "quality" to sell.

If we don't talk about quality, someone else will.

In recent years there has been a spate of magazine rankings of colleges and universities. *U.S. News and World Report* has its "America's Best Colleges," *Business Week* annually ranks the best b-schools. *Money Guide* premiered "America's 10 Best College Buys" in fall 1990. Everyone in higher education realizes that the methodology used to generate these rankings is openly suspect. Nonetheless, the issues sell out—indeed, *U.S. News* begins its 1990 issue by saying "The annual *U.S. News* survey of 'America's Best Colleges' is one of the magazine's most widely read and quoted features." These rankings are a wake up call. They will not go away because there is far too much at stake in an era of $100,000 college degrees. The public's perception of our ability to cause quality and communicate quality is being challenged in a way that it never has been before. In *Money Guide*'s "America's Best College Buys" issue, for example, an article begins: "[C]olleges, which once enjoyed the public's confidence, have created an education marketplace where caveat emptor is the rule. As the competition for applicants has heated up, schools have done their best to camouflage their imperfections."[15] In another article in the same issue, Roland King, a marketing consultant states: "We're forcing people to make what is probably the biggest decisions of their lives—next to getting married—with less hard information than if they were buying a $20 toaster."[16] The quality story will be told, one way or another. Either it will be told by us or it will be purchased at the newstand for $3.95.

The strategic management of quality provides boundary-spanners with tangible truths.

Rankings or "top ten" lists provide customers with a tangible measure. It is no different than Siskle and Ebert (the Chicago movie critics) reviewing a movie and assigning it "two thumbs up." Telling a customer, a prospective student or a board member, that you are "committed to excellence" or that you offer a "quality education" does not put meat on the bones of the quality story. On the other hand, the process of defining, measuring, and strategically managing quality *necessarily* results in concrete user-based illustrations. It has to because the philosophy I have described in this book is rooted in the understanding and improving of processes through the use of measurement and data. In every area of our institutions, therefore, improving processes yields specific tangible outcomes that can be communicated. There are literally dozens of ways to measure, and then communicate, how effective we are at *changing college students for the better.* Arnold Speert of William Patterson College gave me an example of the kind of tangible outcome that needs to be forthcoming:

> *Casio had a regional contest recently in which they blind-judged college jazz groups. Of the 40 groups that competed, eight of them were from William Patterson and of the eight finalists, five of them were from William Patterson. Casio, I understand, went crazy. We won everything—$10,000 for the music department, each group got Casio equipment, and the winning group got flown out to Anaheim. I think we have the first, if not the first then the second or third best jazz program in the country. And, again, we're talking about a state college in New Jersey, paying state college salary, with nothing more than an uncommon desire to be the best.*

Public relations or admissions officers would love to be able to substitute this kind of quality story for every instance in which they are forced to use the words "excellence" or "quality." Indeed, a recent study involving "nonspecific quality appeals" found that the word "quality" has become so boilerplate that it has virtually no effect on customers' attitudes or intentions. The researchers confirmed what should be obvious to us all: "[R]esults suggest the superiority of communication that explains quality as opposed to just mentioning the word."[17]

Communicating quality is a chance to create real understanding and trust.

In my discussion with John Slaughter, president of Occidental College, we touched upon dozens of "quality" topics. One, in particular, stands out clearly in my mind because he was so adamant about it:

That's one of the problems with higher education. We tend to think that we are detached from the crudity of the real world—that we don't have to do the things that IBM or New York Life have to do. In a competitive environment, it is important for programs and institutions to let people know who they are, what they believe in. It's not so much that I have to stand up and beat my breasts and tell you how great we are, but I need to tell you who we are and where we're going. That's the kind of public relations—the kind that generates understanding—that we need to do.

Slaughter's beliefs are the perfect counterpunch to the lingering notion that using overt communication methods to create an atmosphere conducive to public acceptance of our "products and services" is beneath our dignity. Visibility generates awareness, and from that comes the perception that an institution is alive, doing things, making progress, and contributing to the general well-being of society. The assessment movement is a useful example: While many institutions continue to battle state legislators' and board members' efforts in this area, others see it for what it is—a tremendous opportunity to showcase quality, improvement, and a means to strengthen arguments for various funding initiatives. Assessing talent development is a way to communicate the quality of an educational experience, a way to generate trust in our institutions. Therefore, while quality is something to be treasured, it is not something to be squirrelled away. It is something to be shared, if for no other reason, than for its intrinsic ability to promote goodwill and positive perceptions. All things considered, as Neal Pierce wrote in an article for *CASE Currents,* "it's incumbent on today's colleges and universities . . . to concentrate on developing solutions to societal problems, and then to let the government and the public know about what they've discovered."[18]

Telling the quality story is a two-way exercise that involves both listening and telling.

I discussed the importance of "listening" at some length in Chapter 3, but it needs to be re-emphasized here within the broader context of effective boundary-spanning. Telling the quality story is based upon an institution's ability to develop good listening devices. For example, Dominican College in San Rafael, California has an interdisciplinary graduate program in international studies. Its small size and limited resources have not deterred its director, Françoise LePage. She told me that, "it's possible to be excellent with a core of faculty that is fairly small, but you have to be very, very different and have continual access to ideas." The device that she uses is an advisory board—the Pacific Basin Council. "We are in communication with them weekly, almost daily with some of them. We have about twenty-five members now. These people constantly give ideas as inputs in meetings. Whenever we want advice we get on the phone and call them up. They are an incredible resource and they expand the critical mass in a very real sense," says LePage. So much for the *listening*. Several months after our discussion LePage sent me an editorial from the *San Francisco Chronicle*. It was entitled "Pacific Forum's Time Has Come," and it described Senator Alan Cranston's initiative for a permanent forum of Pacific Basin nations—including the U.S., Canada, Japan, China, South Korea, Indonesia, the Philippines, Malaysia, Thailand, Singapore, Australia, and New Zealand—that would address common interest and security in the region. The final paragraph of the editorial read:

> A newer, closer-to-home effort worthy of private support is the graduate program in Pacific Basin Studies at Dominican College, a unique academic venture which is probably better known throughout Asia—from which it has attracted many students and scholars—then in Dominican's Marin County home. This interdisciplinary program offers a master's degree in international economic and political assessment. The rich, diverse learning experience is designed to provide suitable background for tomorrow's leaders in government, international organizations and corporations, the kind of people, it seems to us, that Senator Cranston's forum will require.[19]

Dominican College's ability to tell its quality story is a direct function of its linking and coordinating efforts—or networking. Some institutions (e.g., Jesuit schools such as Santa Clara University) develop a special relationship with their local communities; two-year colleges, (e.g., South Puget Sound Community College) have shown an unusual knack at using advisory boards; and others (e.g., Stanford University) have developed close linkages with industry. In every case the ability to get close to a customer enhances these institutions' ability to develop quality-causing efforts and to talk about their successes. It is also interesting to note that the University of Wisconsin–Madison, while initiating its Total Quality Leadership Program (highlighted in Chapter 2), organized three boundary-spanning groups: an advisory team of experts from public and private organizations to meet on a formal basis, corporate sponsors to aid with training resources and consulting, and an external network of other "individuals, including other universities and colleges implementing Quality, private consultants and corporations, the City of Madison, state agencies, and public sector agencies across the nation." Again, the emphasis is on listening before telling.

The communication of quality is a self-validating process that enhances pride and self-esteem.

Two primary themes that have permeated this book are (1) building pride and (2) using feedback loops to help people make course corrections. While external boundary-spanning activities are designed to tell the quality story, such efforts have an inside payoff as well. John White, for example, spoke with me about his first days as president of Nebraska Wesleyan University. In the process of doing an admissions plan he concluded that the school was a lot better than people—*his own people*—thought it was. According to White, "They did not have a very high view of themselves as a faculty. In fact, the institutional self-image was extremely poor." He decided that this was because most of the faculty had never worked anywhere else and, consequently, didn't have anyone to compare themselves to. While the resulting recruiting efforts were directed at traditional student groups, he found that there was a significant effect on other groups as well:

> *One of the most valuable things you can have, certainly for recruiting and for other external constituencies, but also internally, is third-party validations or endorsements. We looked real hard for it. We found that the National Center for Educational Statistics keeps track of the production of Ph.D.s. Well, we produced more students that went into doctoral programs in the sciences in the last 60 years than any other school in our state—including Creighton which is five times as big as we are. So we started reminding the faculty of that. There was also a study done of Ph.D.s in psychology. We were ranked 41st in the country in terms of undergraduate programs whose students went on to gain Ph.D.s in psychology. And we were tenth, above a number of very prestigious schools, West of the Mississippi. If you don't think that made our psychology department feel proud.*

Not only does such information make for exceptionally good advertising copy, it can also be an effective means of building a strong culture of quality. It acts as a mirror that enhances the ability of the quality-causers to judge themselves against external standards of excellence.

The single best means to communicate quality is through customer satisfaction.

Any teacher will tell you that there are several pedagogical paths (all effective) that can be used to accomplish a learning objective. I have always taken my teaching seriously and worked hard to define what knowledge and skills my students needed. Each syllabus, in turn, has been a serious attempt to deliver the goods. I also know that the identical delivery system doesn't work for every student; so it has always been my policy to offer an option. On the first day of a new class several years ago I made my standard introductory offer: "If any of you would like to consider accomplishing my objectives some other way, let's talk." Of course I rarely get any takers. Most students prefer anonymity. This particular class, however, was an exception because several days later a student appeared at my office. She had done a paper in another class that had piqued her interest in an area and wanted to know whether she could use my research methods class to pursue it further. She was very shy and it had obviously taken every ounce of courage for her to make the overture. I read her paper and checked her transcript. The paper was good and her coursework and grades were great—almost straight A's. We proceeded. After three months of solid effort the data were in and analyzed. Instead of just writing a report we decided to draft an article together and spent several additional months doing so. The results were good enough, I felt, to submit them to a journal for consideration. Soon thereafter we received notice that the article had been accepted for publication and later that year it appeared in print. At graduation I had the opportunity to meet my co-author's father. It turned out that he had been concerned about his daughter attending a university because he feared that she'd be trampled by the crowds. According to him, she was smart and a hard worker but she didn't have a lot of confidence. My course and our work together had made a difference. She had changed, "blossomed" I think was his word, and he is still sending reprints of our article to relatives and friends.

Now the flip side: A friend and co-author of mine is the director of market research at a large Massachusetts corporation. She regularly recruits student interns from several local colleges and universities, many of whom are later offered full-time employment. Recently, she discovered that one intern, a senior, was unable to accomplish even the most rudimentary assignment. This was not a case of a student having a few weaknesses in some minor skill areas but, rather, a situation in which she couldn't understand how the student ever made it that far. She wrote a letter to the college president expressing her concerns. No response. Weeks later she began telephoning— he was always out of town, in a meeting or preparing a speech. The calls were never returned. Apparently, customer satisfaction was not in the president's job description. The result? My friend removed the college from the company's job recruiting list. She also continues to tell the story of customer dissatisfaction whenever the opportunity arises.

Quality is, as John Slaughter suggested to me, "a body of sentiment that builds over time." And while overt efforts at telling the quality story in higher education are necessary and completely warranted, we should not forget the power of a story that tells itself. A satisfied customer is like a walking billboard. Whether it is a proud parent of a college senior or a pleasantly surprised employer, the effect is the same. By exceeding peoples' expectations you make a statement—*their needs come first*. All of us feel good when something like that happens in our lives. It's such a contrast to the everyday grind of broken promises, late deliveries, surly secretaries, and unreturned telephone calls. Imagine what would happen if a college or university began to exceed the expectations of its customers—employers, students, alumni, parents, board members, state legislators, local community members. Imagine the stories that would be told and retold.

———————◆———————

By the way, there is virtually no mention of communicating quality in any of the strategic quality management literature. It does not make Deming's fourteen points, and it is scarcely mentioned by either Juran or Crosby. On the other hand, in May, 1990, a group of 300 communicators from across the country converged in Houston for a conference sponsored by the American Productivity & Quality Center to discuss the communicator's role in the quality improvement process. After reading through the conference proceedings I came away with a basic conclusion to apply to higher education: We must understand our customers' requirements much better and we must work hard to develop a distinctive vision of how we can best satisfy those needs. We have to define the processes that underlie our services and generate sound measures that enable us to change and grow. We need to strip away ego-bruising policies, drive out fear, and empower everyone to contribute to never-ending improvement. We need to cause quality on our college campuses. And after adopting the philosophy and mastering the tools, we should tell our quality story tirelessly to everyone who will listen.

Notes

Chapter 1: The Incline of Quality

1. Cited in Beth Kobliner, "How to be a Smart College Shopper," *Money Guide America's Best College Buys* (Fall 1990): 12.
2. Cited in Robert A. Rosenblatt, "U.S. Medical Spending Soars 11% During 1989," *Los Angeles Times,* 21 December 1990, A4.
3. Cited in Jean Evangelauf, "1991 Tuition Increases Expected to Outpace Inflation, but Some Private Colleges Will Slow the Upward Trend," *Chronicle of Higher Education,* 6 March 1991, A1.
4. Kenneth W. Harrigan, "Ensuring Quality is Job 1 at Ford," *Business Quarterly* (November 1989): 94.
5. Robin Wilson, "Undergraduates at Large Universities Found to Be Increasingly Dissatisfied," *Chronicle of Higher Education,* 9 January 1991, A1.
6. David A. Garvin, *Managing Quality: The Strategic And Competitive Edge* (New York: The Free Press, 1988), 9.
7. Mary Walton, *The Deming Management Method* (New York: Putnam, 1986), 11.
8. Ibid., 19.
9. Robert W. Galvin, Speech delivered at the *1st National Symposium on the Role of Academia in National Competitiveness and Total Quality Management* (Morgantown, W.V., July 1990), 144.
10. Mary Walton, *Deming Management at Work* (New York: Putnam, 1990), 85.
11. Lee Cheaney and Maury Cotter, *Real People, Real Work: Parables on Leadership in the 90s* (Knoxville, TN: SPC Press, 1991), 9.
12. John A. White, Speech delivered at the *1st National Symposium on the Role of Academia in National Competitiveness and Total Quality Management* (Morgantown, W.V., July 1990), 47.

Chapter 2: Strategic Quality Management on Campus

1. *Oxford American Dictionary,* s.v. "paradigm."
2. Roger Rollin, "There's No Business Like Education," *Academe* (January–February 1989): 17.

3. Allan W. Ostar, "The Faculty's Leadership Role," *Chronicle of Higher Education,* 26 September 1990, B5.

4. *Discovering the Future: The Business of Paradigms* by Joel Barker is available through Charthouse Learning Corporation, Burnsville, MN.

5. Tom Peters, *Thriving on Chaos* (New York: Harper & Row, 1987), 279.

6. Robert M. Pirsig, *Zen and the Art of Motorcycle Maintenance* (New York: Bantam, 1974), 225.

7. David A. Garvin, *Managing Quality* (New York: The Free Press, 1988), 40–46.

8. Harold L. Enarson, "Quality—Indefinable But Not Unattainable," *Education Record,* 64 (Winter 1983):7.

9. Philip B. Crosby, *Quality Is Free* (New York: McGraw-Hill, 1979), 38–9.

10. Jersey Gilbert, "Money's College Value Ranking," *Money Guide: America's Best College Buys* (Fall 1990): 72.

11. Joseph M. Juran, ed., *Quality Control Handbook* (New York: McGraw-Hill, 1974), 2.

12. Lewis B. Mayhew, Patrick J. Ford, and Dean L. Hubbard, *The Quest for Quality* (San Francisco: Jossey-Bass, 1990), 25–6.

13. Cited in Mary Crystal Cage, "For a Powerful State Senator in Colorado, 'the Student Comes First,' " *Chronicle of Higher Education,* 19 December 1990, A22.

14. Pat Hutchings, "Assessment and the Way We Work" (Speech delivered at AAHE Conference on Assessment, Washington, D.C., June 1990).

15. "Interview with Robert Maynard Hutchins," *Chronicle of Higher Education,* 8 February 1977, 14.

16. David Glidden, "A Loss of Community, and of Education Graduates," *Los Angeles Times,* 6 September 1990, M5.

17. Henry Mintzberg, *Structure in Fives: Designing Effective Organizations* (Englewood Cliffs, NJ: Prentice Hall, 1983), 206.

18. Karl E. Weick, "Educational Organizations as Loosely Coupled Systems," *Administrative Science Quarterly* (March 1976):1–19.

19. Henry Mintzberg, "The Professional Bureaucracy," in *The Strategy Process,* eds. James Bryan Quinn, Henry Mintzberg, and Robert M. James (Englewood Cliffs, NJ: Prentice Hall, 1988), 648.

20. The primary resource for this section is *Transition to Total Quality Leadership at the University of Wisconsin–Madison,* an internal draft plan dated October 1990.

21. The primary resource for this section is *Partners for Progress for 1990–1997,* a North Dakota University System publication dated June 1990.

22. The primary resource for this section is *Total Quality Management* at Delaware County Community College, an internal document dated November 1990.

23. The primary resource for this section is *Implementing Total Quality Management in a University Setting,* an Oregon State University internal publication dated July 1990. See also L. Edwin Coates, "TQM on Campus: Implementing Total Quality Management in a University Setting." *NACUBO Business Officer* (November 1990):26–35. It should be noted that Figure 2.1 and the following text is based

upon "Ten Elements of Total Quality Management Implementation Model" developed by GOAL/QPA, a Methuen, Massachusetts quality consulting firm.

24. Frank Newman, *Choosing Quality: Reducing Conflict Between the State and the University* (Denver: Education Commission of the States, 1987), 10.

25. Ibid., 7.

Chapter 3: Satisfy the Customer: Everything Else Follows

1. Tom Peters, *Thriving on Chaos* (New York: Harper & Row, 1987), 586.

2. Cited in "King Customer," *Business Week,* 12 March 1990, 88.

3. William R. Thurston, "Quality Is Between The Customer's Ears," *Across the Board* (January 1985):29–32.

4. John Harris, Susan Hillenmeyer, and James V. Foran, *Quality Assurance for Private Career School* (Association of Independent Colleges and Schools, 1989), 3.

5. Thomas R. Plough, "Identifying and Evaluating Major Element in the Quality of Student Life," in *Current Issues in Higher Education* (Washington, D.C.: American Association for Higher Education, 1979), 22.

6. Roger Rollin, "There's No Business Like Education," *Academe* (January–February 1989): 14.

7. Allan Tucker and Robert A. Bryan. *The Academic Dean: Dove, Dragon, and Diplomat* (New York: Macmillan, 1988), 102.

8. Jan Carlzon, *Moments of Truth* (New York: Harper & Row, 1987), 72–4.

9. Cited in David A. Garvin, *Managing Quality: The Strategic and Competitive Edge* (New York: The Free Press, 1988), 40. Copyright © 1988 by David A. Garvin. Reprinted by permission of The Free Press, a Division of Macmillan, Inc.

10. This input-process-output format and the others that follow in this chapter are based upon diagrams used by Joseph M. Juran in *Juran on Planning for Quality* (New York: The Free Press, 1988), 18, 34, 62. Copyright © 1988 by Juran Institute, Inc. Reprinted by permission of The Free Press, a Division of Macmillan, Inc.

11. John B. Bennett, *Managing the Academic Department: Cases and Notes* (New York: ACE and Macmillan, 1983), 9. Copyright © 1983 by the American Council on Education and Macmillan Publishing Company, a Division of Macmillan, Inc. Reprinted by permission of Macmillan Publishing Company.

12. Robert H. Waterman, Jr., *The Renewal Factor* (New York: Bantam, 1987), 88.

13. James R. Mingle, *"The Political Meaning of Quality,"* American Association for Higher Education Bulletin (May 1989): 9.

14. Frank Newman, *Choosing Quality: Reducing Conflict Between The State And the University* (Denver: Education Commission of the States, 1987), 8.

15. Lyman Porter and Lawrence McKibbon, *Management Education and Development* (St. Louis: American Assembly of Schools and Colleges of Business, 1988), 69.

16. Anne C. Ciliberte, et al., "Material Availability: A Study of Academic Library Performances," *College of Research Libraries* (November 1987): 513–27.

17. Peter Hernon and Charles R. McClure, "Unobtrusive Reference Testing: The 55 Percent Rule," *Library Journal* (April 1986): 37–41.

18. Howard Schwartz and J. Jacobs, *Qualitative Sociology* (New York: The Free Press, 1979), 272.

19. Waterman, *The Renewal Factor,* 149.

20. Patrick L. Townsend, *Commit to Quality* (New York: John-Wiley, 1986), 141–59.

21. Philip Crosby, *Quality Is Free* (New York: McGraw-Hill, 1979), 133.

22. Jim Cathcart, "Winning Customer Service," *Management Solutions* (November 1988): 15.

Chapter 4: Choosing to Be Distinctive

1. Martin Fishbein, "A Behavior Theory Approach to the Relations between Beliefs about an Object and Attitudes toward the Object," in *Attitude Theory and Measurement,* ed. Martin Fishbein (New York: John-Wiley, 1967), 394. The model is developed as follows:

$$\text{Attitude}_A = \sum_{i=1}^{k} B_i I_i$$

Where:

Attitude_A = Individual's overall attitude toward Object A

B_i = Individual's belief concerning the extent to which attribute i is associated with Object A

I_i = The importance of attribute i to the individual

k = The total number of attributes considered by the individual

i = Any specific attribute

2. Benjamin B. Tregoe and Peter M. Tobia, "Set a Goal and Reach It Step by Step," *New York Times,* 29 October 1989, F2.

3. Daniel T. Seymour, "HODGE-PODGE: Or the Unintended Results from Straying too Far Afield," *Planning for Higher Education* (Fall 1988–89):10.

4. Allan Bloom, *The Closing of the American Mind* (New York: Simon and Schuster, 1987), 337–9.

5. Cited in Alan Deutschman, "Why Universities are Shrinking," *Fortune,* 24 September 1990, 103.

6. Michael E. Porter, *Competitive Advantage: Creating and Sustaining Superior Performance* (New York: The Free Press; 1985), 11–20.

7. J. Wade Gilley, Kenneth A. Fulmer, and Sally J. Reithlingshoefer, *Searching for Academic Excellence* (New York: Macmillan, 1986), 35, 41.

8. Tom Peters, *Thriving on Chaos* (New York: Harper & Row, 1987), 171.

9. Larry J. Williams and John T. Hazer, "Antecedents and Consequences of Satisfaction

and Commitment in Turnover Models: A Reanalysis Using Latent Variable Structural Equation Methods," *Journal of Applied Psychology* (May 1986): 219–31.

10. David A. Nichols, "Challenging Chait on Theory Z," *AGB Reports* (March–April 1982): 6.

11. From *Implementing Total Quality Management in a University Setting,* an Oregon State University internal publication dated July 1990: 15.

12. Nichols, "Challenging," 8.

13. Peter M. Senge, *The Fifth Discipline: The Art and Practice of the Learning Organization* (New York: Doubleday, 1991), 205–32.

Chapter 5: Process, Process, and More Process

1. For an insightful description of systems thinking and its relationship to quality improvement, see Peter M. Senge, *The Fifth Discipline* (New York: Doubleday, 1991), 205–32.

2. Masaaki Imai, *KAIZEN: The Key to Japan's Competitive Success* (New York: Random House, 1986), 5.

3. Jack Lindquist, "Political Linkage: The Academic-Innovation Process," *Journal of Higher Education* (May 1974): 325.

4. Robert C. Nordvall, *The Process of Change in Higher Education Institutions* (Washington D.C.: AAHE-ERIC Clearinghouse on Higher Education, 1982), 43.

5. H.J. Harrington, *The Improvement Process* (New York: McGraw-Hill, 1987), 103.

6. Nancy Rivera Brooks, "Speed of Mail Tracked By Accountants," *Los Angeles Times,* 6 February 1990, A4.

7. Philip B. Crosby, *Quality Is Free* (New York: McGraw-Hill, 1979), 113.

8. Harold Geneen, *Managing* (New York: Avon Books, 1984), 192.

9. David A. Garvin, *Managing Quality: The Strategic and Competitive Edge* (New York: The Free Press, 1988), 169.

10. George Keller, *Academic Strategy* (Baltimore: The Johns Hopkins University Press, 1983), 131.

11. Stuart Terrass and Velma Pomrenke, "The Institutional Researcher as Change Agent," in *New Directions for Institutional Research: Increasing the Utilization of Institutional Research* ed. Jack Lindquist (San Francisco: Jossey-Bass, 1981), 73.

12. For a more detailed examination of these tools please refer to "Doing it with Data" in Mary Walton, *The Deming Management Method* (New York: Putnam, 1986), 96–118, or "Improving the System" in Howard S. Gitlow and Shelly J. Gitlow, *The Deming Guide to Quality and Competitive Position* (Englewood Cliffs, NJ: Prentice-Hall, 1987), 69–96.

13. Imai, *KAIZEN,* 5.

14. Tom Peters, *Thriving on Chaos* (New York: Harper & Row. 1987), 127.

15. Richard E. Kopelman, "Objective Feedback," in *Generalizing from Laboratory to Field Settings,* ed. Edwin A. Locke (Lexington, MA: D.C. Health, 1986), 119–45.

Chapter 6: Involving Everyone in the Pursuit

1. *Accreditation Council Policies Procedures and Standards,* (St. Louis, MO: American Assembly of Collegiate Schools of Business, 1989–90).

2. Cited in Diane Curtis, "Bay Area's CSU Schools Tell of 'Serious' Budget Cuts," *San Francisco Chronicle,* 11 August 1990, A7.

3. Allan Bloom, *The Closing of the American Mind* (New York: Simon and Schuster, 1987), 339.

4. Neal R. Pierce, "A Public Trust," *CASE Currents* (June 1988): 9.

5. Jan Carlzon, *Moments of Truth.* (New York: Harper & Row, 1987), 3.

6. Cited in Tom Peters, *Thriving of Chaos* (New York: Harper & Row 1987), 343.

7. Thomas F. O'Boyle, "From Pyramid to Pancake," *The Wall Street Journal,* 4 June 1990, R37.

8. John Hood, "Education: Money Isn't Everything," *The Wall Street Journal,* 12 March 1991, A10.

9. Peter Likins, "In an Era of Tight Budgets and Public Criticism, Colleges Must Rethink Their Goals and Priorities." *Chronicle of Higher Education,* 9 May 1990, B1–2.

10. Cited in Patrick L. Townsend, *Commit to Quality* (New York: John Wiley & Sons, 1986), 57.

11. Lawrence Sherr, speech delivered at *The Association of Instututitional Research Annual Forum* (Louisville, KY, May 1990), 6.

12. James L. Bess, "Miscast Professors," *Change* (May–June 1990): 20.

13. John A. Centra, "Maintaining Faculty Vitality Through Faculty Development," in *Faculty Vitality and Institutional Productivity* eds. Shirley M. Clark and Darrell R. Lewis (New York: Teachers College Press, 1985), 151.

14. Cited in Kenneth C. Green and Daniel T. Seymour, *Who's Going to Run General Motors?* (Princeton, NJ: Peterson's Guides, 1991), 27.

15. Brian Dumaine, "Who Needs a Boss?" *Fortune,* 7 May 1990, 52.

16. For additional information on quality circles in higher education see David A. Nichols. "Can Theory Z Be Applied to Academic Management?" *Chronicle of Higher Education.* v25.1.1982.p.71; Larry C. Holt and Thomas E. Wagner. "Quality Circle: An Alternative for Higher Education," *CUPA Journal* (Spring 1983):11; Liz McMillen, "College Employees Try 'Quality Circles,' to Improve Administration, Curriculum," *Chronicle of Higher Education,* 11 December 1985, 21.

17. Pat Hutchings, "Behind Outcomes: Contexts and Questions for Assessment." *AAHE Forum,* June 1989, 30.

18. Peter M. Senge, *The Fifth Discipline* (New York: Doubleday, 1991), 141.

Chapter 7: Pride: The Engine of Success

1. Jan Carlzon, *Moments of Truth* (New York: Harper & Row, 1987), 135.

2. Philip Crosby, *Quality Without Tears* (New York: McGraw-Hill, 1984), 15.

3. Ibid., 19.

4. Christine Licata, *Post-tenure Faculty Evaluation: Threat or Opportunity?* (Washington D.C.: Association for the Study of Higher Education, 1986).

5. Dan R. Dalton, David M. Krackhardt and Lyman W. Porter, "Functional Turnover: An Empirical Assessment," *Journal of Applied Psychology* (December 1981): 716–21.

6. Richard M. Steers and Richard T. Mowday, "Employee Turnover and Post-Decision Accomodation Processes," in *Research in Organizational Behavior* eds. L.L. Cummings and Barry M. Staw (Greenwich, CT: JAI Press, 1981), 235–281.

7. Howard S. Gitlow and Shelly J. Gitlow, *The Deming Guide to Quality and Competitive Position* (Englewood Cliffs, NJ: Prentice-Hall, 1987), 179.

8. Yvonna S. Lincoln, "Indigenous Efforts at Individualizing Program Review: A Case Study," Paper presented at the annual meeting of the *Association for the Study of Higher Education,* San Antonio, Texas, 1986, 16–17.

9. Carolyn Mooney, "Faculty Generation Gap Brings Campus Tensions, Debates Over Rating of Professors," *Chronicle of Higher Education,* 27 June 1990, 1.

10. Beverly T. Watkins, "Colleges Are Said to Offer Little Help to Senior Professors," *Chronicle of Higher Education,* 29 March 1989, 29.

11. Allan Tucker and Robert A. Bryan, *The Academic Dean: Dove, Dragon, and Diplomat* (New York: Macmillan, 1988), 85.

12. Ibid., 85.

13. Tom Peters, *Thriving on Chaos* (New York: Harper & Row, 1987), 371.

Chapter 8: It's all in the Attitude

1. Cited in John J. Goldman, "Universities Rated 'F' for Inability to Help Solve Society's Problems," *Los Angeles Times,* 7 August 1990, A5.

2. A. Parasuraman, Valerie A. Zeithaml, and Leonard L. Berry, *A Conceptual Model of Service Quality and its Implications for Future Research,* The Marketing Science Institute Working Paper No. 84–106 (Cambridge, MA: The Institute, 1984), 13–14.

3. Valerie A. Zeithaml, Leonard L. Berry, and A. Parasuraman, *Communication and Control Processes in the Delivery of Service Quality,* The Marketing Science Institute Working Paper No. 87–100 (Cambridge, MA: The Institute, 1987), 2.

4. Philip Crosby, *Quality Without Tears* (New York:McGraw-Hill, 1984), 74–84.

5. Cited in Howard S. Gitlow and Shelly J. Gitlow, *The Deming Guide to Quality and Competitive Position* (Englewood Cliffs, NJ: Prentice Hall, 1987), 32.

6. Annetta Miller, "Perrier Loses Its Fizz," *Newsweek,* 26 February 1990, 53.

7. Crosby, *Quality Without Tears,* 5.

8. Ibid., 5.

9. Cited in Anne Hinman Diffily, "Partnerships 101," *CASE Currents* (May 1989): 8.

10. Oscar F. Porter. *Undergraduate Completion and Persistence at Four-Year Colleges and Universities* (Washington DC: National Institute of Independent Colleges and Universities, 1989), iv.

11. Cited in Lorna Miles, "Learn From Experience." *CASE Currents* (September 1988):26.

12. Alan Deutschman, "Why Universities are Shrinking?," *Fortune,* 24 September 1990, 106.

13. Mary Jo Kealy and Mark L. Rockel, "Student Perceptions of College Quality," *Journal of Higher Education* (November–December, 1987): 692.

14. Tom Peters, *Thriving on Chaos* (New York: Harper & Row, 1987), 120.

Chapter 9: A Culture of Quality

1. Pat Hutchings and Ted Marchese, "Watching Assessment: Questions, Stories. Prospects." *Change* (September–October 1990):12. Reprinted with permission.

2. Cited in Hutchings and Marchese, "Watching Assessment.":14.

3. For example, see William G. Ouchi and Alan L. Wilkins, "Organizational Culture," in *Annual Review of Sociology* (Palo Alto, CA: Annual Reviews Inc., 1985), 457–83.

4. Terrence E. Deal and Allan A. Kennedy, *Corporate Cultures* (Reading, MA: Addison Wesley, 1982), 195.

5. Burton Clark, *Academic Culture* (New Haven, CT: Yale Higher Education Research Group/Report No. 42, 1980), 3.

6. George D. Kuh and Elizabeth J. Whitt, *The Invisible Tapestry* (Washington DC: ASHE:ERIC Higher Education Reports No. 1, 1988).

7. Cited in Ibid., 15–16.

8. Cited in Alan L. Wilkins. "Organizational Stories and Symbols," in *Organizational Symbolism,* ed. Louis Pondy et al. (Greenwich, CT: JAI Press), 81.

9. Deal and Kennedy, *Corporate Cultures,* 16.

10. Harrison Trice and Janice Beyer, "Studying Organization Cultures Through Rites and Ceremonials," *Academy of Management Review* (October 1984): 655.

11. Ibid., 657.

12. Wilkins, "Organizational Stories," 81.

13. Ibid., 89.

14. Burton R. Clark, "The Organizational Saga in Higher Education." *Administrative Science Quarterly* (June 1972): 183.

15. Cited in Kuh and Whitt, *The Invisible Tapestry,* 65.

16. Lin Bothwell, *The Art of Leadership: Skill-Building Techniques that Produce Results* (Englewood Cliffs, NJ: Prentice Hall, 1983).

17. Edgar Schein, "Coming to a New Awareness of Organizational Culture," *Sloan Management Review* (Winter 1984): 3.

18. Thomas J. DeLoughry, "Colleges Fear Graduation-Rate Data Could Be Turned Against Them," *Chronicle of Higher Education,* 31 October 1990, A16.

19. R. Eugene Rice and Ann E. Austin, "High Faculty Morale," *Change* (March/April 1988): 51.

Chapter 10: Telling the Quality Story

1. James Risen, "LeSabre's Success Proved Point for GM: Quality Sells," *Los Angeles Times,* 23 January 1990, D1.

2. Jan Krukowski, "What do Student's Want? Status," *Change* (May–June 1985): 22–23.

3. Alexander W. Astin, Kenneth C. Green, and William S. Korn, *The American Freshmen: Twenty Year Trends* (Washington. DC: American Council on Education, 1987), 88.

4. Ernest Boyer, *College: The Undergraduate Experience in America* (New York: Harper & Row, 1987), 3.

5. Ibid., 14.

6. George D. Kuh and Michael D. Coomes, "What Prospective Students Really Need to Know about Quality," *College and University* (Winter 1984): 167–8.

7. *Special Advisory for College and University Presidents* (Washington, D.C.: Council for Advancement and Support of Education, 1988), 1.

8. Ibid., 5.

9. Larry Gordon, "Increases in Cost of College Again Outstrips Inflation," *Los Angeles Times,* 27 September 1990, A25.

10. Jean Evangelauf, "Fees Rise More Slowly This Year, but Surpass Inflation Rate Again," *Chronicle of Higher Education,* 3 October 1990, 1.

11. Donald Faulkner, "College Public Relations," *Journal of Higher Education* (February 1961): 84.

12. Robert H. Miles, *Macro Organizational Behavior* (Glenview, IL: Scott Foresman, 1980) Also please see a more specific discussion of the topic as it relates to communication in higher education in Robert D. Gratz and Philip J. Salem, "Communication Across the Boundaries," in *Maximizing Opportunities Through External Relationships* ed. Daniel T. Seymour (San Francisco: Jossey-Bass New Directions in Higher Education Series, 1989), 93–111.

13. Robin Wilson, "As Competition for Students Increases, Admission Officers Face Dismissal if They Don't 'Win and Keep on Winning'," *Chronicle of Higher Education,* 31 October 1990, A1.

14. R. Russell Shunk, "Presidents Must Not Make Their Admissions Officers Scapegoats or Victims of the Losing Coach Mentality," *Chronicle of Higher Education,* 14 November 1990, B1.

15. Beth Kobliner, "How to Be a Smart College Shopper," *Money Guide* (Fall 1990): 12.

16. Cited in Denise M. Topolnicki, "The Big Campus Come-On," *Money Guide* (Fall 1990): 20.

17. Stephen B. Castleberry and Anna V.A. Resurreccion, "Communicating Quality to Consumers," *The Journal of Consumer Marketing* (Summer 1989):24.

18. Neal Pierce, "A Public Trust," *CASE Currents* (June 1988): 14.

19. "Pacific Forum's Time Has Come," *San Francisco Chronicle,* 22 April 1989.

Annotated Bibliography

BLOCK, PETER. *The Empowered Manager: Positive Political Skills at Work.* San Francisco: Jossey-Bass, 1987.

A highly readable set of ideas for administrators at any level of the institution. The book explores the human relations side of quality improvement.

CARLZON, JAN. *Moments of Truth.* New York: Harper & Row, 1987.

The president and CEO of Scandinavian Airlines describes how he restructured his company so customer needs take priority. The emphasis is on leadership strategies and improving quality in a service industry.

CHAFFEE, ELLEN E., "Managing for the 1990s." In Larry W. Jones and Franz A. Nowotny, eds. *An Agenda for the New Decade.* New Directions in Higher Education, no. 70. San Francisco: Jossey-Bass, 1990.

Presents a number of the key ideas in quality improvement for administrators in colleges and universities.

CHEANEY, LEE and MAURY COTTER. *Real People/Real Work: Parables on Leadership in the 90s.* Knoxville, TN: SPC Press, 1991.

An engaging series of stories and anecdotes about quality in everyday life. A non-statistical, easy reading book that sets the stage for quality improvement programs.

COATE, L. EDWIN. "TMQ on Campus: Implementing Total Quality Management on Campus." *NACUBO Business Officer* (November 1990): 26–35.

Oregon State University has been a leader applying quality improvement principles to higher education. This article documents OSU's planning process and offers a number of conclusions and recommendations based upon first-year experiences.

CORNESKY, ROBERT A., *Improving Quality in Colleges and Universities.* Madison, WI: Magna Publications, 1990.

Each of Deming's points for managing quality and productivity are discussed in terms of their application to higher education.

CROSBY, PHILIP B. *Quality Is Free.* New York: McGraw-Hill, 1979.

The premise of this book is that doing things right the first time adds nothing to the cost of a product or service. One of the most readable and quotable books on quality improvement.

CROSBY, PHILIP B. *Quality Without Tears.* New York: McGraw-Hill, 1984.

A practical guide to achieving quality. This book focuses on the human side of the quality movement by emphasizing the importance of reducing the amount of "hassling" in a work environment.

DEMING, W. EDWARDS. *Out of the Crisis.* Cambridge: MIT Center for Advanced Engineering Study, 1986.

Deming's classic. It contains full explanations of his now-famous fourteen points for management.

GARVIN, DAVID A. *Managing Quality: The Strategic and Competitive Edge.* New York: The Free Press, 1988.

A Harvard business school professor writes for managers, elaborating the history and nature of the quality concept and illustrating its impact with a comparative study from industry.

GITLOW, HOWARD S., and SHELLY J. GITLOW. *The Deming Guide to Quality and Competitive Position.* Englewood Cliffs, N.J.: Prentice Hall, 1987.

Good explanation of each of Deming's fourteen points with discussion of how each point fits into the overall philosophy. The book also has questions for self-examination and implementation pitfalls.

HARRIS, JOHN, SUSAN HILLENMEYER, and JAMES V. FORAN. *Quality Assurance for Private Career Schools.* New York: McGraw-Hill, 1989.

Sponsored by The Association of Independent Colleges and Schools, this monograph enumerates applications of Deming's fourteen points to education. There are also sections devoted to student outcomes assessments, organizing information, and leadership.

IMAI, MASAAKI. *KAIZEN: The Key to Japan's Competitive Success.* New York: Random House, 1986.

"Kaizen" means commitment to the continuous improvement of quality. The volume compares Eastern and Western management styles and gives brief introductions to a wide array of conceptual and practical tools.

ISHIKAWA, KAORU. *What is Total Quality Control?: The Japanese Way.* Translated by David J. Lu. Englewood Cliffs, N.J.: Prentice Hall, 1985.

A comprehensive how-to book and Total Quality Control implementation program that is characterized by Ishikawa as "a thought revolution in management."

JURAN, JOSEPH M. *Juran on Planning for Quality.* New York: The Free Press, 1988.

This volume offers a very structured description of Juran's "quality trilogy"—quality planning, quality control, and quality improvement. It is advanced reading based upon Juran's experiences with over fifty major manufacturing and service organizations.

JURAN, JOSEPH M. *Juran on Leadership for Quality: An Executive Handbook.* New York: The Free Press, 1989.

In this companion volume to *Juran on Planning for Quality,* the author applies the concepts of planning, controlling, and improving to quality leadership. He gives specific criteria for choosing project-by-project improvements and for selecting teams to carry them out.

MILLER, RICHARD I., ed. *Adapting the Deming Method to Higher Education.* Washington, D.C.: College and University Personnel Association, 1991.

Various authors suggest ways to apply Deming's principles to sixteen areas in higher education management.

RYAN, KATHLEEN D., and DANIEL K. OESTREICH. *Driving Fear Out of the Workplace.* San Francisco: Jossey-Bass, 1991.

Drawing on interview data from people in 22 companies, the authors examine the presence of fear in organizations (one of Deming's key principles). They offer a practical vision of what manager-employee relationships can be when people do not feel threatened about speaking up.

SCHERKENBACK, WILLIAM W. *The Deming Route to Quality and Productivity: Road Maps and Road Blocks.* Rockville, MD: Mercury Press/Fairchild Productions, 1988.

An elaboration on each of Deming's fourteen points with insights and explanations drawn from the author's experiences at Ford Motor Company.

SCHOLTES, PETER R., ET AL. *The Team Handbook: How to Improve Quality with Teams.* Madison, WI: Joiner Associates, 1988.

This is a comprehensive book on helping teams work together to make improvements. It is filled with step-by-step instructions, illustrations, and worksheets.

SENGE, PETER. *The Fifth Discipline: The Art and Practice of the Learning Organization.* New York: Doubleday, 1991.

A wonderful book for detailing the principles of systems thinking. Most of the material can be directly related to strategic quality management—for example, process improvement, shared vision, and team learning.

SEYMOUR, DANIEL, and CASEY COLLETT. *Total Quality Management in Higher Education: A Critical Review.* Methuen, MA: GOAL/QPC, 1991.

Benefits and frustrations, implementation strategies, and future plans are among the issues explored in this research report based upon detailed data collected from 25 colleges and universities that are using TQM principles.

SHERR, LAWRENCE, and DEBRA J. TEETER, eds. *Total Quality Management in Higher Education.* New Directions for Institutional Research, no. 71. San Francisco: Jossey-Bass, 1991.

In addition to chapters devoted to the theory of total quality management and the role of institutional researchers in TQM implementation, this source book also has case studies from Oregon State University, Delaware Community College, and Virginia Polytechnic Institute and State University.

TOWNSEND, PATRICK L. *Commit to Quality.* New York: John Wiley & Sons, 1990.
The first five years of Total Quality at the Paul Revere Insurance Company are described. A good case history of TQM implementation in a service industry.

WALTON, MARY. *The Deming Management Method.* New York: G.P. Putnam's Sons, 1986.
Written by a newspaper reporter, this book contains three major parts: part one gives an overview and short biography of Deming; part two describes Deming's fourteen points in straightforward style; and part three enumerates a small set of cases.

WALTON, MARY. *Deming Management at Work.* New York: G.P. Putnam's Sons, 1990.
Most of this follow-up book concentrates on six successful organizations that use quality principles: Florida Power & Light; Hospital Corporation of America; Tri-Cities, Tennessee; United States Navy; Bridgestone (USA) Inc.; and Globe Metallurigcal Inc.

In addition to these books and articles, there are a number of other sources that can be consulted for additional reference material:

The Quality Press Publications catalog (1991) is available through the American Society for Quality Control (ASQC), 310 West Wisconsin Avenue, Milwaukee, WI 53203. Most of the books discussed above are included in the ASQC catalog. The catalog contains sections on human resources management, service quality, and target industries. It also offers audiotapes and videotapes, and is fully annotated.

SPC Press publishes a series of books from introductory levels to advanced "how tos." Their catalog is available by writing to: SPC Press, 5908 Toole Drive, Knoxville, TN 37919.

A Total Quality Management (TQM) Resource Bibliography has been compiled by Susan Ziemba at the Center for Business and Industry, Northern Essex Community College, Haverhill, MA 01830. This exhaustive listing includes not only texts but also videos/films, magazines/newsletters, and bibliographies. It is not annotated.

GOAL/QPC, a management consulting firm, produces a catalog that includes both general references as well as books and monographs published through GOAL/QPC Press, 13 Branch Street, Methuen, MA 01844. Additionally, GOAL/QPC distributes a software program (QFD/CAPTURE) that includes a glossary of terms, tutorials, and a relational database.

A newsletter that networks higher education institutions having an interest in Total Quality Management is organized and distributed by William A. Golomski and Associates, 59 East Van Buren Street, Chicago, IL 60605-1220.

Another newsletter, National Quality in Education Consortium newsletter, links people interested in the role of academia in national competitiveness and Total Quality Management. Contact Professor Forrest Gale, Defense Systems Management College, Room 202, Bldg. 202, Fort Belvoir, VA 22060-5426.

Index